MOUNTAINS
BEYOND
MOUNTAINS

BEN RANDALL

MOUNTAINS BEYOND MOUNTAINS
First published March 2022

Content warning:
This story contains references to sexual abuse and violence.

Some names have been changed to conceal identities.
The author does not advocate any methods used herein
to contact or meet with victims of human trafficking.
Vietnamese characters are presented without diacritics.
Prices quoted in the text are given in US dollars,
unless stated otherwise.

ISBN (PDF): 978-0-6454487-0-2
ISBN (Paperback): 978-0-6487573-9-9
ISBN (epub): 978-0-6454487-1-9

Learn more at
www.sistersforsale.com

For Mike, Krista, and little Finn

N

Kunming
120km
(75mi)

Beijing
2,160km
(1,342mi)

Wenshan

CHINA

YUNNAN

Hop
Tien

Jinping County

Ha
Giang

Jinshuihe

Nanxi

Muong
Kuong

Pa Nam
Cum

Hekou

Bac
Ha

HA
GIANG

Sapa

Lao
Cai

Lai
Chau

▲
Fansipan
3,147m
(10,326ft)

LAO
CAI

LAI
CHAU

Red River

DIEN
BIEN

YEN
BAI

Yen
Bai

Dien Bien Phu

VIETNAM

Tay Trang

SON
LA

Hanoi
80km
(50mi)

→

Ho Chi
Minh City
1,120km
(695mi)

LAOS

0	25	50	75 km

0	25	50 mi

MONGOLIA

N

LIAONING

Beijing
Tianjin
Bo Sea

HEBEI

SHANDONG

Yellow Sea

Lhasa (Tibet)
950km
(590mi)

JIANGSU

Nanjing
Shanghai

Chengdu

Litang

SICHUAN

CHINA

ANHUI

Lushan
1,474m
(4,836ft)

East China Sea

HUNAN

Dali

Kunming

Guilin
Yangshuo

YUNNAN

GUANGXI

GUANGDONG

TAIWAN

See map one

Nanning

Guangzhou
Dongguan
Shenzhen

MACAU HONG KONG

Hanoi

VIETNAM

South China Sea

LAOS

THAILAND

0	200	400	600 km

0	200	400 mi

CONTENTS

"We need to stop just pulling people out of the river. We need to go upstream and find out why they're falling in."

- Desmond Tutu

"It is impossible to realise our goals while discriminating against half the human race. As study after study has taught us, there is no tool for development more effective than the empowerment of women."

- Kofi Annan

"Unto the woman He said, 'I will greatly multiply thy pain and thy trevail; in pain thou shalt bring forth children; and thy desire shall be to thy husband, and he shall rule over thee."

- Genesis 3:16

INTRODUCTION

'Mountains Beyond Mountains' is the fourth and final part of the incredible true story behind the multi-award-winning documentary, 'Sisters for Sale'.

Young women on the border between Vietnam and China find themselves caught between a violent custom and a vicious criminal underworld.

Investigating the mysterious disappearances of his local friends May and Pang, an Australian filmmaker uncovers a human trafficking crisis and sparks an amazing series of events.

Betrayed, kidnapped, and forced into marriage with strangers, May and Pang – still only teenagers – are forced to make the heartbreaking choice between their baby girls and their own freedom.

Following its premiere in Italy in November 2018, 'Sisters for Sale' won awards and acclaim at film festivals around the world for exceptional filmmaking and courageous storytelling. It has now been translated into more than a dozen languages – an extraordinary feat for such a small production.

'Sisters for Sale' is a five-year story. Each of the books can be read independently: reading the first three parts is not essential to understanding part four.

In the first book, 'Every Stranger's Eyes', Ben meets May and Pang, learns of their subsequent abductions, and returns to Vietnam determined to do everything he can to find and help them.

Part two, 'Suspicious Minds', covers Ben's fascinating and eye-opening investigation in Vietnam, in early 2014.

The third part of the story, 'The Man's Machine', follows the desperate search for May and Pang in China.

The author, Ben Randall, is an Australian activist and acclaimed documentary filmmaker whose writing was shortlisted for the prestigious 2021 Richell Prize.

Ben's work has been seen and heard by millions of people around the world via new and traditional media - including CNN, Discovery Channel, Newsweek, TEDx, VICE, ABC, CBC, Channel NewsAsia, VTV, Walk Free, Freedom United, Imgur, and Reddit.

The 'Sisters for Sale' books and documentary are part of 'The Human, Earth Project', a non-profit grassroots organisation founded by the author in 2013.

All sales help fund the fight against the global human trafficking crisis. Additional contributions make a real difference and are always welcome at sistersforsale.com.

MOUNTAINS BEYOND MOUNTAINS

PART FOUR OF THE INCREDIBLE
TRUE STORY BEHIND THE ACCLAIMED
'SISTERS FOR SALE' DOCUMENTARY

LIST OF CHARACTERS

There were many people involved in this story – and while this list might appear intimidating, it's not nearly as confusing as it seems, I promise. If you do get lost, you can always come back here.

At the centre of the story is a group of ten teenage Hmong girls from the town of Sapa, in the mountains of northern Vietnam:

– May (a bright, fearless girl who had been trafficked into "marriage" and motherhood in Shandong province, China),
– Pang (a moody girl who had been trafficked into "marriage" and motherhood in Guangdong province, China),
– Vu (a survivor of human trafficking who had escaped a forced "marriage" in China),
– Chan (a very intelligent girl, who had now become my closest Hmong friend in Sapa),
– Zao (May's cousin and closest friend, who had behaved very strangely and suspiciously during my earlier investigations),
– Chu (a sweet, serious girl, now studying in the provincial

capital, Lao Cai),

    – Little Chu (a cheerful girl, now married in Sapa),

    – Ha (May's cousin),

    – Cho (May's elder sister, who had first been trafficked and then returned to China voluntarily under suspicious circumstances),

    – Shu (a survivor of human trafficking who had escaped a Chinese brothel).

Other members of the Sapa Hmong community, some of whom are yet to be introduced, are listed here alphabetically:

    – Bao (Pang's mother, a widow),

    – Big Zao (Vu's aunt, also a survivor of human trafficking),

    – Dinh (May's eldest sister, now married with children),

    – Dung and Lung (May's mother and father, respectively),

    – Gom (another friend of May and Pang's, one of Sapa's "bad girls"),

    – Khu (another survivor of human trafficking, one of Sapa's "bad girls"),

    – Ling (another survivor of human trafficking),

    – Lucky Charm (a young Hmong man),

    – Ny (Gom's sister, one of Sapa's "bad girls"),

    – Sung (Chan's partner),

    – Zy (another friend of May and Pang's, a notorious gossip, and one of Sapa's "bad girls").

Others who play a role in the story, listed alphabetically:

    – Aamir (a Kashmiri who had assisted my search for May in China),

    – Aart (a retired Dutch psychiatrist living in Sapa),

    – Anemi (a Swiss journalist based in Hanoi),

    – Charlie (a Texan who had assisted my search for May in China),

    – Georges (the French founder of Alliance Anti-Trafic,

based in Ho Chi Minh City),

– Marinho (a European cameraperson who had accompanied my search in Vietnam and China),

– May's middlemen (a middle-aged Chinese Hmong couple; the wife had been arrested during my time in China, while the husband remained at large),

– Michael (the Australian founder of Blue Dragon Children's Foundation, based in Hanoi),

– Qiuda (a Chinese friend who had assisted my search for May and Pang in China),

– Sebastien (a Frenchman whom May had a romantic interest in),

– 'X' (an anonymous rescue worker for Blue Dragon Children's Foundation).

I'LL TAKE YOU THERE

9th October 2014

Bao was one of the loveliest, most kind-hearted people I knew.

A middle-aged woman with sun-browned skin and a silver tooth gleaming in her smile, Bao had large liquid eyes that shone with love and trust. Her small, seemingly delicate figure remained unbent, despite having endured years of sorrow and a lifetime of unrelenting physical hardship.

Bao lived in a village between the mountains outside the town of Sapa, in the rugged borderlands of northern Vietnam. I'd always looked forward to seeing her – but not this time.

I'd first met Bao earlier that year while I'd been investigating the disappearance of her daughter, Pang. Pang was a friend of mine who had been kidnapped from Sapa.

That first meeting with Bao had been an emotional one, as she spoke of the years of heartbreak and uncertainty that had followed the sudden loss of her daughter. The local police had shown no interest in Pang's case and Bao had very few resources of her own. A widow who didn't know the world beyond Sapa, she'd felt helpless and very much alone.

After our meeting – against all odds – I'd found Pang

where she was being held captive a thousand kilometres away in a distant region of China. It was the first time that any of Pang's friends had seen her in over three years, and Pang had been overjoyed to have that all-too-brief contact with the world she'd once known.

I'd returned to Sapa with photographs of Pang to show Bao. While no photographs could ever replace a stolen child, I'd believed that Pang herself would soon follow.

I'd helped plan Pang's rescue – but in her desperation to escape, Pang had run away and crossed the immensity of China alone, attempting to reach Sapa by herself. She'd very nearly succeeded, too, having come within a stone's throw of the Vietnamese border before vanishing completely.

The last time I spoke to Pang, she was lost somewhere in the mountainous borderlands, in the hands of another suspected human trafficker. I could hear the confusion in her voice.

"I really, really don't want to stay here, so I coming back," she'd told me. "But... I don't know where is here."

And then she disappeared.

For three days, I'd been trying to call Pang – but I hadn't heard anything from her, nor had anyone else. Her phone still rang, and my heart sank a little further with the distant buzz of each unanswered ring.

After years of captivity and a fleeting moment of freedom, Pang had almost certainly been trafficked again. The final photograph I had of Pang in China now seemed destined to be printed on her missing-person poster.

Bao knew nothing about her daughter's escape. She believed Pang was still captive but otherwise safe with the man who'd bought her, a thousand kilometres away. I hated to be the person to break Bao's heart all over again with the news that her daughter had leaped from the proverbial frying pan into the fire – but Bao deserved to know the truth.

After making the half-hour motorbike ride from Sapa, I was told that Bao was at a wedding somewhere in the centre of the village. With a gnarled, indigo-stained finger, a local woman pointed out the path for me.

The idea of tearing Bao away from a wedding celebration only to smash her world to pieces made me feel worse than I did already. I parked my motorbike and, with a heavy heart, began following the path.

It was a rough dirt track littered with fallen leaves and lined with thick, towering stands of bamboo that creaked and swayed in the breeze moving overhead. Flickering shadows and sudden lashes of glaring sunlight swam through the dust around me. Having taken only a few steps along the path, I was startled to see Bao come rushing headlong towards me from the opposite direction.

With her thick black hair tied up beneath a brightly-coloured scarf, a large woven basket strapped to her back, and her flushed and sweating face framed by silver hoop earrings, Bao was in a state of great excitement – but I didn't speak her language, and couldn't understand what she was saying.

A cluster of local women in their dark traditional costumes quickly gathered around us, but nobody spoke enough English to tell me what was happening. Bao was chattering excitedly on her phone, and passed it to me. The voice on the other end was a familiar one that I hadn't expected to hear again.

It was Pang.

Pang had just called to tell her mother she was somewhere on the border, but didn't know where. She believed she was in a region three hours' journey by motorbike from Sapa and had asked Bao to come and find her – but Bao didn't have a motorbike, she couldn't ride, and she'd never travelled so far in her life.

Pang knew I was in Sapa, and knew that I could help. She'd told her mother to find me.

Bao wasn't even sure how she'd get to Sapa, much less find me there – but by chance, that was the moment I'd arrived in her village. Just as I'd come looking for Bao to bring her terrible news, she'd come looking for me to bring me far better news.

It was a deeply surreal moment as Bao stood there looking at me, her large dark eyes shining with anxious excitement, a rapid series of conflicting emotions struggling for possession of her face. I saw flashes of her smile trying to break through, as if she was awaiting my permission to feel the sudden surge of hope welling up inside her. I don't know what mixture of emotions registered on my own face.

"I've got a bike," I said, in gestures as much as words. "Let's go."

In that moment, it felt like a perfect ending to Pang's story – but of course, real life is never quite perfect, and Pang's story was still far from its end.

TELL IT LIKE IT IS

I've always been a great believer in the power of storytelling.

I'm fascinated by the stories we tell each other and the way they alter our realities. They shape our moral sense, motivations, and expectations, and so change the very essence of our lives. The power of stories can bring us closer or convince us to slaughter each other.

Stories stand at the very heart of our culture – and every culture – in every sphere from history to politics, religion, law, philosophy, psychology, commerce, art, and entertainment. They determine our roles in society and how we interact with one another.

In the West, there is one great story above all others that we particularly love to tell each other. This story centres on an individual who perseveres against all odds, overcomes all obstacles, and ultimately succeeds in achieving what they most desire. While the individual changes from one story to the next, the story remains fundamentally the same.

As this one great story approaches its end, its characters move forward with determination, resolute in their purpose. Its various threads converge and become interwoven. The story wraps up neatly, ends happily, and leaves each of us with renewed faith in the inherent justice of the world.

Each time you hear it, this story tells you – the reader, the watcher, the listener – that you can do anything you want, if only you want it badly enough.

The various protagonists of this story, and anyone who might resemble them, become our cultural heroes. Even royalty and those who have never known anything but unimaginable privilege twist their stories to fit this pattern.

As the present recedes into the past, we keep it alive – collectively and individually – in the form of stories. Even these stories, the true stories of our own lives, are so very often sculpted to fit the pattern of our one great story. While the objective facts remain unchanged, we can select and skew them in any number of ways, and interpret reality however we please.

If you achieve any great personal success, it's almost obligatory to reveal the challenges you've faced to show how you, too, persevered and overcame the odds stacked against you. How you, too, believed as everyone else doubted; how success came to you because you earned it. You'll offer your personal testimony as further proof that this one great story at the heart of our culture represents an eternal, undeniable truth.

...Does it, though?

The pattern of this one great story is ingrained within each of us. Each new generation of storytellers – and we are all storytellers – has repeated this pattern, often without realising that there are other stories and other ways of telling them.

Even those who recognise the pattern still tend to follow it, because this one great story is the story that we as audiences most want to hear. It gives us all a sense of latent power and makes us feel better about the world we live in. It gives us hope and comfort, keeps us believing in ourselves, and motivates us through life.

It's a beautiful story. On some level, however, most of us are aware that our one great story is merely a myth, an enticing deception. It's a mirage, a mermaid's song. It has never reflected the true nature of reality – and, in fact, stands in direct contradiction to the vast majority of our lived experience.

We won't all achieve what we want in life, and we won't all die happy and successful. Many of us will fail, and keep failing, and die failures, no matter how hard we try. These are the facts, but they don't make beautiful stories.

We find ourselves caught in a glaring contradiction between the stark realities of our lives and the one great myth we want so desperately to believe in. While other cultures teach acceptance of suffering and death, Western religions try to overcome this contradiction by extending our one great myth beyond death and perceptible reality.

If you stand firm and keep believing, they tell us – no matter how challenging your life might be, and regardless of any evidence to the contrary – then you will receive a glorious reward at the end of your story. As countless saints and martyrs show us, the more suffering you endure, the greater your story and glory will ultimately be.

While it's an enticing thing to believe, many of us have become too sceptical for these all-too-perfect promises. No matter what we do, many of our own life experiences will never conform to the pattern of our one great myth. Does that make our experiences any less valid, any less true?

Because there's a darker, more destructive side to our one great myth. The myth at the heart of our culture tells you – every day, in countless forms – that any failure is your own personal failure. If you fail, then you and your story will be left to fall like garbage beside the glorious path of Western civilisation. We choose to blind ourselves to the possibility of failure, and these stories remain untold.

Even those of us with no religious beliefs suffer crises of faith in our one great myth – but the myth refuses to tolerate our doubt. According to the myth and the infinitude of stories it spawns, those who doubt are condemned to mediocrity or failure. The doubters are supporting characters included as examples of what not to do, whose fates stand in stark contrast to the hero's glorious triumph – unless, of course, doubt is woven into the story as yet another obstacle to be overcome on the path to success, further strengthening the myth.

And so the myth leads us back to itself and, even during times of prolonged and hopeless failure, we cling desperately to our belief in it. We imagine future successes, telling ourselves that our stories aren't yet over and that any failures are only temporary setbacks – or else we go back and reframe our stories to convince ourselves that we have in fact already succeeded in some unforeseen way.

After heartbreak, we comfort ourselves with romantic films and the timeless love they promise. After bankruptcy, we highlight the lessons we've learned and envisage our return to greater wealth. After the death of a loved one, we focus on their legacy and the life that still goes on.

When we can find no way to twist our stories to fit the myth then they become a source of shame to us, and we bury them.

We're a society in denial of even the most basic facts of reality. Perhaps this is why it is so difficult for us to imagine environmental collapse, even as it unfolds around us – but calling a thing by another name doesn't change its fundamental nature. When our culture's one great story centres around escaping reality, how does our denial alter our reality?

The story that follows has been a very difficult one for me to share. It has taken me years to find a way to tell it without betraying the very essence of the story itself.

It's a story of my kidnapped friends May and Pang, and of my attempts to help them. At first glance, through Western eyes, it seems to be a story of failure, because it doesn't fit the pattern of our one great myth. On closer inspection, however, it's not immediately obvious what it was that failed.

Up to this point, my own part in the story has conformed almost perfectly to our one great myth. I'd persevered against incredible odds, held fast to my beliefs while those around me doubted, and achieved my seemingly-impossible goal of finding both May and Pang at opposite ends of China.

It would have been easy to tell the rest of the story in the same way, and I very nearly did. It wasn't a matter of temptation, to make myself seem more heroic than I really am; it was simply a matter of unquestioned cultural habit. That's just how we tell stories.

It would have been a wonderful story, too, and it would have all been true – but it wouldn't have been the whole truth. Far from it.

Finding May and Pang in China wasn't the end of the story: not even close. By pretending it was, by skipping through what came afterwards in a giddy rush to reach a neat and satisfying conclusion, I would have had to deny the dips and swerves of the most extreme emotional rollercoaster of my life, and set aside some vital truths that are so rarely shared.

No doubt you would have preferred this story to have ended happily with May and Pang returning home immediately after I found them in China. So would I: but that's not how it happened.

This is where the river reaches the delta, where the linear becomes fractal and the way ahead is no longer clear. This is where the rushing stream loses itself in myriad murky channels, where sweet waters turn salty and surge back against themselves. In a sense, this is where the story truly begins. Where it ends, exactly, is more difficult to say.

May and Pang came from another culture, with another great story that was central to their lives. That story took a very different form, and might best be summarised as: *Men lead, and women follow*. It's a very simple story, simple enough to have penetrated every fibre of their beings, though it was to make their lives anything but simple.

Perhaps that's why our shared story came apart: we tried to combine two mutually-exclusive cultural narratives. Is there any real hope for a woman from May and Pang's culture to get what she truly wants, if she is not permitted to play anything more than a supporting role in her own life?

Beyond this point in the story, rather than converging, the various threads quickly unravel. Rather than forging ahead with unshakeable determination, the central characters become lost and confused. Rather than reinforcing your faith in the inherent justice of the world, this story may very well do just the opposite. It's not an easy story, but it's an important one, and the message it holds concerns us all.

So here it is, as challenging as it might be. It is indeed a story of failure – but not our failure. May, Pang, and I each succeeded in getting what we wanted, more or less.

Ultimately, it was our stories – our cultures – that failed us.

MOUNTAINS

8th July 2014

On 8th July 2014, after a thirty-three hour journey, I stepped off the train in New Delhi, India.

It had been four years since I'd met my Hmong friends May and Pang in their hometown of Sapa, in the mountains of northern Vietnam... Three years since both girls had been kidnapped in separate incidents and sold across the border into China... Two years since my own life had fallen apart, and – without having the means to do so – I'd decided to return to Asia to search for May and Pang... Almost a year since I'd given up my home and full-time job in the Canadian Rockies to begin that search... And six months, to the day, since I'd received news of May's first contact from China.

Those six months had been the most relentlessly intense six months of my life. After struggling to uncover the truth of May and Pang's mysterious disappearances in Sapa, I'd followed a trail of crumbs to distant parts of China where each girl had been forced into so-called "marriage" and motherhood.

May and Pang's connections to the outside world were so tenuous that the success of my search had hinged on the tiniest of details – a string of digits, a pair of incomprehensible syllables, a little phone credit, and a few chance encounters.

Incredibly, after a series of rushed and risky decisions, I'd located Pang in Dongguan – part of the largest urban conglomeration on the planet, home to sixty million people. Of the two girls, Pang had been the easier to find by far.

I'd come halfway around the world and given everything I could in search of May. I'd always hoped but never realistically expected to find her. I'd anticipated dead ends, expulsion, perhaps imprisonment or something worse – but somehow, after forty days in China, I had actually succeeded in meeting with May in Shandong province, far to the north. Shandong lay halfway between China's capital, Beijing, and its largest city, Shanghai – a city whose name is synonymous with kidnapping.

My search had been complicated by the betrayal, sabotage, and attempted blackmail perpetrated by Marinho, the European cameraperson who'd been helping me film May and Pang's stories to raise awareness of human trafficking.

In finding May, I'd believed that the hardest part of my journey was behind me – but I'd never been more wrong in my life. Some peaks appear deceptively close, only to reveal themselves to the climber as a series of false summits.

May was caught in a horrifying situation, with her life controlled by three older men: her highly unpredictable and occasionally violent "husband" in China, her callous and domineering father in Vietnam, and her sister Cho's husband who lived in the Chinese borderlands and had very unexpectedly been pulling strings behind the scenes.

By finding May and Pang in China, I'd given each girl a dilemma no mother should ever have to face: the heartbreaking choice between her baby girl and her own freedom.

After wrestling with her decision for five weeks, May had gradually hardened in her resolve to leave her child in China and return home alone to Vietnam. She'd asked to be rescued in early August, immediately after her daughter's first birthday.

While Pang seemed less certain, she'd also asked to be

rescued at the same time, so that she and May could return to Vietnam together.

I'd spent the year working closely with Michael Brosowski, founder of the Hanoi-based Blue Dragon Children's Foundation, which rescues trafficked girls from China.

The plan had been simple enough: if I could find May and Pang in China, and if they chose to come home, then Blue Dragon would rescue them. All I had to do was step away and call the cavalry.

I felt fortunate to have survived China and, after six long months, I desperately needed to rest and rebalance – but the situation had now spiralled out of control.

A Chinese act of territorial aggression in the South China Sea had sparked waves of deadly riots across Vietnam. Hundreds of foreign-owned factories were damaged or destroyed, at least twenty-one people were killed, and industrial parks were left looking like war zones. Protests against both China's aggression and the Vietnamese reaction had erupted around the globe.

It was the closest the two countries had come to war in decades, and security in China was extraordinarily high. May was two and a half thousand kilometres from Vietnam – further than any rescue Blue Dragon had yet attempted – and under those circumstances, it was simply too risky for them to operate so deep within China.

I'd reluctantly realised that the initial phase of May's rescue – getting her away from her "husband" and bringing her south to the borderlands – would be up to me. From there, Blue Dragon would arrange her return across the border itself, and provide any support she needed in Vietnam.

I'd never imagined I'd be personally involved in rescuing May, and the very idea terrified me. I'd just survived the most intense experience of my life, and now I was to go back to China to do something ten times more dangerous. I wasn't ready for it, but there was nobody else. Whatever happened next was to be the best or worst news of the entire project – and possibly our lives.

A few days earlier – at the beginning of July – I'd gone to Mamallapuram, a quiet beach town in southern India, to take my first break from the project all year. I'd thought of it as a time to make plans and mentally prepare myself for May's rescue, which was scheduled for the following month. Almost immediately, however, I'd received some startling news that had sent me straight back to work.

With her spirits soaring in anticipation of her return home to Vietnam, May had become cocky, and she was terrible at keeping secrets. May's "husband" knew that I'd found her in China – he'd seen me there. He didn't have to guess our next move: in the course of an argument, May had brazenly flaunted her intention to return home.

Not only did May's "husband" stand to lose the teenage "wife" he'd purchased, but if he was caught with a trafficked girl, he also risked prison time. Now it seemed he was planning to wash his hands of May by selling her again – and this time, her fate could be far worse than forced "marriage". There was a very real danger that May would be sold into prostitution, surrogacy, or even for her organs.

With the great demand for women in China, not only would May's "husband" rid himself of a dangerous liability, but he could benefit by her sale. He'd told May he was sending her to another city, supposedly for work. May didn't know where she was being sent, or when, but it seemed imminent.

I'd spent a huge amount of time, money, and energy – and risked my life – to find May in China. If she was sent away, I'd have to start again from scratch – and if we lost contact with her, there was nothing we could do to help her. We might never hear from her again.

After ten long months on the road together, Marinho and I had parted ways just two days earlier in southern India. I'd come rushing north to Delhi to arrange a visa and a flight back across the Himalayas: there was no time to lose. We had to get May away from her "husband" before he got rid of her – but things started going wrong almost from the moment I stepped off the train.

I thought I'd seen how complex and challenging the world of human trafficking could be, but my journey had only just begun. The answers to so many of my questions – about May, the men who'd sold her, the men who controlled her, and the mysterious insider who had betrayed her in Sapa – still lay ahead.

I'M YOUR PUPPET

It was my seventh trip to Delhi, and I hadn't particularly enjoyed any of them.

I associated Delhi – the second-largest city in the world, a vast and teeming hive of twenty-five million people – with gridlocked traffic, grinding poverty, and the pervasive stench of human waste. It was the kind of place you visit out of necessity, not for pleasure. I'd spent over three weeks there in 2011, when I'd been swindled by a local secondhand car dealer.

Delhi (of which India's capital, New Delhi, was only a part) didn't seem to have improved in my absence. The sticky heat of the monsoon didn't make it any more pleasant, nor did the disturbing news I received upon my arrival.

During my time in China, May, Pang, and I had all been in regular phone contact. May, in particular, was a highly sociable person who had been held in isolation for far too long. She'd been thrilled to be able to call me, and we'd spent many hours speaking together in secret.

Since my departure from China four weeks earlier, I'd had much less contact with May and Pang, who were no longer able to call me directly. When I could, I'd call both girls via the Internet, but the connections I'd found in Nepal and India were often very poor quality and wouldn't even support a phonecall. Even when I could find a reliable Internet connection, it had been difficult to reach May – her number was often inaccessible, and I could no longer add credit to her account so that she could reliably receive my calls.

Before I'd left China, May had asked me to put her in contact with Sebastien, a French friend she'd met in Sapa four years earlier – and I had, though I'd had mixed feelings about doing so.

Sebastien knew May personally, had a reasonable understanding of her current situation, and could now call her more easily than I could. To some degree, he'd now stepped into the gap left by my departure from China.

If May told him anything of particular interest, Sebastien would pass that information to me, which was much appreciated – but he was a strange ally. I was concerned about the connection between May and Sebastien, and the things they spoke about.

When they'd met in Sapa, May had fallen head over heels for Sebastien, despite the fact that she'd been a child and he was almost twice her age. Even now, four years later, May evidently saw Sebastien as her ideal partner, and was overjoyed at the thought of meeting him again. Sebastien seemed to have encouraged May's feelings with his carelessly over-affectionate behaviour.

I believe Sebastien's heart was in the right place, but he still spoke thoughtlessly to May and their conversations were rife with misunderstandings. He didn't seem to fully grasp the gravity of May's situation or the pressure she was now under, and May held him in such high regard that she obsessed over every word he said.

During my time in China, I'd been gradually talking May through her myriad fears and concerns about returning home to Vietnam. While many of those fears were irrational, the fact that they were causing May distress meant they deserved to be taken seriously.

Rather than talking May through her fears, Sebastien seemed to respond with a casual, unthinking sympathy that only seemed to validate and magnify them. At times, he'd further added to May's distress by creating new and irrelevant concerns for her.

Once, for example, Sebastien had offered to take May travelling after her return home to Vietnam, and had told her she'd need a passport. May had called me immediately afterwards, anxious that she didn't have a passport and didn't know how to get one. At a time when May was wrestling with major life decisions that would forever alter lives in both Vietnam and China, the last thing she needed to be worrying about was a hypothetical passport application that wouldn't happen for months, if at all.

While these incidents were frustrating, I'd been able to talk May through them, and I felt that Sebastien's help still outweighed any incidental harm.

By the time I arrived in Delhi, I'd been trying and failing to call May for two weeks or more. It was Sebastien who had told me, five days earlier, that May's "husband" was sending her away. Under the impression it would happen "pretty quickly", he told me there was no time to be wasted and that May had to escape before she was sent away. I agreed with his assessment, as did both Michael and X, Blue Dragon's anonymous rescue worker.

I wanted to speak to May directly, to get as much information as I could, and to discuss rescheduling her rescue. We no longer seemed to have the luxury of waiting another month.

I knew it would be a difficult conversation. May's daughter was sickly and had often been hospitalised, and May had wanted to wait until August in the hope that her daughter would grow stronger. That hadn't happened: Sebastien had told me May's daughter had recently been in hospital for another ten days, so I knew May would be reluctant to leave early.

I wanted to explain to May that if she was sent away, we'd lose her location and might not be able to help her at all – and if she was resold, her situation could become unimaginably worse.

On arrival in Delhi, I checked into a guesthouse, logged onto the wifi, and tried to call May – but I couldn't reach her.

Next I tried Pang, and got through. Pang had spoken to May four or five days earlier and had been trying to call her every day since then, but May was uncontactable, which was worrying.

Pang's next piece of news, however, was far more disturbing. For the past six weeks, May had been committed to returning home in early August. Michael and I had been building our plans around that decision, and I hadn't seen any indication that May had been wavering or reconsidering.

Now, however, Pang said May had changed her mind and wanted to stay in China for another seven and a half months, until after the Lunar New Year in February. Just when it had become most urgent for May to get away from her "husband", she didn't want to leave.

I was blindsided. What was the reason for May's change of heart?

My immediate thought was that May had been shaken by her daughter's hospitalisation, and realised she wasn't yet ready to leave her baby girl – but that wasn't the reason at all.

Sebastien had told May he was going to visit her in China. Perhaps it was a joke – Sebastien later claimed it was a miscommunication – but May had taken it seriously. She'd decided to stay in China to wait for him, and wanted to be rescued afterwards.

I could hardly believe it. It was an absurd and incredibly dangerous idea which showed just how complacent May had become in China, and how careless Sebastien could be.

I'd seen how the flutterings of May's teenage heart had wrought huge and permanent changes in the lives of those around her. May's seemingly personal decisions had impacted a growing circle of people in Vietnam and China – and I'd now become one of those people. May was allowing an impractical, misguided desire to see Sebastien to override her very real and urgent need for safety.

Until now, I'd moved forward with a clear, consistent sense of purpose on my journey to find May and give her whatever help she needed. Suddenly, though, I felt like a puppet on a string being jerked around by a distracted child.

I'd been determined to do everything I could to find and help my friends – but only now did I realise how vague the second part of that mission could become. What kind of help did they want? How long would it be until they knew for certain? Was I even in a position to offer that help? I didn't know.

Sebastien had no plans to visit May in China, and it was foolish of him to have ever suggested it. We had more than enough trouble from May's "husband" and father without having to worry about this.

"I think there is some confusion about what I said," Sebastien told me. "I don't have plans to go visit her in China and ruin any chance of escape for her. I said if it was to take longer for her to leave, I would go and visit her, but I don't have any immediate plans to go to China."

I asked Sebastien to call May back and clear up the misunderstanding, but he said he'd broken his phone. Even if he could call her, I wasn't sure he could be trusted to clearly convey that message.

I had to talk to May as soon as possible – but I still couldn't reach her. Like a puppet, I was left hanging on the line.

YOU CAN'T ALWAYS GET
WHAT YOU WANT

Delhi's Chinese embassy was located in an unusually leafy and spacious district with sandbagged machine-gun nests in the nearby subway station.

For both of my previous visits to China, I'd applied for and received my visa at the Chinese embassy in Hanoi. Over the past decade of living and travelling around the world, theirs was one of the most complex visa application processes I'd been through.

It was part family tree, part job application, and part travel plan. Among other things, you were required to share the details of all immediate family members; your occupational, educational, and health information; an exhaustive itinerary including all hotel names and addresses; plus you had to tell them who would be paying for your journey. On both occasions, after providing all the requested information, the staff had still sent me away for further documentation before finally granting me a visa.

At the embassy in Delhi, I discovered that the process was even more convoluted. This time, to receive a thirty-day visa, I also had to supply proof of thirty days' worth of confirmed hotel reservations, proof of return flights, a diplomatic note from my embassy, and proof of funds or a letter from my employer – none of which gave any guarantee of actually receiving a visa.

I realised it would be far quicker and easier to fly into Hong Kong and arrange my visa there, so that's what I decided to do. That would also give me a chance to reconnoitre the current security situation on the bus route north to Shandong province.

The question was the timing. Michael, X, Sebastien, and I all agreed it would be best if May got away from her "husband" as quickly as possible – but it wasn't our decision. The decision was May's, and only she could make it.

While I'd been in China, and May and Pang had each faced the incredibly painful dilemma between her child and her own freedom, I'd been careful not to influence them with my own opinions. Instead, I'd helped them to examine their options and had answered their questions as honestly and as fairly as I could.

There were two reasons for this approach.

Firstly, May and Pang had spent years being coerced and manipulated by the people around them. I'd come to Asia to offer them any freedom I could, and it would have been deeply hypocritical of me to pressure their decisions in any way.

While I'd heard May and Pang's stories in more detail than anyone, I could never know how it felt to have lived their experiences. What might have seemed like the best option from my perspective wasn't necessarily what May and Pang would have chosen for themselves.

My second reason for not influencing May and Pang's decisions was a more selfish one. If I pressured either girl into a choice she later regretted, or if I helped make their situations worse, I'd never forgive myself.

Now, although I had my own opinion about the timing of May's rescue, my approach was the same: it had to be. If I pressured May into leaving her child before she was ready to do so, if she returned to Vietnam only to regret the decision I'd pushed her into, it would be disastrous for both of us.

Although I didn't enjoy the feeling of being a puppet at the beck and call of May's caprices, it was better than the alternative.

May and Pang's traffickers hadn't merely taken away the girls' freedom: they'd taken away any hope of May and Pang ever living normal lives, and left them with only hard, heartbreaking options.

These teenage girls, who had never received the benefits of even the most rudimentary formal education, had been forced to reduce a phenomenally complex problem to a binary "yes" or "no", a "stay" or "go" – and now May needed to select a date to turn her world upside-down.

What made it especially difficult was that May wasn't used to making her own decisions. During her three years in China, she'd barely been allowed to make any decisions at all, and any major life decisions had always been made by the men who dominated her life.

When asked what she wanted, May's immediate habitual response was to ask herself what her father and "husband" would want her to do. Even when she knew that their decisions were actively harming her, she'd often still submit herself to them. This deep-rooted compulsion to comply with the demands of the men in their lives was part of the reason why Hmong girls were so easy to traffic in the first place.

I believed that May had every right to determine her own future – and while that concept excited her, she wasn't accustomed to thinking in those terms. It could take a great deal of time and patience to understand what May actually wanted for herself.

I finally succeeded in reaching May on the phone. She flatly denied Pang's story about having changed her mind and wanting to remain longer in China for the sake of Sebastien.

May said she didn't want to postpone her rescue – but she wasn't ready to leave her daughter just yet, either. She told me the same thing she'd been telling me for months: that she wanted to be rescued in early August, immediately after her daughter's first birthday.

While I wasn't convinced that May's decision to keep waiting was the best one, I accepted it – and, in some ways, that decision worked well for me personally.

May could fall pregnant or be sent away at any time. I knew I'd be worried about her until she was safe at home – but I also knew I wasn't yet ready for the challenges ahead. My long journey had taken its toll on me, and I needed time to recover my strength and balance.

Before my return to Asia, I'd been working in the Canadian Rockies, sometimes for over a hundred hours per week – but even then, there had still been times I could clock off and forget about work. Now, my work had become all-consuming, and there was no getting away from it: I'd barely clocked off since coming back to Asia ten months earlier.

I booked a ticket to fly to Hong Kong on 5th August, which gave me three and a half weeks to relax in India beforehand. If we were lucky, the tensions between Vietnam and China would ease in that time, and security in China might also relax – but August lay in wait with a few surprises of its own.

KISS OF LIFE

Over the past ten months, I'd been sharing the details of my work via a blog on 'The Human, Earth Project' website.

For the safety of everyone involved, I'd become more secretive during my investigation and search in Vietnam and China. Many people connected to Sapa were now aware of my work, and there was a chance that any information I shared publicly would reach the traffickers.

(While that might have seemed overly cautious, I later learned that at least one trafficker was indeed following my work – but that's another story.)

I'd only hinted at May and Pang's planned rescues on my blog – but I was never more tight-lipped than during my three-and-a-half-week break in July and early August. Besides a cryptic reference to "terribly cruel and predatory" human behaviour, I'd said almost nothing.

I now realise I've never really told anyone what happened during that time, not even my closest friends. What began as a personal story collided with and ultimately changed the project entirely – and it all began in a little restaurant in the chaotic heart of Delhi.

One afternoon, two things happened in that restaurant

that sent my life spinning off in a very unexpected direction.

By then, I'd spent a total of four years in Asia. During the first year, I'd suffered the long-term traveller's typical series of stomach illnesses, and on one occasion had been rushed to hospital with a severe intestinal infection.

After that first year, though, my gut had become incredibly robust. By my third year, I was drinking the local water in most places I went. I was glad to do so, because it reduced my dependency on plastic bottles and removed another barrier that stood between myself and the locals.

I'd never even considered drinking the local water in such a huge city as Delhi, though, and certainly not during a monsoon when the drains were overflowing with sewage.

Each time I sat down in that particular restaurant in Delhi, I'd be given an English menu card and a metal cup filled with local water. I didn't know where that water came from, or how trustworthy the pipes and tanks might be – so each time I sat down, I'd take the menu card and set the cup of water aside, untouched.

On this particular afternoon, two other foreigners wandered into that little restaurant – a dark-eyed Argentinian beauty named Isabela, and her red-headed Spanish friend. We fell into conversation and soon found ourselves sharing a table.

Four years earlier, when I'd first been living in Sapa, my Vietnamese friends and I had spent several long nights struggling to stay awake through the early morning hours to watch World Cup soccer matches.

Now the World Cup was on again, Argentina had reached the grand final, and Isabela and I were both looking for somewhere to watch the game later that evening. We decided to join forces, and were discussing possibilities.

I've never been good at focusing on more than one thing at a time. I must have been a little distracted by Isabela's crooked smile and the sense that she'd become interested in more than just soccer. At a certain point in the conversation she paused and gave me an odd look.

"Do you drink the local water here?" she asked.

I told her I didn't – then I looked down at the cup of water I'd just taken a long, unconscious swallow from. Having come that far I didn't see any reason to stop, so I finished the cup and took another.

Those two cups destroyed me. It took me weeks to recover and regain my strength, and my stomach has never been the same. That was the less impactful of the two things that happened in the restaurant that afternoon.

After her friend made a tactful exit, Isabela and I spent a long evening chatting and exploring the city. Jumping over a fence, Isabela tore a huge and rather embarrassing hole through the middle of her baggy fisherman's pants. She spent the rest of the evening with her scarf wrapped around her middle.

On finding a bar that advertised the World Cup final, we made ourselves comfortable and had a drink or two. Hilariously, the bar shut at midnight – just minutes before the game began – so Isabela and I had a last-minute scramble to find another screen before kickoff.

We ended up watching the game with the night staff in the lobby of a local hotel, then Isabela invited me back to her guesthouse to help with her scarf.

Isabela was lovely, and we had a wonderful time together – but I only had a few weeks of freedom and certainly wasn't going to spend them in Delhi. For years I'd wanted to visit Kashmir and Ladakh, high amongst the Himalayas on India's ragged northern edge. It was the right season, I had some time, and Isabela readily agreed to join me.

Isabela and I travelled north along some of the world's highest and wildest unpaved roads into a barren, jagged land of upheaval and erosion, where the phenomenal power of nature was written in the loops and whorls of the tortured rock. Vast glaciers huddled between towering walls of broken stone, and silvery ribbons of water slid and tumbled down the sides of misty valleys into broad, sullen brown rivers. Dusty trucks and buses crawled like tiny stubborn beetles through a hostile, seemingly endless maze of mountains.

In a world away from the world, we encountered the life that lingered in the crevices: green oases filled with humble flat-roofed buildings and joyful prayer flags. Hulking fortress-like monasteries stood guard over communities of black-haired mountain folk with centuries of tears and laughter etched into their wind-pinched faces.

In Leh, Isabela and I rented a motorbike. We rode out amongst the mountains and hiked to temples on high serrated ridges where gleaming golden Buddhas smiled knowingly down upon us. I would have loved to explore further, but my time was rapidly ticking away.

After two weeks in the mountains, Isabela and I reached Kashmir's summer capital, Srinagar. I have photographs of the two of us nestled together there in a gondola on Dal Lake. I don't know what Isabela was feeling or what she might have been hoping for – we never had that conversation, and never spoke those words – but in those photos we're glowing like a couple on the very cusp of love, and I know that I felt happier than I had in a long time.

It had been two years since my separation from Dominique. I never thought I'd meet anyone who could make me feel that way again, but there was something special about Isabela.

Then, literally overnight, it all came apart. Some love stories are epics, some are only fleeting, and others are cut tragically short.

On the night bus from Leh to Srinagar, I remember catching a terrifying, vertiginous glimpse of a steep rocky slope plunging thousands of metres into the inky darkness below. Our bus was inching along the very edge, and I couldn't help but wonder what might happen to us if we tumbled over.

I soon found out.

KASHMIR

Cupped in the Vale of Kashmir and surrounded by water, its skyline broken by the spires of mosques, Srinagar is a city of over a million people. Isabela and I spent five days there, in a cute little guesthouse on the shore of Dal Lake. Having long since stitched her pants, Isabela wore her scarf over her head as a sign of modesty and respect for local customs.

Isabela and I walked and talked, exploring each other's minds as we explored the streets and markets of Srinagar. We were befriended by a local man who invited us for a magnificent luncheon at his family home, and to his sister's wedding. It was a beautiful time.

There was just one thing in Srinagar that made me feel uncomfortable: the owner of our guesthouse had a middle-aged brother who often hung around pestering us. From the moment we'd met I sensed something incredibly slimy about him, and I couldn't understand how Isabela didn't notice it too.

My embarrassment at having spent my time with Isabela going back and forth between the bedroom and the bathroom had been somewhat lessened by the fact that Isabela was also having trouble with her stomach. When the brother heard her mention it, he offered his help in the form of a complimentary massage.

I told Isabela I didn't think the man was trustworthy, and didn't think it was a good idea. Ultimately, though, the decision was Isabela's, and she decided to take the chance. She hoped to learn something about local healing or massage, and thought the fact that the man had a wife and children would somehow guarantee his good behaviour.

Isabela's approach to travel was very similar to mine. She loved to connect with the locals and experience as much of their culture as she could. Unfortunately, the fact that she was a woman made that more difficult and dangerous for her.

For Isabela, trusting this man seemed to have become a point of pride. She took pride in being a tough Latina who could handle herself around sexually aggressive men, and wasn't at all worried about this smiling middle-aged family man. She felt I was being overly suspicious and wanted to prove me wrong, to show me that he wasn't really a creep – but sadly, she was mistaken.

On what would become our final evening in Srinagar, the locals were celebrating Eid al-Fitr to mark the end of Ramadan. The owner of our guesthouse also owned a second guesthouse a few minutes' walk further around the edge of the lake. The occupants of both guesthouses had been invited there at sunset for a celebratory feast with the owner's extended family.

Isabela and I had spent a long, lazy afternoon in bed, and had both eventually fallen asleep. It was the last truly restful sleep I was to have for a long time.

Isabela woke before I did and, not wanting to disturb me, had gone outside to work on a macramé necklace in the last of the afternoon light. The owner's brother had found her there, and had again offered to massage her stomach.

Isabela thought it was a good idea, and he led her to one of the empty rooms upstairs, where he told her to lie down on the bed. Dusk was falling but the brother didn't turn on any of the lights. While Isabela found that a little unsettling, she knew I was just downstairs so she could call out if anything went wrong.

It was growing dark by the time I awoke. When I saw Isabela was gone, I assumed she hadn't wanted to miss the beginning of the Eid al-Fitr celebrations and had gone ahead of me. I quickly dressed and left.

The celebrations had already begun, and the second guesthouse was a bustle of excitement. I was one of the last to arrive. The owner's family hurried me inside and before I knew it, I had my shoes off and was sitting cross-legged at one end of a crowded room while the women filled my plate.

Everyone else from our guesthouse was already there, but I couldn't see Isabela – and, more disturbingly, I couldn't see the owner's brother, though his wife and children were all present.

Whatever Isabela chose to believe about the owner's brother, I didn't trust him at all. I excused myself at the first opportunity and hurried back around the lake.

I was crossing a small bridge just before the guesthouse when I ran into the owner's brother coming the other way. I'd never concealed my dislike for him, so there had always been a certain distance between us – but now he grinned and greeted me warmly, calling me his brother. At that moment I knew something was terribly wrong, and that I'd come too late.

The guesthouse was deserted, and I found Isabela alone in our room. She was in a bad way. She took a shower and began sharing her story, though she was still struggling to make sense of it herself.

It had started as a massage, but by degrees the brother had turned it into something far more terrifying. He'd been confident and in full control of the situation, as if playing a game he'd mastered through regular repetition. The room had been dark, Isabela had felt trapped, and she hadn't known how to escape.

She now felt guilty and ashamed, as if she'd been responsible for what had happened. She seemed to think that the onus had been on her to stop the man: that until she'd drawn a clear line, he had the right to do whatever he pleased with her body. She blamed herself because she'd been too frightened to call out or tell him to stop.

I gave Isabela what support I could, but didn't really know what to do. I felt a helpless fury, and imagined that's how Marinho had felt after his partner had been assaulted in Europe.

My first instinct was to confront the brother and contact the police. Neither of us imagined for a moment that it was an isolated incident. It was clear that this man was abusing his position at the guesthouse to regularly assault women – and if we didn't act, others would be targeted.

Isabela understood that, and agreed with me – but it was her decision, and she didn't want to make a fuss. She'd been hurt, and the last thing she wanted was to become more deeply entangled with the source of her pain. She just wanted to get away, and didn't have the strength in that moment for anything more. She said she didn't want to cause any trouble for the man's wife and children.

My sense of justice was enraged but I understood and accepted Isabela's decision: ultimately, I wanted her to do whatever she felt was best. While it may seem defeatist, the sad fact is that Srinagar was an isolated, strongly patriarchal community, and I suspected that a police report would lead nowhere.

The owner's brother was there the next day as we were checking out. He stuck close to us, trying to read the situation, trying to see if we'd cause any trouble for him. Out of respect for Isabela, I didn't say anything, but I'm sure he must have realised I was seething with a barely-restrained anger for him.

Perhaps the most upsetting part was seeing both the perpetrator and victim united in their silent pretence that nothing had happened. The brother had taken what he'd wanted and left Isabela hurting – and now she'd only satisfied him further with the knowledge that he'd gotten away with it.

The brother was gloating, smirking – and, as we turned to

leave, he wanted to take my hand. I just couldn't pretend any longer. In a low voice only the three of us could hear, I told him to get the f*ck away from me.

Isabela gave me a sharp look, but the owner's brother just kept grinning at me. I very rarely believe in violence as the solution to any problem, but if Isabela hadn't been there, I would have happily broken every last one of those teeth.

THERE'S NO WAY OUT OF HERE

For the past two months – since I'd first met with May in China, and confirmed her decision to return home – Michael and I had been wrestling with an enormously complex, almost insoluble puzzle.

A broad range of difficulties and very real dangers were set against the backdrop of an ongoing political nightmare. We examined the problem from every possible angle, weighing one risk against another.

At the centre of it all was May – very alone, and very far from home in a country notorious for its mishandling of human trafficking, where the roads, rail lines, and access points were now being very closely monitored by the local authorities. How were we to bring her home?

One of my first questions had been whether a rescue was really necessary.

"As a victim of human trafficking, wouldn't the Chinese authorities have an obligation to assist May's return home?" I asked.

"The problem is proving it," Michael told me. "Police might be sympathetic... or not..."

This was terrain Blue Dragon knew better than anyone.

Over the past seven years, they'd rescued dozens of trafficked Vietnamese girls from China. These rescues had all been led by a single heroic figure – X – whom I'd had the honour of meeting in Hanoi three months earlier.

When bringing girls home from China, X liaised with the authorities on both sides of the border to ensure the handover was done legally. In China, he worked with certain contacts at the border, but he was usually on his own beyond the immediate border region.

Human trafficking cases can be very delicate and complex. Not only were the Chinese authorities notorious for their stifling bureaucracy and high levels of corruption, they seemed to have little understanding of human trafficking, especially in rural areas.

The result was a somewhat surreal situation in which, after a rescue, X would have to evade the Chinese authorities he didn't know and couldn't trust in order to reach those he did.

Pang had a Chinese identity card, which her "husband's" family had arranged via a corrupt police connection. If Pang could escape her "husband" and his family, she could use the card to travel freely in China.

May had also been given a Chinese identity card – but hers was an obvious fake and had long since expired. If she was caught by the police, anything at all could happen to her. With no valid identification and no proof of having been trafficked, it was very likely she'd be prosecuted as an illegal immigrant.

"Once you report to [the Chinese authorities]," Michael said, "the matter is totally in their hands, and there's nothing anyone can do."

When my trafficked friend Big Zao had approached the Chinese police for help to return home, two officers had driven her six hours to another city and simply left her there, without handing her over to the local authorities or giving her any paperwork to make her onward journey easier. I've heard stories of other survivors being imprisoned for months in squalid conditions, and even being re-trafficked, by the

Chinese authorities.

The previous year, the US State Department's Trafficking In Persons report had listed China among the world's worst countries when it came to fighting human trafficking. China holds the same position today, with victims very often being treated as criminals and the authorities themselves perpetrating widespread trafficking.

Michael advised that involving the Chinese authorities in May's rescue would be "extremely risky". May didn't want to involve the authorities, either – not for her own sake, but for fear of what might happen to her "husband" and daughter.

Even though he'd treated her badly and kept her locked up inside his house, May didn't want her "husband" to go to prison – she wanted to protect him. While she referred to him as a "crazy boy" and feared he might one day kill her, May's "husband" was also the father of her baby girl.

If May went home, her "husband" would be the only one left to take care of their daughter. She didn't want him punished: she just wanted to go home knowing her child was being looked after.

Sadly, it was unrealistic that May's "husband" would ever be punished for his crimes, especially in the absence of May's testimony. If the authorities became involved, they were far more likely to side with a Chinese national than an illegal alien, further reinforcing the power May's "husband" held over her.

With mounting tensions between China and Vietnam, Michael said that security in China was now "very high", and X had to be "extremely careful" in planning any rescue operations.

"Escape is extremely difficult at the moment," he told me. "It is very, very hard to get from China to Vietnam and vice versa."

When X had rescued my friend Vu from a forced marriage outside Nanjing, they'd spent several long, stressful days travelling through the backroads of China to avoid any scattered checkpoints. May would have to travel much further, under more challenging circumstances.

It would be an overland journey of two and a half thousand kilometres from May's current location back to the Vietnamese border. Checkpoints were a certainty, and the final approach to the border would be the most tightly-controlled section of all, with multiple military checkpoints even under ordinary circumstances.

One of the many things I appreciated about Michael's support was his honesty about Blue Dragon's limitations. He knew there were no certainties, and offered no promises or pretences.

Blue Dragon's team certainly wasn't afraid to take risks: in his Chinese rescues, X had taken more risks than I ever would. When rescuing girls forced into sex work, sometimes X even went so far as to pose as a client, and would enter a brothel himself to get a girl out.

I couldn't imagine what a hair-raising experience it must be to come face-to-face with the criminals who ran the brothels – and as X regularly rescued girls and risked being identified, I didn't want to imagine what might happen to him if he was caught.

Blue Dragon had been so consistently successful with their rescues because they'd learned how to effectively assess and manage risk, and because they weren't afraid to step back and reconsider when they realised the dangers were too great.

Under current circumstances, Blue Dragon was unable to operate beyond the immediate border region. Michael said that if the girls could reach the border, Blue Dragon would "likely" be able to help them cross back to Vietnam. Otherwise, until the tensions between Vietnam and China subsided, there was little more they could do.

THE LAST RESORT

Michael asked if May or Pang were in a position to escape their "husbands" by themselves, or what assistance they might need.

Of the two girls, Pang had far more freedom. She could escape by herself, and had a little money – but it was still a seven-hundred-kilometre overland journey to the nearest border crossing and, even with her Chinese identity card, I wasn't confident she could reach it alone. It would be better if someone could meet her in Dongguan or Guangzhou and accompany her home.

With no valid identification and little or no money of her own, May was in a far more difficult position. She was in a more remote area away from any transport hubs, an incredibly long way from the southern border. What's more, she'd already tried and failed to escape her "husband".

May would need help to escape, and she'd need it soon – and if Blue Dragon couldn't help now, I realised it would be up to me. Suddenly, all of the problems that Michael and I had been discussing in an abstract sense felt intensely personal.

Getting directly involved in May's rescue was far beyond anything I'd imagined when I'd first set out to find her, but I'd come too far to turn back now. I knew May personally, and was more familiar than anyone with her current circumstances and location.

If I was arrested or blacklisted trying to help her, then so be it – but if X was caught, that would jeopardise all of Blue Dragon's future rescues in China.

I'd already committed my time and remaining funds to finishing the 'Sisters for Sale' documentary, but that would have to wait: getting May out of China was both more urgent and more important to me.

Examining the map, I realised there was a way for both May and Pang to avoid the final and most hazardous stretch before the border: there were other authorities in China besides the Chinese.

If May could be brought south, she and Pang could be reunited and taken together to the Vietnamese consulate in Guangzhou.

They were Vietnamese citizens in need of assistance – but the problem, once again, would be proving it. Anything linking the girls with Vietnam had been stripped from them years ago.

May's family would have to supply the necessary paperwork to bring May home – but May's family didn't want her to come home.

May's father Lung had recently told May that if she didn't obey her "husband", he'd never allow her to return home to Vietnam. At the time, the idea that Lung could control May's access to Vietnam had struck me as absurd – but in this situation, he would in fact hold that power.

I knew Lung would do everything he could to pressure May into returning to her Chinese "husband". I didn't know if May would have the strength to resist him at such a delicate moment, and I didn't know if Blue Dragon or I would be able to support her through that process. Once May and Pang were inside the consulate, we might not be able to speak to them at all.

I didn't know how enthusiastic the Vietnamese authorities would be to repatriate the girls, or if they could do so without becoming entangled in a lengthy legal process with China. If I was present, my own role in their story would inevitably be exposed, with uncertain consequences. Any path that led through the Vietnamese consulate would be a path strewn with question marks.

Michael told me that X had rescued girls via a Vietnamese consulate once before, and said it might also work in this case. He reminded me, though, that the biggest challenge was still China's internal checkpoints. All it would take was a single officer to ruin the entire operation. If there were any checkpoints between May's current location and the consulate, our greatest problem remained unsolved.

SLIPPING AWAY

In consultation with Michael, I began sketching out a more detailed rescue plan. First I'd return to the city in Shandong province where I'd recently spent twelve days attempting to locate and meet with May – and then I'd wait.

While "rescue" was the most accurate term for the broader operation, the first phase wouldn't be a rescue at all: it would be an escape. As I'd never identified May's village, she herself would have to get away from her "husband" and come to meet me. It wouldn't be easy, though – May was rarely allowed to leave the house unaccompanied, even to go to the market in her own village.

She'd have to wait and watch for her chance to slip away from the house and make her way to the nearby crossroads where we'd recently rendezvoused.

For the past three years, May's "husband" had been working as a taxi driver at the crossroads. He'd left that job soon after I'd met with May in China, but it wasn't clear what he was doing now, or how much time he was spending at home watching May.

Until May could slip away – which could take days – her "husband" could ruin our plans at any time by confiscating her money and phone, as he'd done before. To avoid arousing his suspicions, we'd have to keep contact to a bare minimum – but once she was out of the house May would have to alert me as soon as possible so that I could come to find her.

Our mutual friend Vu had initially escaped her Chinese "husband" by jumping in a taxi and passing her phone to the driver, who then followed X's directions to a meeting point. May's "husband's" connection with the local taxi network would make her escape more challenging, both to and from the crossroads. To avoid the local drivers entirely, I would bring a taxi from the city to collect May.

The escape plan seemed simple enough on paper, but I knew it would be far more nerve-wracking in reality, and there was no knowing what might go wrong. X had been pursued during some of his rescues. If the locals realised I was taking one of their "wives", it was very possible that they'd band together to take May back – and beat me up in the street, turn me over to the local authorities, or both.

Logistics aside, I knew it would be incredibly difficult for May to abandon a daughter she'd never see again, and I had to be prepared for any last-minute hesitations.

May had been a major investment for her "husband" and his family: how would they respond once they realised she was gone?

First they'd try calling her – and she might also receive threatening phonecalls from the man who'd sold her, as Vu had. Then they'd search the village and the crossroads. May's "husband" would likely alert the local taxi drivers – and perhaps even the local police, if his family had any contacts there.

The next logical move would be to check the long-distance bus and train stations in both nearby cities. May would have to go to one of those stations, and she'd be vulnerable there.

We'd have two options: we could try to rush May out of Shandong as quickly as possible, or she could lie low until the Chinese security situation relaxed and her "husband" and his family had given up any efforts to find her.

I felt it would be best to take things slowly and carefully, one step at a time – but having escaped, I knew that May would be impatient to get back to Vietnam.

In either case, the initial escape would be the easiest step of all: beyond it lay the far longer and more difficult challenge of bringing May south to the border.

DRIVING SOUTH

Without identification, any travel would be dangerous for May.

In China, identification was needed not only to pass any checkpoints, but to check into any accommodation and – at least in theory – to board any long-distance transport.

I didn't expect accommodation to be a problem: I had friends with their own apartments in both Shandong and Guangdong, the two provinces we'd be travelling between.

The real problem would be transport. Air travel was out of the question, and a hired car was too risky. Our remaining options were trains and buses. When May had planned to travel south with her middlemen two months earlier, I wasn't sure who'd bought her train ticket, or how. I'd understood that tickets had to be bought in person, but May had been given hers. I wondered if May's "husband" had also been worried that she'd be caught en route, and if that was part of the reason he'd refused to let her go at the last moment.

I realised there was another possibility, too. May couldn't read Chinese, and her "husband" often made false promises as a means of controlling her. Perhaps he'd never planned to let her go south: he could have given her a ticket to anywhere, in anyone's name, just to placate her, and May would never have known the difference.

Blue Dragon preferred to use buses, which were easier for foreigners to travel on. The journey could be done directly, or in a series of shorter hops between smaller cities as Vu had done – but both options were a gamble.

The second approach would make May seem like she was only travelling locally. It would reduce her chances of having to show identification while buying tickets, but it would also mean she'd have to buy tickets more often.

While I felt the increased complexity only increased the risk, this was X's preferred method, and he knew more about these rescues than anyone.

My trafficked friend Big Zao had been caught at a checkpoint while fleeing China, but was ultimately released. The deciding factor seemed to be that she'd bought her ticket nearby and was presumed to have been travelling locally, whereas a long-distance ticket would have been more suspicious.

A friend in Shandong had a contact he hoped could help with the identity card problem: otherwise, it would be a matter of playing the odds. I could only hope that China's internal security would be relaxed by August.

If I could get May to Guangzhou, she and Pang could be reunited for the first time in three and a half years.

We then faced another decision: to approach the Vietnamese consulate in Guangzhou, or to try to reach Blue Dragon at the border. The first option offered more immediate safety but was likely to be a far longer process, and I was wary of interference by May's father. On the other hand, the run to the border would be a risky one, and we might still need papers from May's family to bring her home.

It felt deeply surreal even to be having these discussions.

I still thought of myself essentially as a backpacker: was I really planning to pit my own scant resources against the entire mechanism of the Chinese state? There must have been a fundamental flaw in the logic, if this was where it had led me.

May's escape and her journey south to Guangzhou, for which I'd be responsible, could take a week or more, and would involve thousands of kilometres of travel. I had no experience with this kind of operation and, for much of that time, I'd have little or no support.

When he'd rescued Vu in China, X had been accompanied by another of Blue Dragon's rescue workers, a man named Thanh. Thanh had already helped rescue enslaved children from several Vietnamese garment factories. Even so, he found himself unprepared for such an intensely stressful and utterly exhausting experience as Vu's rescue, which had involved five thousand gruelling kilometres of bus travel.

When X and Thanh had finally rendezvoused with Vu outside Nanjing, they'd fled the area immediately and had had nothing to eat until the following day. Overwhelmed by the lack of food, the lack of sleep, and the relentless nervous tension, Thanh had collapsed on the ground at a bus station halfway back to Vietnam. He said he couldn't move, and "really, really" needed help. The three of them had been forced to stop while he recovered, and for a time Thanh thought he'd have to leave the operation and fly back to Vietnam.

The rescue we were planning for May would be very similar, but would involve an even longer overland journey. Thanh had been fortunate that X had been there to support him – but I would be alone with May, and entirely out of my depth.

The very idea was harrowing, and the entire operation seemed mad: there were so many ways it could go catastrophically wrong. If the risks had been reasonable, X would have rescued May himself.

X was very likely the most heroic human being I'd ever known, and I stood in awe of all the things he'd achieved. The more I learned about him, the deeper my respect for him ran.

I was told that X always slept on his back with a mobile phone on his chest set to vibrate so that he could respond to calls for help at any hour of the night without disturbing his family. He'd slept that way every night for years, in anticipation of the calls and messages that came all too frequently from China. For many of the girls who were sold to brothels, night time was the only opportunity they had to make contact.

We have a habit of putting our heroes on pedestals, of pretending they're somehow more than human. It relieves us of the burden of trying to follow in their footsteps, of seeing how comparatively weak our own moral strength and determination might be.

But I'd met X face to face. I'd looked him in the eye, and shaken his hand. He was a phenomenal human being – but he was still just a human being. He hadn't been blessed with any extraordinary powers; he'd just done incredible things with what he did have.

I'm sure that X had had many of the same fears and doubts the first time he'd rescued a trafficking victim from China. Perhaps he felt the same way, even now, every time he crossed that border. It was easy to tell myself I could never do the kinds of things X had done, and maybe that was true, but there was only one way to find out.

What gnawed at me most was the uncertainty. I'd led an unusual life, and had taken plenty of risks – but always with my own life, not with other people's.

I would have willingly taken all the risks upon myself to guarantee May and Pang's safe return home, but that was impossible. There were no guarantees here, and there was a very real danger that any effort of mine would only make May and Pang's situations worse.

I'd once stayed overnight at the base camp on the north face of Mount Everest. I'd been there with my then-partner Dominique, who had been struck suddenly by severe altitude sickness.

The only road back to the safety of lower altitudes was a rough mountain road which would first take us even higher. In the middle of the night, we faced the dilemma between remaining where we were or running the risks of a long tough journey through the darkness over high mountain passes.

There were no safe options: whatever we chose, someone I cared for deeply would be in serious danger. Now, I found myself facing a very similar dilemma.

How could I live with myself if I brought more tragedy into May and Pang's lives? It would be beyond devastating to have offered them hope only to see it all snatched away at the last moment.

But what was the alternative? For May, at least, escape was a matter of urgency. Someone had to get her out of there, and there was nobody else... Was there?

REACH OUT

I was acutely conscious of my own limitations: I had to be.

While I had knowledge, resources, and contacts that could help May and Pang, in other ways I knew I'd only make their escape from China more complicated.

May and Pang both lived in untouristed areas where foreigners went rarely, if ever. As a Westerner, I'd been extremely conspicuous during my search for the girls there, and would be again during a rescue. As I couldn't speak Chinese, even the most basic aspects of travelling in China could be a challenge – and, as a foreigner, there were so many things there I just didn't understand. I might not know how to overcome any obstacles we encountered, and wasn't the best person to be making those kinds of decisions.

What I needed was an intelligent, adventurous, trustworthy, English-speaking Chinese person – and I had one.

My friend Qiuda had been one of the most enthusiastic supporters of my project from the very beginning. He'd told me numerous times he'd be honoured to help in any way that he could, and in fact he had already helped in many ways.

As a local who could blend in and speak the language, Qiuda's involvement could very well mean the difference between success and failure. Our combined knowledge and skillsets would be ideal for the work ahead.

I wrote to Qiuda asking if he'd be willing and able to join me. I explained May and Pang's situations and sketched out my plan to help them reach the southern border region, from where I hoped Blue Dragon could take them home. If Qiuda could arrange a week off work, I'd cover all costs.

Qiuda's response was both surprising and sobering. The following comments have been taken from a series of emails he sent me explaining why my plan was doomed to failure.

"My dear friend," he said. "I do respect all your efforts and admire all your achievements so far. What you've done shouldn't be called a miracle, for you know how much effort it has taken, and what a long tough journey it has been. It's not easy to make it so close to victory. But with all due respect, I have to say that the plan you've proposed would turn it into a disaster."

While the rescue plan might seem viable from my point of view, Qiuda assured me it wasn't. He'd been raised in Communist China and he understood its control-based social management principles.

"You have no idea how many pairs of eyes are watching you," he told me. "ID checking is so frequent and so prevalent all across the country for rising terrorist threats and social crises, you never know when and where your ID will be checked!"

In May's situation, "one simple enquiry from any policeman in any town would be devastating. What should I tell the police if they ask me who May is and what we are doing? Ben, if that ever happens, only one time, we will all be done."

If Qiuda and I were caught with May or Pang – and he was certain we would be – the authorities would demand to know why he hadn't reported the situation at the first opportunity. It was "quite possible", too, that Qiuda himself would be suspected of trafficking the girls – which would be personally catastrophic for him, even if he was later cleared.

"Once I become a suspect, no one can save me," he said. "You can't, either."

If I wanted to handle the case in a legal way, Qiuda said he'd be happy to help me make a police report and liaise with local authorities. Otherwise, I was on my own.

"I'm afraid you won't be able to find any Chinese to make this trip with May," he told me. "It has nothing to do with time or money."

Qiuda was concerned that I wanted to rescue May because I wanted to make myself some kind of hero. I was surprised and a little saddened that Qiuda believed I'd take such risks for the sake of feeding my own ego. He told me I was already a hero and didn't have to prove anything to anyone.

"May was taken in an illegal way, why do you want to rescue her in an illegal way?" he asked. "Why do you wish to hide her from one town to another and let her worry about unpredictable ID checks, huddled up in strange buses suffering a long tough journey, rather than asking the Vietnamese embassy staff to rescue her and bring her home by air? Why do you wish to sneak her over the border with the risk of being detected by patrolling soldiers rather than let them escort her home?"

I was confused by some of Qiuda's comments. I'd never suggested sneaking May across the border: it seems he'd misunderstood Blue Dragon's role. The notion that the Vietnamese embassy would be directly involved in a rescue on foreign soil seemed odd, too. He even raised the possibility of approaching the Chinese media with the story, which is something I never would have considered.

Qiuda suggested I use the threat of involving the Chinese authorities as a "bargaining chip" with May's "husband". I said that the authorities were far more likely to side with the "husband", and the fact that May's "husband" would have legal possession of her child made the situation far more complicated.

"You are not rescuing a Jewish family from Nazi Germany,"

Qiuda told me. "We are not the Taliban, she is not an American corporal. May wasn't sold to a remote undeveloped village deep in an unknown mountain range. She's in Shandong, one of the richest provinces in northern China. The police there will definitely stand on your side, or on the side of the law."

The idea of entrusting May's rescue to the Chinese authorities had been the very first to be eliminated, and for good reason. Qiuda's praise of the Chinese police stood in stark contrast to every other opinion I'd encountered – including later comments made by Qiuda himself.

In an email he sent me five years later, Qiuda explained that the Chinese authorities had very little incentive to help a trafficked girl. He said this was particularly true in smaller communities, where government representatives were all local people, and the buyer of a trafficked girl was likely to be someone they were connected to personally. An officer's desire to preserve their own position in the local community would outweigh their sense of duty to the distant national government, and would certainly outweigh any sense of obligation to a foreign girl with no legal status.

Even if the authorities were willing to investigate a trafficker, Qiuda assured me that few locals would cooperate for the same reasons. It would be "regarded as betrayal to the local community," he said. "The whole community is united and closed in a stubborn way." If the victim was a Chinese girl, she might receive more sympathy, but an illegal alien would be helpless.

These later comments fit with everything else I'd heard – so why had Qiuda been so insistent that I place my trust in the Chinese authorities?

"I kind of work for the government now," he admitted. By asking Qiuda to break the law, I'd asked him to take far greater risks than I myself would be taking.

If I was caught, I'd most likely be arrested and interrogated before being blacklisted from the country – but that wouldn't affect the rest of my life. As a citizen, the repercussions for

Qiuda would be far more severe. The Chinese government controlled his life, including his career.

While I understood and respected Qiuda's decision, his messages were disheartening – not because I believed he was wrong, but because I was afraid he was right. Although I didn't agree with his comments about trusting the local authorities, everything else he said rang true.

Blue Dragon and I had ruled out all other options as impractical, and now Qiuda had dismissed my last remaining hope as destined for disaster. Even if I could find a local who was willing to assist with the rescue, I couldn't ask them to stake their future on such a hazardous operation.

I was still willing to take the risks – but if there was no reasonable hope of success, and a very real possibility that I'd only make May and Pang's situations worse, then the whole plan seemed futile and foolhardy.

I'd begun this work because I was certain it was the right thing to do, and I'd relied on that sense of what was right to guide me – but the further I went, the less certain it all seemed. The correct path wasn't always clear, and now it had become murkier than ever.

"My friend, please think twice before you make any moves. For yourself, and for May," Qiuda said. "Good luck with the last battle."

CAN'T TAKE MY EYES OFF YOU

In early July, when I learned that May's "husband" was planning to send her away, I informed Michael immediately. Michael felt the news was "definitely a concern", and that if May wanted to come home "it should be sooner rather than later".

"The "husband" knows he has done wrong, knows he can be in trouble and needs to protect himself," Michael said. "It might be that he's planning to re-sell May to someone else, to get his money back before she escapes."

Michael and X reassessed the security situation and had some excellent news for me. Blue Dragon still couldn't rescue May – but could likely organise something they referred to as an "assist".

Rather than me having to get May and Pang all the way to the border region before handing them into the care of Blue Dragon, Michael believed he could now arrange for a "contact person" to take over from Guangzhou.

My greatest challenge, then, would be bringing May nearly two thousand kilometres south from Shandong province to Guangzhou. While Michael agreed that bus travel seemed like May's safest option for coming south, he and I had conflicting opinions on how it might best be done.

We both knew that, as a Westerner, I'd only draw unwanted attention to May by travelling with her on public transport. I felt it was best if May and I each bought separate tickets for the same bus – ideally, I'd be sitting close enough to keep an eye on May without being seen to travel with her.

In that situation, though, if May was caught at a checkpoint, Michael said it would take only one glance between us to reveal our connection and further complicate matters.

I couldn't understand what difference that would make, or why I'd want to hide my connection to May if she was in trouble. It was far too late to pretend I wasn't involved.

Michael felt it would be safer if May and I travelled on separate buses and met only when necessary.

I could see an advantage in my going ahead to scout out the route for checkpoints – but travelling separately seemed to open all kinds of disastrous new possibilities.

If May tried to make the journey south in one stretch, she might disappear into the hands of the authorities at any point along the two-thousand-kilometre route, and we might not know where to begin looking for her. On the other hand, if she tried to make the journey in a series of shorter hops, the entire operation would become incredibly complicated.

Instead of having to arrange just one rendezvous at a familiar location in Shandong – the crossroads – May and I might have to arrange multiple additional rendezvous at unfamiliar locations between Shandong and Guangzhou. We could very easily spend hours waiting for each other at all hours of the day or night. I had no friends in this region we could turn to for assistance or accommodation, and it would be only too easy to lose ourselves and each other in Chinese bus terminals, where neither one of us could read the signs.

In China, a fertile young woman like May was a valuable commodity in high demand. She was also a village girl, and Sapa was the biggest "city" she'd ever navigated alone. If May could have disappeared from such a cosy little town where she could speak the language and had a support network of friends and family, then how much more vulnerable would she be if she was alone and lost in China?

May wouldn't be able to read her ticket or the signs around her, and she wasn't literate or tech-savvy enough to get the information she needed via her phone. She could always ask for help, but a young woman with a foreign accent and no luggage who spent hours lost or loitering around bus terminals would already draw far too much unwanted attention from both security and any opportunistic traffickers. I couldn't imagine how my presence nearby might make that situation any worse.

Ultimately, though, I knew my reaction was more emotional than logical. I'd come so far to find May, and would be going much further to help her escape. I couldn't imagine simply putting her on a bus and watching her disappear when she was still so far from safety.

Michael had the patience of a saint in responding to my endless questions. I'd come to trust his judgement to such an extent that, in disagreeing with him, I came to seriously doubt my own judgement. Was there something here I wasn't seeing? That was very possible: I'd certainly made plenty of mistakes over the past six months.

In any case, I considered it to be Blue Dragon's operation, not mine. I told Michael I'd defer to his judgement – but even as I said it, I wondered if it was true. Once I'd helped May escape, would I really be capable of letting her go so easily? Or would I insist on getting on that bus with her, regardless of what Michael might say?

I didn't know – and, ultimately, I was never in a position to find out.

When I'd first conceived the project, I'd envisaged it as a vast game of chess against life itself. As Michael and I mapped out our strategies for May and Pang's rescues, it felt more than ever as if we were plotting our moves against unseen opponents: but the game we'd planned for wasn't the game we ended up playing.

Ultimately, what disrupted our meticulously-constructed plans wasn't the Chinese authorities, or anything else we'd reckoned on: the problem was me.

At least that's what I believed, for the longest time.

DOWNBOUND TRAIN

While Isabela and I had been in the mountains of northern India, X had been trying to call May and Pang. To avoid arousing the suspicions of the girls' "husbands" ahead of their rescues, Michael felt it was best that we contact the girls as little as possible. I'd stopped calling both May and Pang and had passed the message on to Sebastien, who said he'd stop calling May.

X couldn't get through to May, but he did reach Pang. Pang had been wavering in her decision for months, but now told X she wanted to go home and was ready to be rescued at any time.

Michael said that the situation between Vietnam and China was still "very tense", with "very tight security and some military activity on the border". Blue Dragon was arranging an "assist" for Pang: one of their Chinese contacts would accompany Pang from Guangdong back to the border, where X would meet her and bring her across.

"I don't have a timeframe yet, but should do soon," Michael said.

Disturbingly, Pang had told X the same story she'd told me three weeks earlier: that May didn't want to be rescued in August, but wanted to stay in China until the Lunar New Year, in seven months' time.

I was confused. We were receiving two contradictory narratives, one from May and one from Pang. Had there been a miscommunication, or was one of the girls being dishonest with us? If so, which one – and why?

During my investigation in Sapa, I'd often heard conflicting stories, and hadn't always known who to trust or what to believe. Blue Dragon and I now found ourselves in the same situation – but this time, with May and Pang themselves.

With barely a week remaining until my scheduled return to China, I suggested that X try again to speak directly to May about what she wanted to do – but X still couldn't get through, and Michael wasn't sure what to make of May and Pang's contradictory stories. It was the first time that Blue Dragon had been working with multiple sources of information while arranging rescues.

Every time I'd spoken to May in the past two months, she'd consistently and confidently told me that she wanted to be rescued immediately after her baby's first birthday – but the doubt raised by Pang cast a shadow over the entire operation. It would be senseless for Blue Dragon to arrange May's return home if May was in fact reluctant or unwilling, and was telling different stories to different people.

Isabela was assaulted in Srinagar just one week before my flight to Hong Kong. The following evening, she and I took the night bus south to Jammu, then continued by train to Amritsar. There was a group of teenage boys hanging around taking photos of her on the train. Isabela curled up against the window and covered herself as much as possible with her scarf, but it made no difference.

There was nothing unusual about the situation – it was the kind of casual harassment that women in India endure on a daily basis – but Isabela was feeling fragile, and I was all churned up with a sense of helplessness.

Although it was illogical and I knew there was nothing

more I could have done under the circumstances, I think Isabela and I both had an overwhelming sense that I'd failed to protect her when she'd needed me most.

I felt that I'd failed her, and was still failing her: because I hadn't been there for her, because I didn't know how to offer her the support she needed, and because I hadn't been able to restrain my remark to the owner's brother. It was as if by acknowledging the situation I'd somehow made it real, and Isabela resented that.

I was upset with the teenagers on the train and perhaps overreacted, which only made things worse between Isabela and me. Coming from Latin America, she seemed resigned to being the subject of aggressive male attention. By calling out that kind of behaviour she felt I was only making a pointless and unnecessary fuss.

Isabela wanted to forget what had happened in Srinagar, and my very presence had become a living reminder of it. I could feel her starting to turn on me, pushing me away.

My flight to Hong Kong was leaving from Kolkata, nearly two thousand kilometres away in eastern India. I'd have to allow two days for the train journey to reach Kolkata, and I was rapidly running out of time.

Was May the one playing games with us, and Pang telling us the truth? Or was Pang playing games, and May still waiting to be rescued? I knew that both girls were capable of telling stories, but I couldn't understand why either of them would want to deceive us now.

Should I take my flight back to China, or would I only be wasting my time? Did May still want my help, or was she just jerking me around? I had to speak to her directly, to learn whatever I could and make my decision – and I had to do it quickly.

This was the moment for which we'd been preparing for months. It was the moment for decisive action – but it felt as though everything was sliding backwards, and slowly falling apart.

ON HOLD

The city of Amritsar, near the Pakistani border, is best known for its exquisite Golden Temple. The temple is the most sacred site for Sikh people – it's their Mecca, Temple Mount, Vatican City, Varanasi, or Bodhgaya. It's a lively, magical place with a wonderful sense of community.

The Sikh not only tolerate but warmly welcome non-Sikhs to visit, eat at, and even sleep at the temple complex. There were mixed dormitories reserved for foreigners like ourselves. While they were bustling hives where beds were pushed together to form what were essentially long, communal mattresses, the dormitories were more comfortable than the accommodation available to many of the Sikh pilgrims, and they offered the incredible experience of living within the temple complex.

I'd spent almost a week there three years earlier, and Isabela and I both wanted to stay there now: it seemed like a good place to heal. I quickly realised, however, that I'd need an Internet connection and space to work, so I took a hotel room nearby while Isabela remained at the temple.

During my search for May in Shandong province, I'd been assisted by a group of foreigners and locals who lived in the same area – including a Kashmiri named Aamir, who had been acting as my proxy since I'd left China. If May particularly wanted to speak to me, she could call Aamir, and Aamir would relay the message to me.

Aamir was the first person I contacted now. He said that May had recently called him two or three times, worried that she hadn't heard from me lately. He tried calling her back for me and said her phone was ringing, but she wasn't answering.

Isabela came to visit me at the hotel but there were strange new spaces between us which I didn't know how to navigate. What had been so sweet and simple between us had dissolved into an emotional quagmire of guilt, shame, frustration, anger, disappointment, resentment, wounded pride, and self-disgust.

Isabela acted as if I'd left the dormitory because I was too precious for a little discomfort, which might have been funny under other circumstances. I'd never really told her much about my work and tried now to explain what was happening with May, but I couldn't understand it myself.

Forty-eight hours before my flight, with just hours left to make my decision, I finally succeeded in reaching May. We spoke for forty minutes.

Since I'd left China and was no longer available to talk May and Pang through any concerns they might have had, both girls had become overwhelmed by fears for their long-term security if they left their Chinese "husbands".

While neither girl wanted to remarry, they'd both come to accept it as necessary, and May had become fixated on Sebastien as her one great hope for a brighter future. Once again, she was trying to understand Vietnam's passport application process, and even how to arrange the paperwork to marry a foreigner. Having realised that these processes were more complex than she'd first imagined, she'd become disheartened.

While May's family rarely called her themselves, it seemed they'd passed her phone number to other Hmong people in Sapa who had begun calling her regularly. I wasn't sure who those people were, but they seemed to be discouraging May from coming home.

May was upset that Sebastien hadn't called her lately. I explained that Blue Dragon – "my friends in Hanoi" – felt it was better that Sebastien and I both stopped calling for a while, so that May's "husband" wouldn't get too suspicious before her rescue.

May was furious. If she couldn't talk to Sebastien, she said she'd change her number and wouldn't talk to any of us.

In any case, May told me a rescue had now become impossible. She was still committed to going home and to leaving her daughter in China – but said she was now being watched too closely, and could barely step outside without being accompanied by her "husband" or his father.

While I'd been in Shandong, May's "parents-in-law" had repeatedly told her that she'd be expected to fall pregnant again before her daughter was eighteen months old: they wanted a boy this time. Recently, however, May's "in-laws" had inexplicably stopped pressuring May into having a second child. While May celebrated this as a victory, I was far from convinced, and felt sure there was something more sinister underway.

May's "husband" was still planning to send her away. May still had no idea where she was being sent, or what type of work she was supposedly being sent away for. It all struck me as terribly suspicious, and I knew that Michael shared my doubts.

While I considered it the worst news of all, a danger far worse than a second pregnancy, May had taken her "husband's" statement at face value. She was looking forward to being sent away, and saw it as an opportunity to have more freedom from her "husband" and his family.

May's "husband" had told her he'd send her away after the Lunar New Year in February, and May believed that our best chance of a rescue would be after she was sent away. She wanted to put the rescue on hold for another seven months.

I asked May why her "husband" was waiting until after the Lunar New Year, but she didn't know and didn't much care.

She was blissfully unaware of the dangers, and I was deeply concerned about how complacent she'd become in China. I found her attitude alarming, and deeply frustrating: it was like trying to reason with a child.

I didn't tell May the whole truth. I didn't tell her that I was afraid she'd be sold as meat for the brothels, or even butchered for her organs. I didn't know how to say any of that to a teenage girl who was already living in such difficult circumstances. I did say that the situation was unlikely to turn out the way she was hoping and could potentially get much worse for her, but May didn't grasp my meaning and I just couldn't make it any more explicit.

I felt that May wasn't being entirely honest with me, either. She made no mention of her hope that Sebastien would visit her in China, though it seemed that had been the deciding factor in the postponement of her rescue.

Even if May was now being permitted only a few minutes alone outside the house and never outside the village, I was sure we could find some way to get her out of there. It seemed far better to act immediately than to wait until after May was sent away, when we'd lose her location and possibly all contact.

There was a very real chance that May was about to disappear, along with any hope of ever helping her. I told her how I felt, but she'd already made her decision – just as Isabela had made her decision in Srinagar. I had a terrible sense of foreboding, of watching another tragedy unfold in slow motion. I felt certain it would end badly and May would get hurt, perhaps killed, but I didn't know what else I could do to prevent it. Even if it was the worst choice she could possibly have made, it was still May's choice.

If we tried to take May out of Shandong before she was ready, it wouldn't be a rescue: it would be human trafficking.

TELLING STORIES

May confessed that Pang hadn't been telling me the whole truth, either: Pang was telling different stories to different people.

Pang wasn't yet ready to burn her bridges, and wanted to leave China with her "husband's" permission. She'd told her "husband" she wanted to go back to Vietnam to visit her family, and would soon return to him in China. She'd told X and me that she wanted to go back to Vietnam forever, and I assumed she'd told her mother in Sapa the same thing.

None of that was surprising – but there was another story Pang had kept hidden, and shared only with May. May told me on the condition that I wouldn't mention it to Pang, who would recognise its source and consider it a betrayal.

After months of indecision, Pang was suddenly resolved to return home to Vietnam. I didn't know what had changed, and May provided the missing piece of the puzzle.

A month ago, Pang had begun speaking to a Chinese Hmong stranger who lived in the borderlands of Yunnan province. It wasn't clear how this young man had first gotten Pang's number, but he now spoke to her on a daily basis. Without ever having met her, this stranger was now telling

Pang that he loved her and wanted to marry her.

It all sounded highly suspicious. Traffickers feed on desperation, and Pang was in a desperate situation. The man perfectly fit the profile of a trafficker and was telling Pang all the things traffickers typically said to lure their victims, however implausible they might be. In their conversations, Pang was pretending she had no "husband" or child.

It was the timing that struck me as particularly odd. Why had this man contacted Pang now, just as she was planning her escape?

The middlemen who had sold Pang to her "husband" were Chinese Hmong people living in the Yunnan borderlands. With the clear intention of selling Pang a second time, they'd told Pang that if she had any trouble with her "husband" she could always come back to them.

These same middlemen had first connected Pang to a network of other Vietnamese Hmong trafficking victims she now spoke with regularly in China. It would have been very easy for the middlemen to monitor this network and learn if any of these young women were thinking of escape, as Pang was.

Pang loathed the middlemen, and would never have returned to them voluntarily. It was plausible that the middlemen had passed Pang's number to an accomplice who was now working to lure her back to them.

This stranger could tell Pang whatever she wanted to hear and, for the cost of a few phonecalls, the middlemen would have another saleable product worth thousands of dollars. They wouldn't have to pay any kidnappers, or worry about any trouble from the authorities: Pang had long since slipped into the shadow world of human trafficking. The middlemen wouldn't even have to go and collect her: Pang was desperate enough to self-deliver. She was easy money.

The price of a trafficked girl depended on her youth, beauty, virginity, and docility. Pang was now several years older, no longer a virgin, and known to be uncooperative. As with May, if Pang was sold a second time, it was very possible she'd be sold into something far more horrifying than "marriage" – but she seemed oblivious to the dangers she faced.

While Blue Dragon was planning Pang's rescue, Pang had been secretly making plans of her own. According to May, Pang was planning to go back to Sapa for a few weeks or months to see her family and friends, and to see if the local community would accept her return. If not, she would skip back across the border to meet this stranger in Yunnan – and if she liked him, she intended to marry him. If all else failed, Pang planned to go back to her "husband" and child in Guangdong province.

A woman in May and Pang's culture very rarely owned land or property of any real value, and so she spent her entire life dependent on the men around her – first her father, then her husband, and perhaps later her sons. Without a man, a woman had no place in society: there was no provision in traditional Hmong culture for an unattached woman.

May and Pang's Chinese "husbands" had done horrific things to the girls – but they had the entire weight of May and Pang's culture on their side. By leaving their "marriages" – however false and abusive they might be – the girls would be putting themselves into a position their culture refused to recognise. Before the girls got out, they wanted to know there was some way for them to get back in, to find acceptance in the eyes of their people again.

May and Pang's uncertainty about going home rested on an even greater uncertainty about marriage. While I'd been thinking in terms of freedom, May and Pang were thinking in terms of long-term security – and culturally, that meant finding a man to marry.

No self-respecting Hmong man would commit to marry a woman who had not only been trafficked, but was still living with the man who'd bought her – and so May and Pang found themselves caught in a Catch-22. Before they left their "husbands", the girls needed certainty – but so long as they remained in China, they would never have that certainty.

May and Pang's desperate need to attach themselves to a man had driven the girls into situations that only left them more vulnerable to harm and exploitation. May had pinned her hopes on Sebastien, choosing to prolong a dangerous and abusive situation for his sake, while Pang was looking to a seeming trafficker for her own salvation.

I'd told Pang that Blue Dragon and I could help her if she was certain she wanted to go back to Vietnam. She wasn't certain, and never would be, but she wanted our help anyway – and so she'd lied. Pang was not only lying about her marital status to this strange man who supposedly wanted to marry her, she was also lying to us – the very people who were trying to help her. She was telling us what we wanted to hear, and planned on taking advantage of our assistance.

I could understand that, but it didn't mean I liked it. What upset me most was not the fact that Pang was deceiving us, but that she didn't seem to have learned anything from her experiences over the past three and half years. In her desperation to believe this mysterious stranger, Pang didn't seem to have considered how improbable it was that he should suddenly appear in her life promising to give her the one thing she needed more than anything, exactly when she needed it.

There was nothing I could do. There was nothing I could say, even – I'd promised May I wouldn't.

HEART ON A STRING

In central China stands Lushan, a sacred mountain which is famed for its beauty – but it is a fluid and notoriously inaccessible beauty. Lushan is obscured by mist and clouds for most of the year – and, with a cluster of high peaks, the mountain can change shape dramatically depending on where the observer stands. As Su Shi's renowned thousand-year-old poem declares, it is impossible to know Lushan's true shape when you're in the middle of the mountain.

(I'd once driven past the very foot of Lushan, in a sleeper bus on my journey north to search for May – but in the darkness I hadn't seen it at all.)

Two very different paths now stretched ahead of me – one led towards China, while the other remained in India – and it was impossible to know where either path might ultimately lead me, or what the outcome might be for May and Pang.

I had just a few rapidly-disappearing hours to make my decision. I'd have the rest of my life to gather new perspectives and wonder what I might have done differently – but for now, I was in the middle of the mountain. I didn't have the information I needed to make my decision – but I still had to decide.

Throughout our long journey across Asia, Marinho and I had ascribed our many successes to "luck and persistence", a phrase which had served as an unofficial motto for the project. We'd been fortunate in many ways – but so much of our success had depended on being in the right place, ready for action, when all the stars aligned.

During my time in China, May had told me it would be impossible to find and meet with her. She'd been half right – while I'd never identified May's precise home location, we'd identified the nearby crossroads, and I had succeeded in meeting her there. As ever, it had been a matter of luck and persistence.

Now, May told me it would be impossible to rescue her, but I wasn't convinced. The problem seemed to be her strange new reluctance, which seemed to stem from a desire to see Sebastien again, rather than any more tangible barriers to her escape.

In recent months, I'd spent countless hours on the phone with May and had come to know her better than ever. If I was right there in Shandong and May knew that I could help her go home at any time, if she understood that Sebastien was never really coming to visit her in China, then I was sure she'd feel differently and would seize her opportunity. We could get her home, and Sebastien could visit her in Vietnam.

At any other time, I would have heard May say "impossible" and taken it as a challenge – but this time was different.

I'd told myself I'd do whatever I could to help May. But if May herself didn't know what she wanted – or, worse, if she was concealing the truth from me – then what was I to do? My funds were rapidly disappearing, and I'd already committed myself to finishing the 'Sisters for Sale' documentary. I couldn't spend the rest of the year hanging around waiting for disaster to strike, or for May to change her mind again.

During my search in China, I'd found myself having to lie to both May and Pang, and had hated doing so. Now it seemed as if both girls were lying to me, or at least omitting crucial facts. Not only had May changed her mind, it seemed she'd changed it a month ago and had since been deceiving me.

I'd always reacted strongly to any situation in which I felt powerless. Perhaps that's why I'd felt such a compulsion to help May and Pang in any way I could – because I knew how powerless they were in China, and I had a sense of how horrible that could feel.

In giving May and Pang the option of going home, I'd given them a little more power over their lives – but I'd also lost some of my own. I felt annoyed by May's behaviour and began to resent the control I'd given her over my life. I hadn't come all this way just to be her puppet and, after what had just happened with Isabela, I couldn't face the prospect of standing helplessly by as someone else I cared about fell prey to some horrific new tragedy.

In any case, if I was to be hanging around, treading water for weeks or months, it would be far more expensive to do so in China, and far more complicated in terms of visas. What if I got a Chinese visa only to waste it waiting uselessly, and couldn't get another?

Michael was concerned that I might have influenced May or Pang's decisions to leave China, and rightly so. I assured him I hadn't – but, in voicing that belief, I began to question it.

May had told me countless times how desperately she wanted to return home, and I'd given her that chance – but was it really so simple?

May and I had spent many hours discussing her options, on the phone and in person. I'd done my best to keep my own opinions out of the conversation, but was that really possible? Had I – unknowingly, and unintentionally – pressured May into making a decision she wasn't ready for?

Over the following months, in preparation for scripting the documentary, I was to listen back through all of our recorded conversations. I felt that I'd done a remarkably good job at remaining impartial, and even at playing the devil's advocate when necessary, arguing against my own interests.

Even so, I realised it was impossible not to have had some influence on May and her decision. We're all particles in motion, constantly influencing each other's trajectories in large and small ways. May had certainly influenced mine.

What everyone else had celebrated as a phenomenal success – my meeting with May in China – I'd come to see as a mistake on my part, with potentially fatal consequences for May. As a direct result of my actions, May had been set on a more perilous path than ever. For better or for worse, she and I were now connected, and I felt a deep and lasting responsibility for whatever might happen to her.

I had no right to make May's decisions for her – but I wasn't convinced that May was acting in her own best interests, either. She didn't seem to understand the dangers that now surrounded her. Perhaps she was merely deferring her decision, believing she had time – but that in itself was also a decision, and an extremely risky one under the circumstances.

I examined my motives and found them pure. What I wanted for May – for her to come home – was unquestionably the best thing for her safety. But was it necessarily the best thing for her happiness, or long-term security? I didn't know, and I wasn't sure that she did either. There didn't seem to be any way of knowing – and May's journey to safety would only place her in more danger.

At a time when we all needed to be certain, nothing was. Doubts came creeping in from all directions, and I felt lost.

I was just an ordinary person with no particular training or qualifications who had been accelerated through an incredibly steep learning curve. The idea of my going to rescue a human trafficking victim from China seemed just as mad to me as it would to you, had you been in the same position.

In my meeting with May, I'd been both lucky and persistent – but before we'd succeeded, there had also been a series of failed meetings. This time, we'd have only one opportunity

– and the risks would be far higher, for a much longer time and a much greater distance, for everyone involved. There were so many ways it could all go terribly wrong.

In China, I'd taken risks that could have easily gotten me killed, and I felt lucky to have survived. How long could I expect my luck to last?

I remembered how difficult it had been to picture my friends as victims of human trafficking, and it was just as difficult to picture myself as someone who might now free them from it.

I could have come up with any number of reasons not to go back to China. Ultimately, though, I knew it came down to Isabela. I didn't know what still remained between Isabela and me, but I wanted to see if there was still something left we could salvage. If I left things as they were, I knew I'd never see her again.

I'd asked myself how far I'd go for my friends, and I finally had an answer to that question. This was as far as I was willing to go, at least for now. I tore up my ticket and went back to the temple to be with Isabela. If May wouldn't take her freedom, then I wanted mine.

DRIFT AWAY

Almost immediately, it was clear that I'd made a mistake.

Amritsar's Golden Temple complex became the scene for the most disorienting separation I've ever experienced. It seemed almost to happen in slow motion: Isabela simply drifted away. She retreated into herself, and was soon beyond my reach.

We never spoke about it: there was nothing to say. She began spending less time with me and more time with other people she'd met in the temple. We ate and slept at different times and, before long, we barely saw each other.

Within days, whatever connection Isabela and I had once shared had evaporated completely, leaving only a mess of residual emotions. We'd arrived in Amritsar as a couple and left separately, as strangers. Isabela was still there in the temple when I left, but emotionally she was long gone from me. I can't remember if we even said goodbye, or how.

I didn't blame her. Isabela and I had never defined our relationship, and she didn't owe me an explanation or anything else. I was sorry I couldn't give her the support she needed, and I understood why she had to step away, but that didn't make it any easier.

A month later, in September, Kashmir was hit by devastating floods which lasted weeks and killed hundreds of people. The hotels and guesthouses around Srinagar's Dal Lake were all swamped and forced to close. In the midst of the tragedy, I felt glad that women might be safe from that particular predator, at least for a little while.

In mid-September, I sent Isabela a brief message about the flooding. By that time, she was already back home in Argentina. We've barely spoken since.

I never told anyone how I felt about Isabela because I never knew how to feel. On the rare occasions I'm reminded of her, I still feel conflicted over what we shared, how it fell apart, and what it might have been. There was so much we never knew about each other and never had a chance to find out. After my separation from Dominique, it had taken me years to find someone else I could feel so close to – and it was all over in less than a month.

Although 'The Human, Earth Project' was first established to raise awareness of human trafficking, its focus has gradually shifted towards women's rights. That was partly because of the realisation that May and Pang's stories were so deeply rooted in the broader mistreatment of women, and it was partly because of Isabela, and Kashmir.

WORRIED ABOUT YOU

I'd passed the information from May's latest call to Michael, who had discussed it at length with X.

To their credit, Michael and X weren't bothered by the news that Pang had been deceiving them. If she wanted to escape her "husband" and come home, they would help bring her back: everything else was secondary. While the tensions between Vietnam and China still created "serious difficulties", they felt confident they could bring Pang home.

"We can get Pang back to Vietnam whenever she is ready," Michael told me.

Michael had asked me not to share the details of Pang's planned rescue with anyone – not even Pang herself, nor her family in Sapa. While that might seem strange, I understood and fully agreed with his reasoning.

Blue Dragon were hoping not only to rescue Pang, but also to imprison the men who had kidnapped her from Vietnam. Like May, Pang had a habit of furiously blurting things to her "husband" which only harmed her own cause. Pang was also in regular contact with her mother, Bao, in Sapa.

A careless word could ruin Pang's rescue, be disastrous for her personally – and, if news of her impending return began circulating in Sapa, her kidnappers could be given a chance to slip away.

The key detail that did have to be discussed with Pang, of course, was the timing of her rescue – but after her recent enthusiasm, Pang was suddenly hesitant.

"Pang is telling us she wants to wait another month before coming back," Michael told me. "It seems there is no urgency, which makes this case completely different to all the others we have worked before. We will stay in contact, and we're ready to go at any time."

Michael said that having conflicting sources of information had made May and Pang's cases "much more complicated" than the cases Blue Dragon generally handled. They decided the best approach was to separate the threads and deal with each in isolation.

"We're going to treat Pang and May as totally separate cases, and will deal with them individually," Michael told me. What that meant in a practical sense was that Blue Dragon would handle Pang's case, including all communication with Pang, while May would be my responsibility – at least until she reached southern China. I stopped calling Pang altogether.

"Please keep me posted on Pang's situation," I said. "I'll be in touch with any further news of May."

Before leaving Amritsar, I went back to the hotel and tried to call May again. Her daughter's birthday had come and gone. I wanted to tell May I couldn't wait another seven months for a rescue, and that it would be far better for her to go home as soon as possible.

I called May in the middle of the afternoon, a time when she was generally home alone. Somebody answered the call but it was a poor connection, and I'd already begun speaking before I realised it wasn't May: nobody else had ever answered at that number before.

May took the phone, but I didn't want to speak with her while there were others present, and in any case the connection made it difficult. I said I'd talk to her another time.

I called the next day, mid-morning: another time of day I'd considered safe. Again, it was a bad connection – and again, a male voice answered the phone. Flustered and unprepared, I quickly hung up, realising how suspicious that must have seemed.

May had told me she was being watched constantly. I'd thought she'd been exaggerating, to convince me that a rescue was now impossible – but I now realised she'd been telling me the truth.

Now that May's "husband" had left his work as a taxi driver, it seemed he was home far more often. It wasn't a large home, and May had few opportunities to be alone while he was there.

May's "husband" and his family were working class people in a highly-competitive country with a scanty welfare system. It struck me as bizarre that May's "husband" had suddenly quit a job he'd held for years, abandoning his only source of income without replacing it – but there was a very simple and sobering explanation.

May had been a major investment for the family – and by selling her, they could recoup a great deal of that money. Their priority now was protecting their investment.

If they sold May, they'd no longer have to worry about the loss of money and the potential threat to their own freedom she'd come to represent. They wouldn't have to worry about money for a while, either: they'd be turning an imminent loss into a substantial gain.

Had they already found a buyer? I didn't know, but it seemed crucial to get May out of there as soon as possible.

Over the following week I tried several times to contact May, but couldn't get through at all. It was too dangerous to keep calling: May's "husband" knew too much and could easily take her phone, her only link with the outside world.

Were there any other possibilities for helping May I hadn't yet considered?

In China, May had given me a copy of her wedding DVD. Perhaps it held enough clues to determine her location more precisely – but I'd have to be on the spot in Shandong to make sense of them, and I'd be far too conspicuous in rural areas where Western people never went.

I even considered the idea of involving the Chinese authorities, though I knew how risky that would be. I had photographs of May and her "husband", as well as audio recordings of May saying their Chinese names. If I gave that information to the Chinese police, surely they could find her – but then what would happen?

I began second-guessing myself. What if I was wrong, and May's "husband" hadn't yet decided to sell her? If I stopped trying to call May and she made no move to escape, then perhaps his fears would subside.

I didn't know what to do. Should I book another ticket to Hong Kong, and get back to Shandong as soon as I could? Or should I – at least for the moment – sever my connection with May, removing the threat I posed to her "husband" and his family, and thereby removing their need to resell her?

Whichever way I turned, I would be exposing May to danger. Again, I found myself in the middle of the mountain – and again, I did nothing.

I felt as though I should have pushed on at all costs, that I should have gone back to China to do whatever I could to help May – but I just didn't have the strength anymore. I had nothing left to give.

When I'd arrived in India, my head had been a shambles, and I'd given myself three and a half weeks to sort it out. Instead, I'd only added my heart and stomach to the list. I'd been left in tatters by eight weeks in China, two cups of tap water, and one middle-aged Kashmiri man.

At the risk of making May feel that I'd abandoned her, I decided to stop trying to call her. I chose to wait, never imagining just how torturous it would prove to be. With every passing day, anything might happen to May, and I might never find out.

My imagination, of course, was only too eager to fill in the blanks. With every passing day, all of the worst possible things happened to May, over and over and over again.

AIN'T NO SUNSHINE

I left a message with Aamir, asking that if May called him, he should tell her I couldn't wait until February, and that if she wanted to leave China she should go now. But it seemed May could no longer make calls, and Aamir heard nothing from her.

Our tenuous connection to May had been severed.

I'd never found out exactly where May lived. If she couldn't make it to the crossroads, if we couldn't even speak to each other, then there was nothing we could do to help her: she was beyond our reach.

I blamed myself.

When May warned me that she'd change her number if she didn't hear from Sebastien, I didn't consider it a credible threat – not at all – but it did show me how much his contact had meant to her emotionally.

And so I'd found myself caught. I trusted Blue Dragon's judgement and wanted to comply with everything they asked of me – but ultimately, I'd come back to Asia to help May in any way I could. Who was I to say she couldn't speak to her friends, to try and control her life like so many others had? How was I to balance her need for safety with her emotional needs?

As ever, I felt it should be May's choice. Although Michael had told me it was dangerous, I'd told Sebastien to go ahead and call May, and had called her myself – but Michael had been right, and I'd only made May's situation worse.

Ten weeks earlier, when I'd met with May in China, everything had seemed so hopeful. We'd all been working together towards a common goal: May, Pang, Michael, Qiuda, Sebastien, Marinho, and I. The future had been so promising – but now everything had fallen apart, and so had we. Those of us who still remained were working at cross purposes, hiding crucial facts from one another, and I was as guilty as anyone else.

Not only did May and Pang's "husbands" have physical possession of the girls, they had both Hmong culture and the Chinese legal system on their side. What resistance could we possibly offer, if we didn't even know what we were fighting for? What May and Pang so desperately wanted, even more than their freedom, was the acceptance of their community: and that was something we just couldn't give them.

I retreated to McLeod Ganj, a largely Tibetan community in the Himalayan foothills above Dharamshala, and checked into a room at the edge of town. It was a quiet place amongst the clouds, with monkeys chattering and birds of prey wheeling over vast green valleys. For two weeks, it rained biblically on an almost-daily basis.

I had a sickening sense of *déjà vu*. Exactly three years earlier, I'd been in Kathmandu, a thousand kilometres further along the chain of the Himalayas. That's where I'd first heard of May's abduction and had done nothing in response. I'd fumbled for excuses, telling myself I didn't understand what had happened, I didn't know where May was, I didn't know what I could do. I told myself it had nothing to do with me.

Now, all of those excuses were gone. I had a far better idea of what had happened to May, where she was, and what I could do about it. I'd become deeply involved with it all – and still I did nothing.

There was nothing I could do for May where I was, on the wrong side of the Himalayas. I kept telling myself I should go back to China – it was my only real hope of helping May, the only way to salvage something positive out of this mess. But I just couldn't do it: I'd reached a limit within myself.

Marinho and I had recorded dozens of hours of interviews and phonecalls in Vietnam and China. I began trawling through and transcribing them in preparation to begin scripting the 'Sisters for Sale' documentary. I started cataloguing the masses of accumulated footage, and worked on the project's website.

Mostly, though, I just lay in bed and watched old movies, and only left the room to eat. Occasionally, when the weather permitted, I'd muster the energy to go walking in the mountains, but before long I'd be back again, staring mindlessly at the screen.

There are creatures in the depths of the ocean that are held together only by the immense pressure upon them. Once that pressure is removed, they lose their shape and function, and simply fall apart.

The pressure I'd felt in trying to help May and Pang had shaped my life and given me purpose. Now that pressure had been removed – now that I no longer had any contact with either May or Pang – I didn't know who I was supposed to be, or what I was supposed to do. My life felt like a shapeless mess.

I'd been playing an unfamiliar game with unknown rules against unseen opponents – and if I lost that game, terrible things would happen to my friends. I simply didn't have the strength to continue, and couldn't imagine how Michael and X did that same work for years on end.

I'd considered the possibility that my journey might end with expulsion, imprisonment, or worse: but to have all the pieces and fail to put them together just seemed absurd.

I watched movies to distract myself, but it didn't work. Ultimately, the stories I saw were all the same story. It was the same story I'd been hearing all my life, a story I knew so well it might as well have been coded into my genes. It was a story that told me that success was my responsibility, and that any failure was mine alone.

DON'T CARRY IT ALL

As a child, I was a voracious reader, and would read anything I could get my hands on.

Among the stories I loved best were true, firsthand accounts of people who had experienced unique events far beyond the bounds of ordinary life. Explorers who had crossed mountains, deserts, and oceans to the very limits of human endurance; officials who had battled every type of criminal; ordinary people who had survived every conceivable catastrophe.

I couldn't have those experiences myself and I didn't want to: I just wanted to know how they'd felt, to draw a cup from the vast well of human experience.

Like so many other stories I absorbed from books, films, TV, and from the people around me, these stories were essentially all the same story: a story of hardship, perseverance, and ultimate triumph. That story became part of me, and became fundamental to my understanding of the world.

I've since come to realise that, while those stories may have been true, they never told the whole truth. They didn't tell the stories of those who failed; they didn't even tell the whole story of those who had succeeded and survived.

So many of these stories were written by a generation

of white men who were raised by former combatants in a post-war world, or else they were written by the combatants themselves. These were men who'd been taught to idealise strength and discipline, who believed emotion was a weakness to be mocked and repressed, and who often had low levels of empathy for anyone unlike themselves. They embodied a form of masculinity we now recognise as being harmful to themselves and those around them.

From their ranks came my teachers, my storytellers, my heroes, those who taught me what it meant to be a man. I built my dreams upon the stories they told me, and the same poison flowed into me.

These stories were a powerful and addictive drug to me: they gave me hope and reassurance in an otherwise chaotic and confusing world. They led me to believe in the unstoppable nature of my own inner strength, should I ever need to dig deep and call upon it.

But now that day had come, and I'd found myself lacking. I'd never realised that by absorbing our one great myth and internalising its lie, I'd taken out a colossal loan against my own future happiness.

While I'd been working in the Canadian Rockies, one of my colleagues had a prominent tattoo that read "Aut viem inveniam aut faciam" – *I'll find a way or make one.* It was a phrase attributed to Hannibal when faced with the seemingly impossible task of crossing Western Europe's highest mountain range with war elephants.

I'd seen that phrase constantly while I'd planned my search for May, and it encapsulated my mentality when I'd returned to Asia.

The belief that I could achieve anything if only I tried hard enough – it was the same unquestioned belief I'd absorbed from all those stories I'd so eagerly consumed as a child.

It took me far too long to realise that belief was not only foolish but absurdly egocentric – like the conviction that the sun revolved around the Earth, or that man held God-given authority over all other life.

It was nonsense masquerading as wisdom, and a moment's thought would have revealed it as a lie – but I'd never wanted to think about it, never wanted to lose the comfort it offered me. In clinging to that lie, I'd lost something far greater than mere comfort: I'd lost the ability to see the world as it truly was.

Drive and determination were certainly great advantages, but they guaranteed nothing. Those stories had somehow convinced me that if I threw my entire weight against the world, the world would yield first – but the universe in motion is inconceivably larger and more powerful than any of us.

You can very easily drive yourself to the very limits of your mental and physical health and still fail. Far too many people do exactly that – and far too often their stories remain untold, so that others can keep clinging to our great comforting lie.

Now that lie had almost wrecked me, driving me far beyond the point at which I should have stopped for the sake of my own well-being. When I most needed support, the only advice our one great myth could offer me was: *Try harder.*

Our myth refused to recognise the impossible, or acknowledge any extenuating circumstances: it saw only human weaknesses, which belonged to those who failed. Nowhere in our mythology does anyone give up without being punished by fate.

Just as it convinced people to sacrifice themselves on battlefields, or to spend every waking moment working for other people, our one great myth had convinced me that the path to success and happiness led through pain and hardship.

The stories we're told revolve around one magical redemptive moment when all adversity suddenly falls away, and all the pieces fall neatly into place.

Far too many of us are left waiting endlessly for that moment – and the worse our situations become, the more desperately we hold on, telling ourselves that the darkest hour comes before the dawn. Restless and unbalanced, we push each other onwards towards that promised moment that arrives rarely and briefly, if at all, before flitting away again.

When I'd failed – as we all inevitably fail, in one way or another – that failure was magnified by a sense of guilt and shame that the failing was all mine.

Our one great myth kicked me when I was down, told me everything was my fault, and shunned me when I most needed something to believe in – yet I went crawling back to it, without seeing how abusive our relationship had become.

The myth assured me that if I'd tried harder, that if I'd been a stronger, smarter, better person, then I would have found some way to succeed. In the shame of failure, when I most needed the support of others, I locked myself up in silence and bore defeat alone.

I began seeking out the flaws in my own behaviour and picking apart anything I'd done that was less than perfect. I was disgusted with myself for having wavered, for having become distracted, for allowing doubt to cloud my judgement. I'd called May too often, and aroused the suspicions of her "husband". I'd made poor decisions, and taken badly-calculated risks. I'd failed, and deserved to fail. I was fundamentally flawed – and that was my fault, too.

For years, my greatest regret of the entire project was not taking that flight back to China. I was unable to see what little difference it would have made, and how little control I truly had over May's situation. I was furious with myself for not being as strong as I'd wanted to be, for failing at what felt like such a crucial moment.

I tried to tell myself that May had chosen to remain in China, and I'd only done what she'd wanted. I tried to tell myself that, until I rested and rebalanced, I was in no state to help anyone. I tried to tell myself that I'd already gone far beyond what anyone might expect of me.

None of that made any difference, of course: facts were no match for the myth.

It took me years to forgive myself, to realise that the failure wasn't mine, to understand there was no shame in having discovered my limits. It took me years to see the toxicity of a culture that refused to consider me good enough until I'd pushed myself to breaking point, and perhaps not even then. It took me years to see that my story still held validity and meaning – more so, in fact, than the comforting lies we constantly tell ourselves.

It took me years to be able to say, *I needed a rest and I took one*, and to make my peace with that fact.

NEVER CONTENT

But that's not the worst of it: there is another side to our great myth which is still more dangerous.

In a culture where we've enslaved ourselves to a lie, where we blindly worship success and those who succeed, failure can carry a terrible price – but so can success.

Two years earlier, in southern California, I'd told myself I'd do whatever I could to help May, and that I wouldn't back down for anything. That resolution had been made with the purest of intentions, and it's easy to see it as a noble, selfless endeavour, but I've since come to see the secret horror hidden within it.

I'd been prepared to go to any lengths to achieve my goal and avoid a sense of personal failure. I'd known from the beginning it would be almost impossible to find May in China, but some part of me refused to accept it. I'd pursued my goal recklessly, placing my success above all else. I'd cut corners, run inappropriate risks, and endangered other people. Ultimately, it was only a matter of sheer dumb luck that I'd been able to meet with May in China – and even then I'd been unconscious of the danger I'd placed her in.

Yes, I'd risked my life – but that wasn't anything to be

proud of. I'd risked the lives of other people too, including the very person I'd come to help.

While the cost of failure is a deeply personal one, the cost of success is so very often borne by others, and is rarely factored into the equation. I was praised as a hero and inspiration at a time when I was a danger to myself and others. I was applauded for something that had ultimately been a matter of chance.

The fact that I'd found my kidnapped friends in China made a great headline, but whether I'd actually helped them or only further endangered them was a more difficult question. It's so easy to fall for a bold headline and shy away from the finer print: we do it every day. We choose leaders who paint the world in black and white, because it's far easier to believe a simple lie than to grasp a complex truth.

I was now paying the price for my failure, and could only hope that May and Pang weren't forced to pay too high a price for my supposed success.

One reason I'd begun my search for May was because there was something missing within myself. I'd found it easier to look outward than inward, and tried to solve an internal problem with an external solution.

I've since recognised that same relentless drive in others. Those who are spurred most ruthlessly towards success, who are willing to do anything to achieve their goals, are very often those who have been deeply hurt. They don't have the tools or support they need to heal and find peace within themselves, and so they turn outward. They come to believe that their own personal ends can justify any means – and in their desperation to succeed, they very often hurt others and damage the world we live in.

We all play a part in this story, for these are the behaviours that our culture rewards most richly. Someone whose entire existence is focused on accumulating more money than they could ever need or want is neither a healthy nor balanced person – and yet these are the people we praise and idolise as role models, the people we admire and aspire to become.

The myth harms all of us, whether we succeed or fail. It harms even those beyond the bounds of Western culture, and the very systems we depend upon for our survival.

We make these strange and senseless connections between suffering and goodness, between being busy and being fulfilled in life. We worship people's belongings rather than their behaviour.

Of course, there's nothing inherently wrong with the concept of success, or with striving towards a goal. The problem arises when we place success above morality, social responsibility, and our own well-being. I'd acted with the best of intentions – but I'd been trying to solve a problem with the same mentality that had created it.

At the outset of my journey, I'd asked myself what success meant to me. Without having any idea of what my journey might involve, I'd already decided that what I wanted personally took precedence over anyone or anything else I might encounter along the way. I carried with me a sense of purpose that trampled everything in its path.

We so often push ourselves to succeed in one area of our lives to try to redeem our failure elsewhere – in my case, a failed relationship with Dominique.

Rather than supporting and encouraging us on our journeys through life, we have a culture that places unreasonable expectations upon us and makes us feel inadequate for not living up to them. We are hurt, and hurt others.

Even when we do succeed, we don't know how to stop, and we find ourselves chasing the mirage of happiness across an endless desert. Each new success simply becomes one more step in the unending struggle of our lives: as soon as we reach one goal we set our sights on a more distant one, pausing only briefly, if at all, to appreciate what we've achieved. We expend so much energy, and cause so much harm, trying to heal ourselves in all the wrong ways.

When we are driven to succeed at all costs, how can we be

surprised by greed and corruption, by human rights abuses and environmental destruction? When we view material wealth and attractive young lovers as markers of success, how can we be surprised when our daughters become commodified?

True courage isn't trying to find your kidnapped friends in China. True courage is sitting quietly and being honest with yourself about why you do the things you do. True courage is admitting you've made mistakes, and trying to find a better way.

I'd never had that kind of courage, or that kind of honesty with myself. I still had plenty of hurting to do, of myself and others.

SHAKE IT OUT

The momentum that had carried me up to northern India was gone. My inertia grew, and mountains of guilt and shame piled on top. I was out of the game, like a pinball stuck in some obscure corner of the machine.

It took an earthquake to snap me out of it.

Some of the other travellers I'd met in Amritsar had also made their way to McLeod Ganj. One day, during a break in the weather, I went walking with a friend through the mountains high above the town.

We were walking along a narrow path on the face of a mountain when a sudden shock went through us both. It felt as though a titanic fist had slammed into the rocks immediately below us.

I'd never before experienced an earthquake. Being the monsoon, when torrents of water chew away at cliffs and bring them down, my first thought was that the mountainside had fallen away beneath us. I looked down, saw nothing, then turned to look at the rocks above us.

We were completely exposed – there was nowhere to run, nowhere to hide, nothing we could do. My only clear thought was, *Whatever happens next is beyond our control.*

It wasn't the panicked freeze of a deer in headlights: it was a calm acceptance of my own limitations. My heart was hammering, but my mind was clearer and more peaceful than it had been in weeks.

There was a second shock, identical to the first, and then – nothing. It was strangely silent: there were no sounds of falling rocks, no breaking trees, no cries from the valley below. It was almost as if my friend and I had imagined the entire episode, until we saw the freshly-fallen rocks lying further along the trail, and the seething masses of worms crawling out of the earth.

We later learned that the magnitude-five quake had been felt hundreds of kilometres away, and we had been standing just a few kilometres from its epicentre.

The other travellers I met in McLeod Ganj were all on holidays. Most of them had come to study yoga or meditation, and many had adopted the Buddhist mindset of acceptance and non-attachment.

In many ways, that mindset seemed more healthy and balanced than the endless, unsatisfiable striving of Western culture. In other ways, though, it struck me as escapist, an abdication of responsibility.

There were certain things in the world I simply refused to accept – but in that moment on the mountainside, I found complete acceptance. I accepted my limitations, my lack of control, even the potential loss of my life. The quake had jolted me back to the present moment, lifted the crushing weight of responsibility I'd felt, and – by bringing me into sudden confrontation with my own mortality – brought me peace for the first time in weeks.

It was time to get moving. I was no use to anyone up there in McLeod Ganj, least of all myself. I didn't know how my part in the story might end, but I wouldn't let it end there.

My time in McLeod Ganj had made me understand one thing very clearly: that my own sense of freedom and happiness had become deeply interwoven with May and Pang's, however

I might feel about that. Like a Chinese finger trap, I couldn't simply pull away: I was caught, and my only hope of finding release was by pushing deeper.

What happened with May and Pang was largely out of my hands, but not entirely. I couldn't do everything, but I could still do something – and maybe, just maybe, that would be enough.

Six months earlier, I'd been contacted by a Swiss journalist named Anemi, who freelanced for several German-language newspapers and magazines. Anemi was based in Hanoi, knew some of May's friends in Sapa, and wanted to interview me for an article about human trafficking. We hadn't yet had a chance to meet, but had stayed in touch.

In early August, when I was still expecting to go to China for May's rescue, it had seemed that Pang was to be rescued imminently by Blue Dragon. Anemi owned some basic filmmaking equipment and, in my absence, offered to record footage of Pang's return to Vietnam for me, which was much appreciated.

Then Pang had postponed her rescue, and Blue Dragon expected to bring her home in September instead. Anemi was spending September at home in Switzerland, so wouldn't be in Hanoi to record any footage.

An earthquake, of course, hadn't solved all of my problems: I still didn't know what was happening with May, and still wasn't ready for China. With nobody else to record Pang's return, I decided to fly back to Hanoi rather than Hong Kong.

As it happened, I arrived back in Vietnam just as Anemi was leaving, and she was lovely enough to give me the use of her apartment while she was away. We met for the first time when she gave me the keys, and that's where I spent the month of September.

On my first trip through Vietnam, four years earlier, I'd been sick with fever and hadn't particularly enjoyed my time there. That had all changed when I'd met a group of expats living in Hanoi, who'd helped me see Vietnam in a new light.

Now, though, all of my friends had left the city, and it felt just as alien to me as the first time I'd arrived.

A new northwestern highway had been opened, halving the travel time between Hanoi and Sapa to just five hours. It would have been good to visit for a few days and reconnect with my friends there – but I didn't go.

Despite our continual correspondence, I hadn't met with Michael in person for over six months. It was just a short distance from where I was living to Blue Dragon's headquarters, and it would have been great to discuss May and Pang's situations with him – but I didn't do that, either.

I'm sure you've been waiting for this story to take a more positive turn, and so was I. If this was a fictional story, a moment of clarity brought on by an earthquake would have been an ideal moment for a major turning point – but life, unfortunately, is not so simple.

In coming to Hanoi, I'd merely exchanged one monsoon for another. I'd fallen back into a funk and just couldn't seem to shake myself out of it. I'd come there in anticipation of Pang's return – but Pang didn't return, so I spent the month of September alone in an unfamiliar corner of Hanoi, grappling with the 'Sisters for Sale' documentary.

It was the middle of September before I received any news, and it wasn't the news of Pang I'd been hoping for: it was the news about Mike.

SWEET SORROW

In the six months between its conception and its launch, there were only two people I'd told about 'The Human, Earth Project'. The first was my elder brother Nick, who'd built the project's website, and the other was Mike.

Mike was a musician from my hometown in Australia, a close friend of my younger brother who over the years had gradually become a friend of mine. With an irrepressible sense of humour, a magnetic personality, and a heart of solid gold, Mike was the kind of person you couldn't help but admire.

Just as I was looking for a piece of music to accompany the project's launch video, Mike shared an instrumental track he'd recorded – it was called 'Sweet Sorrow', and it was exactly what I wanted.

When I told Mike about the project, not only was he happy for me to use his music, but his early enthusiasm for my work helped give me the courage I needed to push it forward.

What I'll always remember about Mike was how even in the middle of jokes and laughter he could suddenly knock you flat with a spontaneous, heartfelt compliment.

He had a way of seeing the best in people, of making them feel like better human beings and giving them the confidence to be themselves. He helped you see more clearly the kind of person you most wanted to be, and the world was a better place through his eyes.

Soon after the project launched, Mike moved to Whistler, in western Canada. I was then living at Lake Louise, a nine-hour drive further east. Mike and I had made plans for a road trip together, but they fell through – then he met a local woman named Krista and fell head over heels for her.

I visited Mike briefly that July, then he and Krista came to visit me in August, and we'd gone hiking in the mountains. On our last day together, Mike and I had spent hours sitting atop a local peak, looking down over the valley, talking about everything and nothing.

Mike was always laughing, but I'd never seen him in such high spirits as he was that summer. Krista was lovely, and he made no secret of how happy he was with her.

Mike and Krista were hoping to come with me to Burning Man soon after, but they didn't make it. Then I'd left for Asia to begin my search, and I didn't see them again.

From the moment I landed in Asia, the project took over my life, and I'd had far less contact with my friends. My conversations with Mike became brief and rare. I knew that he and Krista had begun living together, but didn't know they were expecting a child.

For eighteen months, 'Sweet Sorrow' had been a motif binding many of our videos, from that original launch video to one I'd edited there in Hanoi just a week earlier. It had become the unofficial theme song for the project – and when the 'Sisters for Sale' trailer and documentary were finally released, it featured in both.

But Mike was so much more than his music – and for those who never met him, I'm sorry that you'll never have the chance.

Three years later, I found myself back in western Canada. I was rockclimbing outside Squamish when a local friend pointed out a jagged two-thousand-metre peak nearby. He told me its name was Sky Pilot, and said it was notorious for killing inexperienced climbers.

I'd never seen the mountain before and hadn't known where it was, but I hadn't forgotten the name. I told him that one of those climbers had been a friend of mine.

Mike had loved Krista, and had loved living with her there in western Canada, which he'd described as a paradise. He'd had so much to live for – including little Finn, the child he never met, who entered the world two months after Mike was so suddenly torn from it.

I was alone on the other side of the world with no home, no partner, no child, and little to look forward to. Over the past six months I'd taken a series of inadvisable and potentially lethal risks. Ironically, in one of his last messages Mike had told me to stay safe.

It might not have been a logical reaction, but in the week following Mike's death, my one recurring thought was: it should have been me. If I could have swapped places with him, I would have – but we don't get to choose these things.

Here's to you, Mike. You were the best of us.

STAY POSITIVE

After all we'd been through and achieved together, I hadn't been comfortable ending my partnership with Marinho on such uncertain terms. I wanted him to feel he still had some part in the project he'd helped build. Now that we no longer had the daily tensions of working together under such intensely stressful conditions, I was hoping to repair the damage that had been done between us.

We seemed to be getting back on better terms – but in September, Marinho began acting erratically and sent a series of confusing, contradictory messages. I noticed he was behaving oddly on Facebook, which had been our most regular point of contact: he removed me, tried to add me again, cancelled his request, then changed his account name before deleting it and disappearing from social media altogether. When I emailed Marinho about his behaviour, his response was equally incomprehensible.

Seven months earlier, Marinho's girlfriend had come to visit him in Sapa. I remembered what he'd told me on the day that she'd left for home: "There goes half of me." I'd had the sense at the time that their relationship was already approaching its end, though Marinho had still seemed unaware of it.

The following month, while Marinho and I continued our work in Asia, his girlfriend had been assaulted in Europe. She had now left him, and he seemed to blame me for their separation.

I knew the separation must have hit Marinho hard, and could empathise with much of what he was going through. I now knew the sense of helplessness and frustration that came from having a partner assaulted, I knew how it felt to lose someone who meant so much, and I knew what it was to feel rudderless, in a transitional phase without a partner, house, or job.

I hoped he was okay: but that didn't mean I wanted him in my life any longer, and I certainly wasn't responsible for his relationship. I had no more patience for Marinho's destructive behaviour and was tired of playing the peacemaker. I severed all connection with him, and we didn't speak again for years.

In a way, I was glad there was a definitive ending between Marinho and me – mostly, though, I just felt hollow. We'd made a great team, so long as we'd been working together – and after having come so far and achieving so much, it was tragic that we couldn't even hold a civil conversation.

The end of our working relationship certainly wasn't the worst thing that happened in September: it was just another item on a rapidly-growing list of things gone wrong.

For the week following Mike's death, I felt paralysed: then I suddenly snapped out of it with new and hardened resolve.

It was time for me to go back to China, to do whatever was necessary to help May. I wasn't doing anything worthwhile in Hanoi, and didn't want to waste any more time hanging around waiting for Pang to decide what she wanted. I'd head back to Shandong, re-establish contact with May, and be there for her when she was ready to leave.

The project had long been a balancing act between trying to raise awareness of human trafficking, and trying to keep a very low profile in the presence of traffickers and of governments known to be hostile to foreign media.

I'd always known there was a risk of my being blacklisted from Vietnam, China, or both. I took what precautions I could, and hoped it wouldn't happen while there was work yet to be done. Now, however, my fears came true.

I submitted a visa application to the Chinese embassy in Hanoi, and returned a few days later for the results. For both of my previous applications, I'd been sent away at this point for additional paperwork. This time, however, I was flatly denied: the Chinese authorities would no longer allow me to enter their country. I was told that a command had been issued refusing me entry because my motives were believed not to be touristic.

They were right, of course, and there was nothing I could do to appeal the decision.

I was furious with myself for not having taken my flight to Hong Kong in early August. I'd assumed that I'd have another chance to return to China later – but I was wrong. I'd been caught out, and might never be able to enter China again.

I might have been denied entry even in August, of course, but now I'd never know. How could I help May if I couldn't get anywhere near her?

Anemi returned to Hanoi on the last day of September. I couldn't get into China and wouldn't stay in Hanoi, so I took a bus to Sapa that very night.

I didn't particularly want to go back to Sapa – but where else was I supposed to go? That was the heart of it all, where May's story had begun and, I hoped, would soon finish.

Sapa had once been my idyllic and carefree home amongst the mountains, and I'd forged connections there I could never forget – but I was staggered by how much the town had changed in the six months since I'd last seen it.

On my first visit to China, I'd taken a long-distance bus to Guilin – a name I'd long associated with fantastic visions of stunning, forested limestone peaks. When I'd found myself disembarking in yet another vast Chinese city of concrete and asphalt, I felt that some mistake had been made. I had a similar sensation now, as I stepped off the bus in the once-familiar streets of Sapa.

The new, faster highway from Hanoi meant that instead of arriving at dawn, my bus had arrived in the depths of the night. It also meant that every weekend, Sapa was now swamped with traffic from the capital, and each weekly wave of tourists seemed larger than the last.

The sounds of construction echoed through the town centre. Brand new hotels had sprung up as if from nowhere, while older buildings sprouted outwards and upwards, like jungle plants striving for the sun.

There were increasing rumours that Sapa would soon have its own airport, and just beyond the town, another major development project was underway that would forever alter the area. A cable car was being constructed to cross the valley and climb Fansipan, Vietnam's highest peak, replacing a challenging multi-day hike with a prepackaged tourist experience. As ever, the lion's share of the profits would fill the pockets of the Kinh majority, while minority groups like the Hmong were pushed further into the margins.

Another thing that hadn't changed was that girls and young women were still being tricked, trafficked, and sold in China. Some returned, but most did not.

The past few weeks had left me with a sense of possibilities shutting down on all sides – with Mike's death, with Marinho, with my Chinese visa, and now with Sapa. I had the feeling that this would be my last stay in Sapa: it was almost time for me to say goodbye to the little mountain town I'd loved.

YOU CAN HAVE HER

It had been seven months since I'd first met with May's father Lung.

In that time, Lung had continually surprised me with the callousness he'd shown towards May, and the depths of his antagonism towards me.

One of the reasons for Lung's animosity was because I hadn't been the first person who had offered to help find May. Others had come, taking May's birth certificate and a few treasured photographs. None had succeeded, or ever returned.

I was no different, Lung told me – but he was wrong. Not only had I met with May in China – twice – but I'd come back to Vietnam bearing photographs and videos of May, her "husband", and their baby girl.

When I arrived in Sapa, I had a large portrait of May and her daughter printed as a gift for May's family. An unreliable laptop battery prevented me from playing the videos for them in their village home, so I invited May's family to join me in town.

Lung himself declined, but his wife Dung and eldest daughter Dinh came to visit me. It was a meeting that revealed the vast and seemingly impassable chasm between their culture and mine.

I had the photos May had sent me from her phone, and the photos and videos from my own meetings with her in China. The jewel in the crown, though, was May's wedding DVD, which she'd brought to our second meeting. The disc had been scratched, but I'd managed to copy almost two-thirds of the 136-minute video to my laptop.

Festooned with tacky effects of lovehearts, flowers, doves, and butterflies, the video unspooled through sequences accompanied by traditional Chinese music and trashy Western dance-pop hits from two decades earlier.

The first twenty minutes focused on the night before May's "wedding". The "groom's" family crowded around a boisterous female MC in a bright red jacket as she led the preparation and blessing of the wedding bed.

The filmmakers had left no doubt as to the purpose of the ceremony, or of the "marriage" itself: they'd superimposed footage of naked crawling babies over the blankets. A poster of two baby boys had been stuck to the wall over the bed – a constant reminder to May not just of why she was in China, but of her own inferior status as a woman.

None of us could understand what was being said in the video and we weren't interested to sit through all 87 minutes, so we skipped ahead. It was more than half an hour until May's first appearance, sitting on a bed all dolled up in red and white. A teddy bear sat beside her, a reminder of how terribly young she was.

The "groom" appeared in the doorway: a large, awkward man almost twice her size wearing a dark grey suit. This was the man who had bought, abused, and repeatedly raped May: the man that May's father insisted she remain with and obey.

To my mind, what May did with her life should have been her own choice, and nobody else's. According to both Hmong and Chinese tradition, however, it was May's father and now her "husband" who made May's decisions for her. I was the alien here: it was my ideas and values that were out of place.

But May's father was basing his decisions on bad information, some of which came from Cho's husband – and some of which came from May herself.

In the space of two years, May's family had lost two daughters to human trafficking, and a son to suicide. It had been a devastating time.

Now May wanted to come home – but until she did, she didn't want her family to suffer any more than they already had. She didn't want to upset them with the knowledge of all she'd suffered and was still suffering – so she lied, and hid the worst of her situation from her parents.

To ease their minds, May told her parents she was living happily in China with a rich man who had a very nice family, a big house, and treated her well. Many of the things she'd told me – especially those regarding her "husband" and the things he'd done to her – she'd specifically asked me to keep secret from her family.

"If you call to my sister, you don't talking about me and my husband," she'd told me. "If you talking about that, my sister call to my family. They will feel very sad."

But by trying to make life easier for her parents, May had made life far more difficult for herself. On hearing that his daughter was safe and happy in China, and unable to see any better options for her in Vietnam, Lung insisted she remain where she was.

And so May found herself stuck with her abuser. May was afraid that if she returned home, her father would judge her as a bad wife for having deserted a good marriage, and would refuse to accept her.

From my perspective, May's "husband" had done wrong for forcing her into "marriage" - but from Lung's perspective, I was the malicious one for trying to give May a chance to leave that "marriage".

Dung and Dinh had plenty of questions about May and her "husband". There were some questions I answered, some I didn't know the answers to – and others I couldn't answer because May had asked me not to.

I was later contacted by a member of the American Hmong community, who interpreted Lung's behaviour in spiritual terms. I was told that his reluctance to welcome May home was rooted in a fear of offending the protective spirits of his ancestors, and a fear for May's eternal soul.

By giving May and Pang the option of returning home, I was accused of threatening both girls with spiritual harm. Having already left their fathers' clan, if May and Pang now left their "husbands'" so-called clans, when they died their spirits would have nowhere to go. They'd become malicious ghosts cursed to wander forever in the wilderness.

Just as in Western religions, it was clear that the threats and promises of the afterlife served to enforce the social status quo here and now. The only approved lifestyle for a Hmong woman was subservience to a man, and any deviation was not only forbidden and shameful in this life, but would be punished eternally in the next.

I'd conducted exhaustive interviews with many members of the Sapa Hmong community, including human trafficking victims, survivors, and their families. My friends had made a special effort to interpret not only the language but also the local culture for me. I'd spent many hours discussing with May and Pang their potential return home and any related concerns.

There was never the slightest indication of any spiritual concern in any of these conversations. When I asked about spiritual beliefs I'd learned about through the American Hmong community, I was told that the culture was different in Sapa.

Lung, in particular, seemed concerned only with practical matters. Did he see himself as the defender of his family's spiritual honour? I doubt it – but if so, the real question is: Why would a family's honour rest on the mistreatment of its women?

If the threat of eternal punishment was part of May and

Pang's calculations, the fact that they would still consider running away from their "husbands" only showed how truly desperate their situations were.

YOU'RE A BIG GIRL NOW

It soon became clear that while Dung, Dinh, and I were watching the same video, we were seeing two very different things. From their perspective, the wedding video only seemed to support the claims May had made about having "married" a good man with plenty of money.

May's "husband" and his family were working-class Chinese. From a Western perspective, their home was a very simple one, and the "wedding" seemed like a shabby, kitschy affair. But for Dung and Dinh, who had never known anything but the poverty and squalor of village life, May's "husband" and his family were indeed wealthy. Their fascination with what I considered trivialities stopped them from seeing what I felt was truly important in May's wedding video.

There were some bizarre scenes I could only interpret as fertility rituals: two boys force-fed bananas to the "groom"; a woman rubbed a pair of hardboiled chicken's eggs on May's face, before feeding them to May and to a baby. The "groom" was encouraged to put his hand up underneath May's dress and he fumbled around between her legs.

It was clear from May's confused reactions that these customs were just as alien to her as they were to any of us. There was one excruciating scene where the MC wanted May to make a simple gesture as part of an otherwise incomprehensible ritual. May, of course, couldn't understand what was being said to her, and it seemed she'd been instructed to smile and nod whenever anyone spoke to her. For the longest time she simply kept smiling and nodding, like an automaton that had reached the limits of its programming, until she finally realised something more was expected of her.

In another scene May was expected to interact with the "groom", but clearly didn't understand what she had to do. It had been very heavily edited, drowned in music and cheesy computer-generated overlays.

I was disturbed not only by the video, but by Dung and Dinh's reactions to it.

Mother and daughter watched with mixed emotions as May was forced into "marriage" with a strange man so far from home – but they seemed disappointed only because they themselves hadn't taken part in the festivities, and overall, they seemed quite pleased for May.

Couldn't they see how desperately lost and confused May was, how much she was suffering? I'm sure they could – but from their perspective, these weren't the key facts. From their perspective, suffering was an inescapable part of life, and May's "marriage" was more successful than they could have hoped for.

For them, the price that May had paid – being kidnapped, taken away from her home and family, sold into "marriage" with a stranger, raped, abused, and denied all reproductive rights – was nothing particularly unusual. Any Vietnamese Hmong woman might expect to pay the same price even for marriage within her own community, and marriage was the price she had to pay to retain the acceptance of that community. A woman might hope for, but couldn't necessarily expect, much more from her marriage. To Dung and Dinh, this was simply the price of being born female.

While I was horrified at the sight of this tiny teenage girl being forced into "marriage" with a significantly older and much larger man, the two Hmong women saw a strong, well-dressed "husband" who would have been a great asset on any farm. They saw a house that was far superior to their own, and marvelled at the relative wealth lavished on the wedding gifts, clothing, and celebrations.

To my eyes, these things were unimportant superficialities in the face of an appalling human rights abuse – but I'd never had to live in a muddy hut without a floor or windows, wearing the same threadbare clothes every day, eating what little I managed to coax from the earth before the killing frosts of winter came creeping back.

Being unimpressed by solid walls, a comfortable bed, a refrigerator, and a colour television didn't make me a more sophisticated person – it only meant I'd had the good fortune to have been born in circumstances where I could take such luxuries for granted.

Yes, May was trapped in China – but they were all trapped. A Hmong woman married in Sapa might pay the same terrible price as May and still spend the rest of her life trapped in grinding poverty with no hope of escape.

Dung, Dinh, and the vast majority of Hmong women in Sapa were caught in that poverty. How could they look at May's life with anything but envy? She'd received more than they ever would, and lived with comforts they could only dream of. While they fought every day to keep their heads above water, May had been lifted to dry land.

On returning to Sapa I'd heard of another attractive young Hmong woman who, despite having heard all the horror stories of trafficked girls and despite all the warnings from her friends and family, had been so desperate to escape her life in Sapa that she'd gone voluntarily to China with a Chinese Hmong man she'd met only the day before. He spoke a different dialect: she couldn't understand him very well, and didn't even know his name.

The police caught the man taking the girl across the river

north of Lao Cai, and her family went there to bring her home – but even then she refused to come back, believing she was to be sold into marriage in China.

When her family realised they couldn't dissuade her, the conversation had become a financial negotiation between her family and her trafficker. With little alternative, the family had accepted twenty million dong ($950) for their daughter and let her go.

May's family didn't live in a world of human rights and high ideals: they lived in a world of harsh and gritty realities. Even to mention a woman's reproductive rights and freedom of choice was to speak from a place of privilege that was completely alien to them.

In a society struggling so desperately to survive, crops, livestock, and a solid roof were objects of undeniable worth. A use could be found for a woman's body, but her happiness was an abstract concept with zero market value.

When Dung and Dinh thought of May in China, it wasn't as a teenage girl who had been kidnapped, raped, and forced into a life of horror. It was as a daughter and sister who would never again have to experience cold, hunger, or seasons of backbreaking labour in the fields. It was as a grown woman who would be clean, warm, and well-fed, and whose children would almost certainly survive. It was more than they themselves could hope for – and in their eyes, whatever price May had been forced to pay was worth it.

So far as they were concerned, May was sitting pretty: all she had to do to maintain her position was to keep her mouth shut and not rock the boat. That was the true reason why May's father loathed me: he was afraid that my meddling would disturb the equilibrium that kept his daughter safe.

Although May had fed him false information, that didn't mean Lung was wrong. From my perspective, everything about May's life was wrong: but Lung was dealing in facts, while I was importing ideals that made little or no sense in Sapa.

The wedding DVD continued with streamers, confetti, and firecrackers. There were speeches, incense, and clouds of floating soap bubbles. There were red money-filled envelopes, candy, and a lengthy ceremony in a crowded courtyard. The "groom" placed a ring on May's finger; the MC grabbed her arm and held it triumphantly in the air as May seemed to struggle with a rapid series of conflicting emotions.

The guests all posed together in the sun and waved to the camera. May stood in the centre of the group with her new "husband", looking unhappy and uncomfortable – and then the video cut out.

SUCH GREAT HEIGHTS

When I'd first launched 'The Human, Earth Project' eighteen months earlier, I'd taken inspiration from Pulitzer Prize-winning journalist Nicholas Kristof. Drawing on his research and extensive personal experience, Kristof asserted that the most impactful type of story was a positive, heartwarming account of triumph focused on an individual rather than a group or broader cause. To try to tell a story that was larger, more complex, or less positive than that, he warned, was to tell a story few would ever want to hear.

The trick was to make audiences feel good, so that they would find supporting a cause "every bit as refreshing as, say, drinking a Pepsi". Kristof's formula was clearly a successful one: his stories had raised tens of millions of dollars for worthy causes around the world.

The pattern Kristof had described was, of course, the pattern of our one great myth – and it had already become clear to me that 'Sisters for Sale' wouldn't fit that pattern. The story was still evolving, even as I tried to sketch it out, but it had exploded into a shapeless mess, just as my life seemed to have. There was no ending and no clear message, and I didn't even know how to start putting it together. While Kristof's pattern presented a clear problem and a clear solution, this story had neither.

Who was the individual at the centre of the story? I'd hoped it would be May – but where was her heartwarming triumph? She was still stuck in China with the man who'd bought her. Even if May was able to overcome her fears, escape her "husband", and return home to Sapa, how was she to find a happy ending there? She would still be trapped by poverty and forced into a life she didn't want by the demands of her family and culture.

It was easy to see why May had placed her hopes in Sebastien – but that was just one more futile dream. I knew that Sebastien would never marry her, and I could barely even imagine what a happy ending might look like for May anymore. Even if she could find one, it could never erase all that she'd been through. It could never counterbalance the endless suffering that saturated her society and weighed down its women.

I'd hoped to tell May's story to inspire action and help protect other young women in danger – but now I saw the contradiction inherent in that goal.

May's story was many things: it was dark, complex, and fascinating, and it revealed a glimpse of the inner workings of the world. But it certainly wasn't the uplifting, comforting, feel-good story people wanted to hear, and there was nothing refreshing about it. I wondered how many awkward truths Kristof had buried while fitting stories to his formula, all the horrific things he'd seen but couldn't share.

The only way to make May's story a happy one was by stripping it of all the complex truths that made it so vitally important and by twisting it into a lie. If I told that story – if I took May's trauma and used it to make other people feel better about themselves – then I'd only be adding to the list of wrongs perpetrated against her. Even if that story succeeded in raising awareness, it would be a betrayal of May herself.

There was no place for May's story in the world we'd

built. We want stories that reassure us that everything's fine, even when it's not. We want happy endings that demand a bare minimum of action on our part, even as greed and inequality run rampant and we drive our planet beyond all sustainable limits. By choosing comforting lies over complex and unsettling truths, we've taken out loans not only against our own future happiness, but against our very survival as a species.

This was no longer a simple little story about May and me: it was a ravenous whirlpool that had drawn in both her culture and mine. We each faced seemingly insoluble problems – May's culture had caught her in a cycle of horrific abuse, and my culture had blinded itself to the truth.

I'd once seen a Khmer film whose protagonist – after being mortally wounded, and having his love taken from him – was taunted with the line: "Now do you see how high the mountain is?"

I'd begun my journey without the least idea of just how deeply challenging it was to become. I'd been willing to pay any price for success – but it was only now, after I'd poured so much time, money, and energy into the project, after I'd ruined my physical and mental health, that I saw what I was truly up against.

The very concept of the project had been flawed from the beginning, and the mountain was far higher than I ever could have imagined. When I'd set out to help May escape trafficking and abuse, I'd unwittingly set myself against her entire culture – in a way that was futile, and perhaps even wrong.

It gets cold up there in the mountains.

THE STATE I AM IN

Mine isn't the kind of family that reaches out for help: mine is the kind of family that stubbornly insists that everything is fine. We don't comfort each other through our moments of weakness: we simply deny their existence and soldier on.

With my head, heart, and guts in ruins, and having had nothing but bad news from the project for four long months, I just didn't know how to go on. On one hand, I felt I wouldn't be free until the problem of helping May and Pang had been solved – and on the other hand, I felt the problem was insoluble.

According to our one great myth, of course, there are no insoluble problems: there are merely people who persist, and people who fail. I felt as though I was inextricably bound to a project whose weight was slowly but surely crushing me.

I barely slept – and when I did, there was no escape for me even there. My dreams were full of death and horror, of being chased endlessly through dark abandoned places where everything seemed to go against me.

At five o'clock one morning, after yet another long, sleepless night, I finally cracked and reached out to my brothers with a long rambling message. I explained the deep sense of responsibility I felt for May, how frustrating her behaviour had been, how it was now almost two months since I'd even spoken to her, how I'd been barred from entering China, how I hadn't even met with Blue Dragon in Hanoi, how numb I'd felt after Mike's death, how disgusted I was by Marinho's attitude, how much I hated begging for money to continue my work, how absurdly misplaced everyone's praise felt, how I hadn't eaten or slept properly for weeks, and how I simply couldn't stand hearing any more human trafficking horror stories, which I'd been steeped in for far too long. I made no mention of Isabela.

"I'm just beyond exhausted," I said. "I look and feel like a zombie. I went to see a friend last week and I can't remember if her jaw actually dropped but she just stood there staring at me trying to find a polite way to tell me I look like shit. This project has taken over my life and there's just no end to it. I gotta get out of here but really don't know where to go and I'll feel guilty as hell if anything happens to May and I'm not around. I don't know how I expect sending this out is going to change anything but I've just been by myself on this for too long."

Why am I sharing these experiences here, when I was so reluctant to share them even with my own family? Because some of us need an occasional reminder to rest and rebalance before we push ourselves too far.

There is something fundamentally flawed with a society that glorifies endless struggle and seeks happiness in a steady, grinding self-destruction. The sense that we need to constantly push ourselves to breaking point to justify our own existence is pure madness, and it's a madness that far too many of us share.

So many of us already have everything we need, except for the ability to appreciate it – yet we still seek structure, identity, and meaning in ceaseless work and hardship. We spend our lives keeping needlessly busy just to assure ourselves we have value as human beings.

Driven by a need to constantly push ourselves to our very

limits, we feel a lingering shame in taking time to breathe, and we refuse to stop until something stops us. We promise ourselves happiness and seek it in all the wrong places, as if it were some prize to win.

You're important, too – and in case you've never heard them, these are the magic words: "I can't deal with this right now: I'm going to take some time out."

For me, this wasn't merely a moment of doubt, another challenge to overcome on the path to success: it was the beginning of a gradual realisation that I'd spent my entire life walking the wrong path, one that would never lead me where I wanted to go.

Of course, there were no miraculous solutions my brothers could offer me: I'd already dug myself too deep a hole. My elder brother Nick told me to get away from Sapa and the project – but I'd tried that in India, and I knew there was no longer anywhere I could go that my sense of responsibility and failure wouldn't follow me.

I'd finally hit rock bottom, and couldn't yet see any path leading back to a better place. I don't know how long I might have stayed there, or what might have otherwise become of me – because things suddenly began to change in very unexpected ways.

SHE'S NOT THERE

I'd been receiving regular reports from Michael about what was happening with Pang – but there hadn't been much to report.

For two months, Blue Dragon had been awaiting Pang's confirmation to bring her home. First Pang had indicated that she wanted to come home before the end of August, and then before the end of September, but both months had passed without anything more definite from her. Michael's messages were peppered with phrases like "nothing certain", "no guarantees", and "fingers crossed".

"Pang is continuing to be a bit elusive," he told me. "She really doesn't seem in any hurry to leave her situation."

Blue Dragon had planned an "assist" for Pang, but she'd had communication difficulties with the Chinese contact who was to bring her to the border, and she wanted to wait until X himself was able to stage a rescue.

I remembered when X had first called Pang, he'd also had communication difficulties with her. I suspected the true problem was not Pang's linguistic abilities but her wary mistrust of the men.

Tensions between Vietnam and China had eased, security

in China had relaxed, and X felt it was safe to resume rescue operations in southern China. On 5th October – five months after the territorial dispute between China and Vietnam had first escalated – X entered China in response to two separate urgent calls for help. Depending on the outcome of those rescues, if X didn't have to go into hiding or rush back to the border, he might have a chance to bring Pang home.

"We won't really know until the last minute," Michael said.

I was stunned by the news Michael sent me the following day. X was close to where Pang was living in China, had an opportunity to rescue her, and had called her to make the necessary arrangements – only to learn that Pang had already run away and was returning across China alone and unassisted.

X said Pang was now just hours away from Lao Cai. I called her directly, for the first time in two months.

"Right now, I coming back myself," she told me.

A week earlier, it seemed that tensions between Pang and her "husband" had finally reached breaking point. Pang had been desperate to get away but, for reasons unknown, said she hadn't been able to contact X. She'd also been trying to call her mother Bao in Vietnam, and had been trying to contact me on my Chinese number which was no longer operational. Frustrated with her inability to reach any of us, Pang had taken matters into her own hands and fled.

"I really, really don't want to stay here, so I coming back," she said. "But... I don't know where is here."

In the past two or three days, Pang had travelled some eighteen hundred kilometres across southern China – but now, having come so close to home, she'd become lost in the borderlands.

Pang believed she was somewhere in Jinping County, a sprawling mountainous region that lay along the Vietnamese border, less than fifty kilometres from Sapa. Looking at the map, I couldn't understand why Pang would be in Jinping – it wasn't on any logical route back home.

The borderlands could be a very dangerous place for a lost

girl. I told Pang to be very careful – and then she disappeared.

X spoke to Pang once more before she vanished. Pang told X she had a new friend who was helping her. X warned her not to trust anyone, and offered to rendezvous with her so he could bring her back to Vietnam safely. Pang said she'd think about it and call him back – but she never did.

For three days, X and I both tried and failed to call Pang: her phone rang, but nobody picked up. Pang didn't call us, or anyone in Sapa, and she didn't come home. Without a location, and without any contact, there was nothing we could do to help her.

Pang was gone.

EVERYTHING HAS CHANGED

As distressing as Pang's situation was, X's presence in China left us with a golden opportunity to bring May home. Michael messaged to say that if we could get May south to Guangzhou within the next two days, X could bring her home.

It would take about thirty hours for May to reach Guangzhou by bus – which left us with less than twenty-four hours to plan and execute her rescue.

None of us had spoken to May for two months. I didn't know how her situation might have changed, or if the break in communication had eased the pressure on her at all.

In mid-September, after six weeks of imagining the worst, I couldn't stand the uncertainty any longer. I'd dialled May's number – but I couldn't reach her. For almost three weeks, I'd been trying and failing to call May.

Before, I'd merely been imagining the worst: now the lack of response from May seemed to confirm it. When I realised I couldn't even enter China, I didn't know what to do.

Over the past two years, I'd asked a lot of people for all kinds of favours with the project – but rescuing May would be a tricky operation that carried very real risks for anyone who got involved, and it was simply too much to ask of anyone.

Ultimately, though, I didn't have to ask.

One of the foreigners who had assisted my search for May in China was a Texan named Charlie. Just two days before Pang disappeared, Charlie had reached out and offered to do anything he could to help May. I gratefully accepted his offer, and we began discussing the details: locations, timing, means of contact, travel arrangements.

The plan was essentially a repurposed, stripped-back version of the plan I'd developed earlier, with Charlie taking my role. He'd arrange to meet May at the crossroads, take her by taxi to a long-distance bus terminal, give her whatever money and information she might need, and send her south to X.

With the more relaxed security situation in China, there no longer seemed to be any need for May to linger in Shandong after her rescue, and I felt more comfortable about her travelling south alone. If Charlie could rescue May and deliver her into the hands of X, it had seemed that Blue Dragon could then arrange a safe and simultaneous return to Vietnam for both May and Pang.

Then Pang vanished, we had two days to get May to Guangzhou, and there was a sudden urgency to the plans we'd been discussing. This was the best chance we'd had to bring May home, perhaps the best chance we'd ever have – but we had to act fast. It didn't have to be perfect: it just had to work.

It was a national holiday in China, Charlie had been travelling, and his phone was dead. It took several tense hours before I was able to reach him, but Charlie then confirmed that he'd returned home and was ready to go at any time.

The only piece missing now was May herself. Could we reach her? Did she think I'd abandoned her? Would she answer, or would her "husband"? Was he still watching her closely? Was he still planning to send her away, or had he already done so? Would she be willing and able to leave the village – and her daughter – at such short notice? Could she get to the crossroads to meet Charlie?

It wasn't even clear if May's phone was still connected to the network. I dialled her number once more – and this time, it rang.

I hadn't felt anything special when I'd first re-established contact with May six months earlier – I hadn't even recognised her voice on the other end of the line. Now, though, I felt an enormous surge of relief when May answered.

Blue Dragon, Sebastien, and I had all worried about what might happen to May if her "husband" sent her away. Now I learned that he had indeed sent her away – but it wasn't at all what we'd feared. In fact, May's situation was remarkable only for being so very ordinary.

May had been sent to work as a waitress in a restaurant not far from the crossroads. She was working twenty-five days a month, from seven in the morning to nine in the evening, and had her phone switched off during that time. She'd only been able to answer my call now because she had two days off during the national holiday.

Now that the family had May's daughter as collateral, and now that the child no longer required May's constant attention, it seemed that May had been sent out to earn money in place of her "mother-in-law", who remained home with May's little girl. It seemed that May's "husband" was also working again, though it wasn't clear what he was doing.

May was exhausted by the long days and nights working in the restaurant, but after being kept inside a small house in a remote village for three years, she was glad to have some interaction with other people. She was earning three thousand yuan ($450) per month, which worked out to less than $1.30 per hour. May was allowed to keep and spend some of this money, though most of it went to her "husband's" family.

May had indeed recovered a measure of freedom, just as she'd hoped: because she was working early mornings and late evenings, she'd been permitted to rent a simple room of her own near the restaurant to save commuting in the dark.

As she now spent only five nights a month with her

"husband", there seemed to be little danger of May falling pregnant again, as she and I had both feared. While May was neither happy nor comfortable – nor, perhaps, even safe – she no longer seemed to be in any immediate danger.

Aside from an unexpected marriage proposal, there are few questions that could possibly carry the weight and pressure of the question I now asked May. I was asking her, at a moment's notice, if she was ready to exchange one life, home, and family for another. For months, she'd expressed a deep desire to return home to Vietnam – but was she willing and able to take that leap within the next twenty-four hours, even if it meant never seeing her daughter again?

At that moment, May was home alone in the village. She was free to move, and a rendezvous with Charlie would be easy to arrange. She was as determined as ever to return home – but said she wanted to wait two more months, because her baby was still too small.

At those words, I felt an overwhelming sense of futility and helplessness: May had told me exactly the same thing, for exactly the same reason, four long months earlier. I began to wonder if May would ever muster the courage to take the leap and do the one thing she said she wanted so desperately to do.

May was, however, able to shed some light on Pang's current situation, and was the only one who knew why Pang had gone to Jinping. She said that Pang had been taken there by the Chinese Hmong stranger – and suspected trafficker – who'd been calling her since July, telling her that he loved her and wanted to marry her.

Pang had originally planned to go back to Sapa first, and if she wasn't accepted there, to cross the border to meet this stranger – but the stranger had convinced Pang to change her plans.

When I'd met with Pang five months earlier, she didn't know how to return home to Vietnam by herself, and had been scared to try. But now, escaping her "husband" alone seemed to have been a deliberate choice that this stranger had talked her into. He'd told her which tickets to buy – not to reach Vietnam, but to come and meet him in Yunnan province.

When Pang arrived in Yunnan she'd finally met this stranger in person, and shared a meal with him. She'd called May immediately afterwards to say she didn't like him after all, and would go straight back to Vietnam.

But even in Yunnan, Pang still faced the same problem: she didn't know the way home.

The stranger said he knew the way to Sapa, and offered to take her there. Pang had accepted, and had expected to reach Sapa the following day: but she didn't. It seemed he'd taken her to Jinping instead.

As the days crept by and there was still no sign of Pang, it seemed certain she'd been sold again by this mysterious stranger.

BODIES

In a sense, May, Pang, and Vu had been very fortunate to have been sold as "brides". Another of their friends – a girl we'll call Shu – had not been so lucky. Shu had been trafficked from Sapa and sold to a Chinese brothel. It had been two long years before Shu had finally managed to escape with two other girls. It seemed they'd returned to Vietnam by themselves.

I'd never known Shu very well. I'd spoken to her during my investigations in Sapa, but she was understandably reluctant to share the details of her story. China was a long time ago, she said, and she didn't want to talk about it.

I was later told that she usually cried at any mention of China, and would never tell anyone what happened there.

Most of what I learned of the girls and women who were trafficked into brothels came not from the survivors themselves, but from those who helped them – particularly Michael and X at Blue Dragon, and Georges Blanchard at Alliance Anti-Trafic. What I learned horrified me, and some readers might prefer to skip over the remainder of this chapter and the next.

When I interviewed Michael and X in early 2014, Blue Dragon had rescued over eighty Vietnamese girls and women from China. Only two of these had been forced into "marriage": the rest had been sold to brothels.

Many girls were taken to brothels on China's south coast, or in nearby Macau or Hong Kong, which were all holiday destinations for Chinese men. There were many sex slaves in that region who had been trafficked not only from Vietnam, but also Laos, Cambodia, Myanmar (also known as Burma), and beyond.

Georges said the sex trafficking networks were principally Chinese – not only in China itself, but throughout Southeast Asia. By far the most dangerous networks were major mafia-style organisations supplying specific brothels. Other networks were smaller, less structured, and more opportunistic: girls would be passed along a chain of middlemen, each of whom would make one or two thousand dollars, for a final sale price of between five and ten thousand dollars. A girl would then be expected to recoup that investment and turn a profit for her owner, one client at a time.

A girl's value depended on her youth and beauty, and most victims were attractive girls between the ages of fifteen and seventeen. While Blue Dragon had worked with boys who had been sexually exploited within Vietnam, they hadn't encountered any cases of boys trafficked into China for sex.

Georges noted that the traffickers were targeting ever-younger girls, including a large number of thirteen-year-olds. Once a girl reached a certain age, she was no longer profitable – and so the younger a victim was, the more profitable years she still had ahead of her.

There was an increase in "virgin trafficking", which seemed partly based on persistent beliefs that having sex with a virgin would bring a man health and happiness. It wasn't merely sex, of course: it was rape and pedophilia.

A girl's virginity could be sold for around two thousand dollars, Georges said – and even before this, she could be forced to perform oral sex for clients. He had personally encountered two girls who had been forced into commercial sexual exploitation at the age of six. He told me of one fourteen-year-old girl who had forcibly undergone plastic surgery on her nose, mouth, and breasts before being commercially exploited, so that she would become "the perfect sex object".

X had rescued girls and women who had been forced to have sex with up to forty men a day, some of whom acted "very brutally". The girls were given no choice whether or not the men used condoms.

I couldn't imagine the psychological impact of being raped up to forty times a day, for years. A single rape can scar a woman for life – and these were only girls. It was too awful to contemplate the kinds of things that could happen to these girls once they were no longer profitable, or visibly infected with sexually-transmitted diseases.

Some girls considered suicide, and many had seen their friends and colleagues take their own lives by leaping from high balconies. The other girls were kept alive by the faint hope that they might someday escape and see their families again. One trafficking victim spent over thirteen years – close to five thousand days – captive in brothels before finally returning home to Vietnam.

When rescuing girls from China, Blue Dragon was responding to specific calls for help. A girl would first have to access a phone – perhaps from a sex worker who had not been trafficked and was working voluntarily in the same brothel. A customer who felt he had a special relationship with a girl might also give her a phone so he could contact her outside of working hours.

Typically, the girl would first contact her family who would then call the police, and the message would be passed to the anti-trafficking organisations.

Blue Dragon had to be very careful with any communication. If a girl was caught with a phone, she could be very severely punished, the phone would be taken from her, and she would often be moved or sold to another brothel. If her captors suspected a rescue attempt, she might even be killed. The girl would have her phone switched on only for limited periods, typically late at night or early in the morning.

Communication was generally text-based, and initial contact was followed by a complex process which could take weeks. Part of that process was building trust with a girl who had every reason to be suspicious of strangers. Before leaving Vietnam, the rescue workers would sometimes have their photo taken together with the girl's family, to show the girl during the rescue as proof of their connection.

Michael described the recent emergence of "fake rescues", which had further complicated Blue Dragon's work. Vietnamese men would make contact with trafficked girls, promising to help them, and possibly even taking payment from their families to do so – before taking the girl and simply reselling her to another brothel.

In one case, within half an hour of X rescuing a girl from a brothel, someone else had contacted the girl's family in Vietnam saying they could bring her home in return for a large sum of money: a brazen attempt to profit from a rescue they'd had nothing to do with. It was presumably one last effort by the traffickers to make money from that girl.

Blue Dragon also had to be sure they were in fact texting a trafficked girl, and not a brothel owner or trafficker who was trying to lure X into a trap. They'd take all possible precautions, speaking with the girl's family in Vietnam to verify any information she gave them, and even then X could never be entirely sure the situation was safe until he was in the middle of it.

At all hours of the night, Blue Dragon's operatives found themselves providing psychological counselling on major life decisions by text message to barely-literate teenage strangers who were being held captive in another country – which wasn't an easy task by any standards.

And, of course, they would also have to piece together any available clues to determine the girl's location, just as I had with May and Pang – which could be a long, laborious, and often frustrating process.

Despite the pervasive stereotypes of girls chained in grubby basements, even sex slaves weren't necessarily held captive twenty-four hours a day. After a time, they'd be allowed a limited measure of freedom: to get a haircut, perhaps, or to eat a meal outside the brothel.

The girls couldn't speak the local language and had no money of their own, so the brothel owners assumed they had no hope of escape, and wouldn't be foolish enough to try. There would be small windows of opportunity when a girl was unsupervised or wasn't being watched very closely, and these were the moments Blue Dragon had to use to their advantage.

X would try to arrange a rendezvous with the girl in a public place – an ideal but rarely practical location would be outside a police station, for example.

Blue Dragon had also helped Vietnamese girls who had escaped Chinese brothels unassisted, but didn't know how to get home. In a foreign country where they couldn't speak the language and had no paperwork, these girls were often afraid to approach the Chinese police for fear of being punished.

Once Blue Dragon had brought a girl back to Vietnam, they worked with communities to remove the stigma that often surrounded sex trafficking survivors. The girls frequently blamed themselves, too, feeling guilt, shame, and a sense of responsibility for what had happened to them.

While the anti-trafficking organisations would provide stable environments and psychological support to survivors, they couldn't erase the trauma the girls had experienced. Alliance Anti-Trafic had worked with many survivors of gang rape, and Georges spoke of one girl who went insane after having been raped by thirty men.

One girl Blue Dragon had rescued returned six and a half years later to thank them for their support. Michael said that while she was a physically healthy and apparently confident young woman, she would always bear the deep psychological scars of the three or four months she'd spent inside a Chinese brothel. She still suffered nightmares about her experience and didn't believe she'd ever marry, because she could never again have that level of intimacy with a man.

DEAD BODIES

A trafficked girl can be used for other purposes besides "marriage" and sexual slavery – and one of these is surrogacy.

A girl being forced into "marriage" with a stranger is essentially being sold for her womb: she's a baby-making machine for a Chinese man who wants a child or children.

Surrogacy takes that concept one step further, dispensing with the farce of marriage altogether. A girl sold into surrogacy will be forcibly impregnated and bear children for a series of unknown men, while she herself remains a captive of the traffickers. Several of these girls are commonly held together on a "baby farm".

Some of these girls are raped, while others are artificaly inseminated. As might be expected, baby boys are sold for a significantly higher price than girls. Sometimes pregnant women are also trafficked, so that their babies can be taken and sold.

A girl's vagina and uterus are not the only parts of her which have value in China, though. Perhaps the most horrific fate of all belongs to the girls who are rumoured to be killed for their organs, which are used for transplants or traditional medicine.

A girl's skeleton, her skin, and almost everything in between has market value. As you might imagine, though, it was difficult to find any firsthand witnesses, and the rumours remained exactly that.

For example, I met one girl from another of Vietnam's ethnic minority groups who had been lured away from her village not by romance but the promise of work. After several months she'd escaped her forced "marriage" in China, and had tried to find her own way home.

She'd been caught near the border and imprisoned for two months by the Chinese authorities while they confirmed her identity and processed the paperwork necessary for her return home. During her time there, the girl was told that she was extremely lucky not to have fallen into the hands of organ traffickers.

Apparently that particular region – which I was never able to locate on a map – was notorious as a centre of organ trafficking. Many people had been killed there, and a lost girl was an ideal victim. The girl believed that human intestines, which were sold and consumed as part of traditional medical treatments, were of particular value. The girl's friend, with whom she had been tricked and trafficked, was still somewhere in China, if she was still alive.

I heard another story in which a trafficked girl had escaped her captors and approached the Chinese police for help. The police had taken her to a room where she was locked up and had quantities of blood drained regularly before she was eventually able to escape a second time.

Whether a girl was sold into "marriage", surrogacy, or for her organs depended on her trafficker's contacts, and who was willing to pay more.

My friend Vu, during her own time in China, had heard gruesome stories of trafficked girls being killed in other ways.

Many of the men who bought Vietnamese girls didn't really want the trouble of a "wife" – they just wanted babies. When a girl had given her "husband" the child or children he wanted, and had nursed them to an age where they were no longer reliant upon her, she was disposable.

Girls could easily be resold to other "husbands" or brothels, or – particularly when they grew older and served little useful purpose – Vu claimed that many were simply pushed in front of oncoming traffic, so that the "husband" could claim restitution from a driver for his "wife's" death or injury. The transaction would be made swiftly, under the threat of criminal prosecution, with the "husband" taking as much money as he could get.

"If they don't want to keep her, they just kill her," Vu said. "The people have to pay you a lot of money."

These were the kinds of stories that came to mind when I caught myself wondering what might have happened to Pang, who had been lost out there somewhere in the borderlands, in the hands of a mysterious and highly suspicious stranger.

ECLIPSE

For three days and nights, I waited for news of Pang – but there was nothing. X came back from China without her.

Michael was deeply puzzled by Pang's recent behaviour. It struck him as bizarre that Pang would have left her "husband" without telling anyone, and that she would have put herself in the hands of someone she'd just met for the first time.

"Too many things don't add up," he said. "There's certainly a danger that she has met another trafficker."

Michael couldn't understand how a trafficker could have manipulated Pang a second time, or why her phone remained switched on but unanswered.

"I wonder if we'll ever know..." he mused.

For the sake of our documentary, I usually recorded my conversations with May and Pang, and would later listen back through them to catch any little details that might have slipped past me the first time. I'd bungled the recording of my final conversation with Pang, though, and had captured only the first ninety seconds of a much longer call. I realised that I'd failed to record what were likely to be Pang's final words to anyone in Sapa.

On my last trip to Vietnam, I'd interviewed a Hmong

man whose niece had been trafficked across the border by two Chinese Hmong men. The man and his brother-in-law had responded in an unusually proactive way: they'd crossed the border and widely distributed copies of the girl's photo in the adjacent region of China.

The strategy had been surprisingly successful. When the middlemen realised they were unable to sell or relocate the girl, they'd switched tactics and called the girl's family with a ransom demand.

The price they asked was more than the man and his brother-in-law could afford – so instead of taking money to the rendezvous, they took the police.

Ultimately, the middlemen were never caught, as they'd sent a bagman to collect the money – but after a two-week ordeal, the girl was recovered and returned home safely.

I had a recent photo of Pang from China, and wondered if we could do something similar. I couldn't get into China personally, and Blue Dragon didn't have any specific contacts in Jinping County, so it would be up to Pang's family to take action.

With what little information we had, however, Michael saw "very little hope" of success. Jinping was a mountainous county, with a dozen small towns and hundreds of thousands of people spread across three and a half thousand square kilometres – and we weren't even certain that's where Pang was.

On 8th October I took my camera and tripod up to Sapa's lake. It was a nice clear evening and, though I didn't have a particularly good lens for it, I wanted to record some footage of the moonrise. I arrived an hour early, and sat watching as the daylight drained from the sky and the lights of Sapa came flickering over the water.

At last, the moon raised its head above the line of mountains across the lake, but something wasn't quite right. I knew it was a full moon – I'd seen it the night before – but now only the thinnest and darkest of slivers slid up into the sky, barely visible against the blackness.

I couldn't understand it, and – never having seen one in my life – it took me several minutes to realise that I'd stumbled into the middle of a syzygy, with the sun, Earth, and moon aligned in a full lunar eclipse. I stood staring for another hour or more as the Earth's shadow slipped away and the gleaming disc of the moon gradually revealed itself.

It was a timely reminder that – every now and then, when you least expect it – strange and serendipitous things can happen.

Pang's mother Bao had no idea that Pang had escaped her "husband", crossed China alone, and had come almost within spitting distance of Sapa – for the first time in three and a half years – only to vanish again.

For the sake of not alerting the traffickers, Michael had asked me not to tell anyone in Sapa about Pang's potential return home – but that no longer seemed to matter. Pang was gone, and I felt Bao had a right to know.

On the morning after the eclipse, I rode out to Pang's village to tell Bao that her daughter had almost certainly been trafficked again.

Bao spoke very little English, and I would normally have taken an interpreter with me. My friends Chan and Chu had interpreted for me during my earlier investigations in Sapa – but now Chan was busy making preparations for her wedding, and Chu was studying in Lao Cai.

I went looking for three other friends but couldn't find any of them. Stopping at the market for a bowl of noodle soup, I found May's eldest sister Dinh doing the same.

Dinh barely spoke any more English than Bao did – but she could help me with another crucial piece of information.

Since the death of her husband several years earlier, Bao's only son had taken control of the family home, and Bao remained there with him. Their home was somewhere high on the mountainside above the village – and if you didn't know exactly where it was, you'd never be able to find it. I'd never been there, so Dinh offered to come with me, to show me the way.

As we entered the village, one of the local women told us she'd just seen Bao at a wedding in a home nearby, and pointed us in the right direction. Dinh and I dismounted and were walking along a dusty path between swaying stands of bamboo when Bao suddenly appeared, rushing towards us from the opposite direction.

Bao was one of the sweetest, most delightful people I knew, and I didn't want to be the one to break her heart all over again with the terrible news I carried.

But I didn't have to: something strange and serendipitous had happened. Bodies were in motion, preparing to align in unexpected ways.

Until a few minutes earlier, Bao had believed that Pang was still with her "husband" and daughter halfway across China – but Pang had just called to say she was somewhere at the border and needed help coming home.

Pang didn't know where she was. She said there was a big bridge, and many Flower Hmong people. It seemed likely she was at the remote Jinshuihe-Pa Nam Cum border crossing, which was a three-hour motorbike ride across the mountains.

Bao didn't know what to do. Her son had a motorbike, but he was away from Sapa for several days. Pang knew I was in Sapa, knew I could help, and told Bao to find me. We met on the pathway in a flurry of excited confusion – and then things happened very quickly.

HERE I AM
(COME AND TAKE ME)

It was then one o'clock. A cluster of local women quickly gathered, debating the best plan of action.

I spoke to Pang directly. We tried to pin down her location, but it was a bad connection and very difficult to hear what she was saying. Bao told Pang to stay where she was: we'd come and find her as soon as we could.

We climbed to Bao's house to get her identity card, and then she borrowed a helmet for the journey.

Neither Bao nor I knew the region Pang was describing, and would be just as lost there as she was. We knew it would be better to go with a local – and, in any case, it would be best to have a second motorbike. I could take Bao to the border, but a three-hour ride back across the mountains in the dark with two passengers wouldn't be an easy one.

Bao made a series of phonecalls and a middle-aged Hmong man named Leng agreed to join us on his own motorbike. Bao would ride with Leng, and Pang would come back with me.

The three of us rode back to Sapa, stopping at the Yellow Dragon so I could pick up my passport, some money, and warm clothing for the journey.

It wasn't clear if Pang was going to try to enter Vietnam via the official border crossing, or if she was going to try to cross illegally. In either case, she was a Vietnamese citizen whose only form of identification was a Chinese identity card. It was likely she'd be caught on one side of the border or the other, with unknown repercussions.

As we were refuelling our bikes in Sapa, Pang called again: she was relocating. Instead of meeting us at Pa Nam Cum, Pang now told to meet her at the major crossing at Lao Cai – which was only an hour's ride away, rather than three.

I didn't speak to Pang directly this time: the conversation took place in Hmong.

Bao and Leng didn't really seem to understand where Pang was or what she was doing, and neither spoke enough English to explain what was happening. Bao simply indicated that we were going to Lao Cai, and I followed.

Lao Cai and Pa Nam Cum lay in opposite directions from Sapa. The fact that Pang would suddenly switch our rendezvous from one border crossing to the other suggested that she was still lost – both physically and mentally – somewhere out there in the mountains.

We began riding towards Lao Cai, but had barely left Sapa when Pang called again. This time, she told us to return to Sapa and wait – so we turned back.

Long-distance buses to Sapa had recently begun operating from a carpark on the outskirts of town. A building had been demolished on one side of the carpark: this was where the locals now parked their motorbikes and sat around on scattered lumps of broken concrete by the roadside, waiting. Bao, Leng, and I did the same.

For reasons I couldn't understand, this seemed to be our new rendezvous with Pang. Had Pang already crossed the border? Was she trying to return to Sapa by bus? Which direction was she coming from – Pa Nam Cum, or Lao Cai? None of it made any sense to me, and I would have much preferred riding through the mountains to find Pang instead of waiting around helplessly for something to happen. I'd done more than enough waiting around over the past few months.

Pang's return still seemed far from certain, and I couldn't imagine what Bao must have been feeling. It had been three years and eight months since Bao had seen her daughter, and she'd never expected to see her again. In that time, her little girl had become a "wife" and the mother to a granddaughter Bao would never see, in a place that was unimaginably far from home.

Bao seemed both scared and excited. She sat fidgeting nervously, anxiously glancing around as if Pang might appear at any moment, from any direction.

There was a surreal yet oddly sweet element to the experience. When we'd first met earlier that year, I'd conducted a lengthy interview with Bao, and knew a great deal about her life and family. While I'd explained my work to her, she knew little about me as a person.

Now, as we sat by the side of the road waiting to see if Pang would reappear, Bao tried to ease her nervousness by making small talk – but the only things she knew how to say in English were the few simple questions that so many of the Sapa Hmong women learned to engage tourists on the street.

And so, in her own sweet, shy way, in the middle of such an emotionally-intense life experience, not knowing what might be happening with her daughter, Bao fumbled out what little English she knew to ask me about my own home and family. I explained as best I could where my parents lived, how old they were, how many brothers and sisters I had, and the fact that none of us had yet married.

Sitting there speaking to Bao and looking into her large liquid eyes, I had a sense of what an intensely private pain Pang's loss had caused for her. The Sapa Hmong women spent their lives surrounded by poverty, abuse, death, and disappearances – yet, from the months I'd spent getting to know May and her friends, it seemed they rarely if ever spoke of the things they'd suffered, and kept those feelings locked deep inside.

Now, with Bao in such a highly-agitated state, I could see her struggling with emotions long buried. I wished we'd shared a common language: I would have loved to have had a very different conversation with her.

As it was, we soon exhausted our shared vocabulary. I wanted to hug Bao and let her know that whatever happened next, I'd be there for her – but with the cultural and linguistic barriers between us, we simply sat and waited like two old friends, the air around us charged and crackling with unspoken emotions.

The shadows lengthened and the other locals gradually dispersed from the demolition site that was our waiting room. More than five hours had passed since Pang had first called Bao, and there was still no sign of her. Bao tried calling Pang, but her phone just rang.

The afternoon became evening, and the evening became night – and still we waited. Then Pang made contact again: she said she was close, and told us to meet her in the centre of Sapa.

Bao, Leng, and I relocated, standing anxiously in the darkness on the pavement above the town square. Pang called to say she was just arriving in Sapa – and then suddenly she was there, standing on the steps outside the church, handing a helmet back to a local man who stood beside her with his motorbike.

CANON IN D

It was seven and a half hours from Pang's first contact to the time she reappeared on the church steps. That long day of waiting was merely the culmination of a much longer wait – which had lasted months for me, and years for Bao.

If there was to be any simple, emotionally-pure moment in this story, it would be this one. Such a dramatic moment might typically mark the end of a fictional story, with smiling faces all around – but reality isn't quite so simple, and Pang's return was really just the beginning.

Somewhere on her long journey home, Pang had bought herself a new outfit. She wore a bright red dress with shining silver buckles, sparkling earrings, and high heels.

I'd never seen Pang so carefully dressed. It had obviously been important to her to make a positive first impression in Sapa, to help ease the shame of her abduction and the uncertainty of the reception that awaited her.

Standing there on the church steps, Pang no longer seemed like a local. She'd clearly been away long enough to forget how impractical a light dress and high heels would be on the cold, sloping streets of Sapa. Having been raised in the mountains, Pang had a much higher tolerance for the cold than I did – but after hours spent riding on the back of a motorcycle, even she had reached her limit.

I was expecting Pang and Bao to run into each other's arms. Instead, Pang stood fiddling uncomfortably with her phone, trying – unsuccessfully – not to cry. Behind her smile she was evidently struggling with a cascade of conflicting emotions.

Pang's anxieties seemed to centre around her mother, which struck me as odd: I couldn't imagine Bao being anything but supportive. She'd been enthusiastic about Pang's homecoming, and – in marked contrast to May's family – didn't seem to have had any reservations about her daughter's return.

While I was over the moon to see Pang back in Sapa, I was surprised and a little embarrassed by how warmly and eagerly she greeted me while she was distant, even dismissive, towards her own mother.

More than ever, I wanted to give Bao the hug that Pang hadn't. I had the sense, though, that both women felt a little ashamed of and overwhelmed by the intensity of their emotions, in a culture where such things are kept hidden.

Pang climbed onto the back of my motorbike and, as we rode through town, she remarked on how much Sapa had changed. I'd been shocked to see it after just six months away, and couldn't imagine how strange it must have appeared to Pang after her forty-four month absence.

Since making contact with her six months earlier, I'd listened carefully to Pang's fears and made it clear that she'd have my moral support whatever she chose to do. It seemed that I'd now become the ally she needed at such an emotionally challenging moment in her life, and I was glad to play that part for her. As we left Sapa on the road towards her village, Pang's reticence quickly fell away, and she began chattering excitedly.

Leaving the motorbikes in the village, we climbed the mountainside to Bao's home. As Bao stepped nimbly ahead, I remained behind with Pang, who struggled up the steep, slippery path in high heels. We both lost our footing more than once on the breathless, seemingly endless climb through the darkness – and then, suddenly, we were there.

Pang was home.

We stood outside for a moment catching our breath, surrounded by the sounds of cicadas, snuffling pigs, and water tumbling down the face of the mountain. Tiny lights lay scattered like so many fallen stars in the valley below, which was magnificent in the gleam of the near-full moon. I wondered if this was how Pang had remembered it during the long years she'd spent dreaming of home.

Pang's sister was there with her four small boys, and a mother and daughter came in from next door. Pang finally seemed to understand that her family was truly happy to have her home. Her lingering fears, and the strange distance she'd held between herself and her mother, quickly dissolved in the warmth of the family home. As everyone sat chatting around the table, there was a moment when Bao and I just sat there grinning wordlessly at each other.

After a simple meal of pork and rice, Leng rose to leave, and I asked Pang how to say goodnight in Hmong.

"I can't remember," she said. "I know only in Chinese."

"You can forget that now," I told her.

"I will," she said. "I'll try to forget."

Bao insisted I stay the night, rather than scrambling back down the mountainside in the dark, and I soon found myself on a rough bed in the loft.

For months, I'd had trouble sleeping. I couldn't sleep this night, either, but for very different reasons. I was buzzing with excitement, overjoyed at Pang's return, and could hardly believe how dramatically everything had changed over the past twelve hours.

Pang's return signalled a return of hope. The crushing weight of failure finally lifted, and I was able to breathe freely for the first time in months.

While Pang herself might have had mixed emotions about her return to Sapa, what I felt was something clean and bright and pure, a euphoria unlike anything I'd felt before.

It was an elation that felt almost like the sensation of falling in love, but without being focused on any particular person – and so it expanded to fill my world and made everything seem beautiful. I don't know how else to describe it.

I have a habit of storing my memories and emotions in other people's music. I had with me my headphones and a portable music player loaded with thousands of songs.

As I lay awake in the darkness in the loft of Pang's family home, I began scrolling through all those songs in search of one that could capture the joy I felt. I tried and discarded dozens of songs: rock, folk, soul, pop, punk, dance, hip-hop, and more. At last I found the warm soaring strings of Johann Pachelbel's 'Canon in D', and listened to it on repeat until I finally fell asleep.

That, to me, will always be the sound of Pang coming home.

WHICH WAY HOME?

The roosters began crowing before two o'clock, and Pang's sister was up splitting bamboo for the fire at four. I was the last out of bed at seven, and was greeted by the sight of Pang wearing her traditional Hmong costume for the first time in years.

I'd interviewed Pang in China six months earlier – and now, sitting outside her family home, she began telling me the rest of her story.

Over the weeks and months that followed, I was to hear Pang tell her story many times. New details gradually emerged, and others were later omitted as she found herself judged for things she'd done. As time passed, Pang depicted herself with increasing courage in her stories – and while she often contradicted things she'd said previously, I've put her story together here as best I can.

Pang had felt "never good" in the life that had been forced upon her in China, but generally tried not to think about what a horrible situation she was in. She said she felt "very sad every day", and didn't want to do anything but sleep. She often consoled herself with the thought that her situation could have been worse – at least she had food, clothing, and somewhere to stay – and with the hope that she would one day go home. She took solace in playing games on her phone, and told herself that when she spoke Chinese well enough to find her way back to Vietnam, she would go.

Pang's "husband" had never treated her kindly. He spent all of his free time drinking and playing cards with his friends, and denied any responsibility for their daughter. He said that if Pang didn't take care of their baby, his mother would.

Pang found herself torn between her desire to go home and her fear that if she left, she would never see her daughter again. If Pang's return to Vietnam didn't go well, she wanted to keep open the possibility of coming back to live with her little girl in China.

What Pang most wanted from her "husband" - the man who'd bought her, and had denied her any personal freedom for years – was the freedom to come and go as she pleased. It seemed like an impossible goal, especially given Pang's nasty temper and her desire to make her "husband's" life difficult in any way she could.

For years, Pang had been telling her "husband" she wanted to go home to Vietnam. Instead of telling her, "No," he'd told her, "Yes, but not yet" – and he used that unfulfilled promise to manipulate her. At first he'd said, "Stay here, we'll have a baby, then I'll take you home to see your family."

"Every year, he say that to me," Pang recalled. "First time he say to me, I little bit believe him. The second time I thinking, he just liar, so better that I don't believe him."

After Pang had given birth to their first baby, Pang's "husband" had only demanded more from her: he wanted Pang to give him two boys and a girl.

"First time I think, 'Okay, I can wait for one more year.' Second time, [after] one and a half year, I asking him, 'Okay, now I have one baby for you already. So we go?' He say, 'No, no, no. Still wait, one more baby.' Oh, you shit. I think, 'Okay, just one [baby] for you only, because I stupid. I born baby for you, but you just liar to me.'"

When Pang had asked her "husband" again about going home, he'd told her, "You can stay here for maybe ten more years, then I'll let you visit your family."

Pang was worried that even if she could leave, she'd never find her way back to Vietnam. She'd asked her "husband" how to get there but he'd only laughed at her, saying, "You're Vietnamese, and you don't know the way to Vietnam?"

She told me how her fury had boiled over when her "husband" had come home drunk late one night. She'd refused to open the door, leaving him standing in the rain for two hours. He'd threatened to kill her, saying she was all alone in China and nobody cared about her – then he'd called his mother to help him. The mother had then called Pang, and Pang had yelled at her, too.

After my arrival in China, Pang had felt a new urgency to go home.

"Every month, every year, I will thinking about, one day I will go home. So when you come to China, I say, 'Oh, this time I have choice, go to Vietnam for sure!"

Pang said she'd wanted to come back with me, but felt we'd draw too much attention together. She was afraid that she'd be recaptured and that I'd be in danger, too.

Pang had also worried that if she came back with Blue Dragon, her "husband" would never allow her to see her daughter again – and so she'd begun formulating her own plan.

By chance, Pang had met some friendly locals who had travelled to Vietnam for a holiday. Seizing her opportunity, she asked them many questions about the journey: how far it was, how they got there, how much it cost, and what documents they'd needed.

Pang was particularly concerned about filling in any paperwork. She'd learned how to write the Chinese name she'd been given and could recognise enough characters to navigate her phone menus, but was otherwise illiterate in Chinese.

The locals had been surprised by Pang's questions.

"They asking me, 'Why you asking me about that? You still very young, why you asking about go? You want to go by yourself, or what?'"

Pang told them, "No, I'm just curious."

They'd told her what she'd wanted to know, and had even written out the details of their route for her. Pang treasured the paper, and thought that if she could only learn to read enough Chinese to understand what was written there, then it would guide her home.

RELEASE

Pang believed she needed two thousand yuan (about three hundred dollars) to reach Vietnam. Her "husband's" family owned a small company and she'd worked there stitching shoes and handbags for global export.

While they never actually paid Pang – her "husband" took the money directly – working for them gave Pang some degree of leverage when she asked her "husband" for money for clothing.

Pang would make a special effort to be nice to her "husband", ask him for a certain amount of money, and then buy clothing of a lesser value, so she could pocket the difference.

In early October, she'd asked her "husband" for some money to buy a new winter jacket – money which added significantly to the amount she had squirrelled away, bringing her much closer to her goal. It was a "very lucky day" for her, she said.

That evening, while drinking and playing cards with his friends, Pang's "husband" had gambled and lost two thousand yuan – the same amount which Pang saw as her own salvation, and had been so painstakingly working towards. Pang had been furious that her "husband" could so casually throw away such large sums, and they'd had a particularly vicious argument.

"I be very mean to him," she said. "I angry with him. I say, 'Okay, just give a little money to me, I go back right now. I don't want to stay here with you any more.' Then he say, 'Oh, shit!' I say, 'Oh, f*ck!' Then he say, 'Okay, you don't care?' I think, 'I don't care. How do I care you for what?' He be very, very angry about this. Me, I also be very, very angry."

Pang's "husband's" friends had warned him that if Pang left, she'd never come back – but he told her he no longer cared, and hoped she'd leave. Pang told him he could go and find some other "very, very young" girl to marry – perhaps another fifteen year old, like she herself had been. He told her, "If you're going, just go – don't worry about me." Pang said she wouldn't worry about him – she'd only be thinking of how "very, very, very happy" she'd be to see her family again.

The day after the argument with her "husband", Pang had been speaking with her friends at work, and crying a lot.

One of Pang's work colleagues was a woman from Guangxi province, which was halfway between Guangdong and Vietnam. She said she'd help Pang buy a bus ticket to go home – which was surprising, given the fact that she worked for Pang's "husband's" family, and presumably risked her job by helping Pang escape. The woman asked if Pang would ever come back to China. Pang said she didn't think so.

Pang felt very alone in China, and her only comfort was her daughter. She knew that if she stayed there, her daughter would one day marry out to another family, and Pang would have nothing to look forward to but a miserable life and lonely death far from home.

As Pang was from Vietnam and her daughter was from China, she felt it was best that they each stay in their own country. She believed her "mother-in-law" would take good care of her little girl.

Pang's "husband" had been trying to call her after their argument, but she refused to speak to him. Once she had her bus ticket, though, she not only told her "husband" about it, but taunted him with it. It was the first of many things Pang had done on her journey home which left me shaking my head in disbelief, amazed that she'd reached Vietnam at all.

"I say, 'Hey, I have the ticket, looking here! I have ticket. Are you jealous?' He don't talking about anything, he don't looking about me. I just say, 'Today I buy the ticket, tomorrow twelve o'clock the bus, so tomorrow I have to go for sure.'"

To my great surprise, faced with the imminent loss of the "wife" he'd paid for and considered to be his property, Pang's "husband" made no effort to take her ticket or to stop her from leaving.

In fact, when he finally seemed to realise she was serious about leaving, Pang said her "husband" began treating her better than ever. Perhaps he believed that a last-minute display of humanity might somehow make up for years of mistreatment.

Pang's "husband" had helped her buy some bottled water, chicken legs, eggs, and other snacks for the journey, and reminded her to take enough warm clothing. Not realising how much money Pang already had, he'd given her more money for the journey, and had even accompanied her to the bus station.

Pang said her "husband" had been genuinely sad at her leaving. He was worried for her safety, because it was a very long journey to be making alone. He told Pang that if she didn't miss him, she would surely miss their daughter, and he reminded her that she could always come back.

Amazingly, it seemed that Pang had achieved all she'd hoped for: not only did she now have her freedom, but she'd attained it without burning her bridges, and still had the option of returning to her daughter if all else failed.

Pang said her "mother-in-law" had also seemed genuinely concerned about Pang's safety.

"You're alone," she warned. "You don't know how to read or write Chinese, and you need to be careful."

Then Pang climbed aboard the bus and was gone.

A few days later, her "husband" had called her in tears, asking her to come back – but it was already far too late.

CAUGHT BY THE FUZZ

That was one version of the story – but Pang later gave a radically different and far more plausible account of events.

She said her "husband" had been so drunk when she'd shown him the ticket that he barely seemed to have noticed, and seemed to have forgotten within a matter of minutes.

"He very drunk, he don't know anything," Pang said. "I say, 'Look, look, look, look!' but I think he forgot already. He go to sleep."

After sneaking out of his apartment the following morning, Pang had bumped into a woman she knew: a friend of her "husband's" family who lived in the same building. The woman had been surprised to see that Pang wasn't going to work that day. Thinking quickly, Pang said she was taking the day off to go shopping in Guangzhou with her "husband's" cousin.

The cousin was nowhere to be seen, and the woman was puzzled. Pang was scared that the woman would call Pang's "husband" to confirm the shopping story and discover it was a lie, which would send her "husband" and his family out in fury after her. The moment that the woman was out of sight, Pang hurried away.

"I just go very faster," she said. "When I go to in the main road I call some taxi."

It was the first time Pang had ever travelled alone. She had no understanding of Chinese geography, and she was scared. She couldn't read the signs or tickets, didn't know how to negotiate China's gargantuan bus stations, and things that might seem obvious to you or me were entirely unfamiliar to her.

"I feel scary," she said, "but when I been to the place I don't know how to go, I just try to asking the people, have some they're also nice."

Pang described her confusion in seeing how many buses there were at Guangzhou's central station, and her delight in matching the number on her ticket to the corresponding bus before it departed. She spoke of her ticket almost as if it were a magical object, opening the long-lost passage home for her.

During the long ride west, Pang was comforted by a series of phone calls to her network of trafficked Vietnamese Hmong friends, including May.

The bus driver saw how lost Pang seemed to be. When they stopped for dinner he was worried that she'd wander off and wouldn't be able to find the bus again when it was leaving. He invited her to eat with him, and even paid for her meal.

"Very lucky!" Pang exclaimed. She described all the food and drink he'd bought for her, and how happy she was.

Curiously, the list of snacks Pang said that the bus driver had bought for her dinner was identical to the list of snacks she said her "husband" had bought for her journey in the first version of the story. Perhaps these were just her favourite Chinese snacks – or maybe Pang wished her "husband" had even just once shown her the same kindness as this stranger.

I was fascinated by the first version of Pang's story, in which she found herself wielding such power over her "husband" at the eleventh hour. For the first time in their relationship, Pang had been the one who got exactly what she wanted, and her "husband" had been the one left hurting. At last he'd shown her the tenderness that had always been missing from their relationship and had treated Pang decently, rather than leaving her to shamefully slink away from a slumbering and uncaring abuser.

I'm sure there are many of us who would change the endings to some of our relationships if we could – and, of course, we prefer happy fictions to complex truths. It seemed that Pang had claimed in fantasy the closure her "husband" would never give her in real life.

Confusingly, though, it did seem that Pang had left Guangdong with much more than the money she'd saved, and must have received or taken more money from her "husband" at some point.

Pang's Chinese identity card was the only thing that could guarantee her safe passage to the border – and, incredibly, she'd forgotten to bring it with her. With no identification, Pang had predictably fallen straight into the hands of the Chinese police.

As the route west crossed into Yunnan province, it passed within forty kilometres of the Vietnamese border. It seems to have been at this point that Pang's bus was boarded by "many policeman asking about the ID card."

Everyone had identity cards but Pang. She tried to lie her way through, saying, "Ooh sorry, because my sister getting baby, she born baby, she say she stomach very hurt, nobody at home now, so I have to go there very faster. When I come here, I do many things, so I forget my ID card."

The police asked if Pang remembered the citizen identity number from her card, but she couldn't, and they took her away. They'd asked her many questions, and searched for her in their system. I'd never been entirely sure if Pang's identity card was genuine, and this was the moment of truth.

Pang told the police she was from Hunan – the province of central China where her "husband's" family came from, and where her identity card had been made using her "sister-in-law's" birth certificate.

If the police were to have any hope of finding Pang's file, she'd have to remember the details from her card, including her legally registered address and her "sister-in-law's" date of birth – all of which, of course, had been written in a language Pang couldn't read.

Pang couldn't remember the details she needed, and the police couldn't find her in their system. They asked if there was anyone at home Pang could call to get the necessary details. Pang could call her "husband's" family – but having just run away from them, how would they respond?

The family wouldn't want to help Pang escape – but if they left her in the hands of the police, her only remaining alternative would be to incriminate them with the truth. As bizarre as it seems, Pang only regained the freedom to continue her journey by the grace of the family that had imprisoned her for so long.

Pang called her "mother-in-law", who sent her a photo of the identity card. At last, the police found Pang in their system: thanks to a corrupt bureaucracy, Pang was officially a Chinese citizen. The police warned Pang not to forget her identity card in future, and they let her go.

LOST IN TIME AND SPACE

Pang never mentioned to me the three months she'd spent in contact with the mysterious Chinese Hmong stranger – and suspected trafficker – who lived in the borderlands. She told me only that May had given her the number of a Hmong man who could help her go home, and he'd called her "two or three times" before she ran away – claims which didn't fit with May's account at all.

The stranger said his name was Ji, and he was twenty-eight: ten years older than Pang, the same age as her "husband". Pang said she was happy to be friends with Ji because he was very nice, and she thought maybe he was a good guy.

"I try to speak with him very well and know [if] he's good person or bad person," Pang told me.

Ji had called Pang often following her escape – asking where she was, and telling her what to do.

"You know you're alone," he said. "You need to be very, very careful. There are many people in China who aren't nice, and they'll lie to you."

Pang had finally met Ji in person when she'd arrived in Yunnan province. He'd come to find her at the bus station, and they'd had dinner together. Ji planned to take her to Jinping, but it was too late in the day and there were no more buses departing, so they'd taken separate rooms in a nearby hotel.

Unable to register at the hotel without her identity card, Pang had been taken to the local police station – but once there, she'd been given the paperwork she needed without any further trouble.

According to May, Pang had considered Ji as a potential husband until she'd finally met him in person, when she decided she didn't really like him after all – but Pang didn't mention any of this. In her version of events, Ji had simply offered to show her the way back to Vietnam, and she'd accepted his offer.

The next day, Pang and Ji had travelled to his village in Jinping – first by bus, and then by motorbike. This was where Pang had vanished, and where her story became hazy.

Though she'd disappeared for three nights, Pang claimed to have stayed in Ji's village for just one night and half a day. She said she'd arrived at Ji's village in the evening and departed in the early morning, so her "half a day" claim made no sense to me either.

Ji had been present when I'd called Pang, and had been amazed to hear her speak English.

"He say, 'How do you speak like this?' I say, 'Do you never know tourist people?'"

Ji said that, like most people in his village, he'd only seen Western people in movies, and had never met any in real life. He told Pang that the villagers would be suspicious of her if they heard her speaking other languages. He warned that they might "catch" her and ask her many awkward questions, which would put them both in a difficult position.

The last time he'd spoken to her, X had offered to bring Pang home safely. She'd told him she'd think about it, and would call him back – but never did. Ji had told Pang to ignore X and let him go back to Vietnam without her. Ji assured Pang that he'd take her home himself, and told her not to answer her phone or make any more calls.

Ignoring X's advice not to trust anyone she'd just met, and completely oblivious to how alarming her sudden disappearance would seem, Pang did what Ji told her.

The borderlands were rotten with traffickers, and I'd suspected Ji of being one of them – but I was wrong. It seemed he was just another young man who couldn't find a partner in a region depleted of marriageable women, one more desperate victim of China's "one-child" policy and the cultural preference for boys. It remained a mystery how he'd first acquired Pang's phone number.

Ji had taken Pang to his family home and had wanted a relationship with her, which his family had encouraged. Pang claimed to have refused him outright, though I suspect the truth wasn't quite so simple.

Having left her "husband", Pang was now in a position her culture refused to recognise. On one hand, she wanted – perhaps needed – the long-term security of marriage and the community acceptance that came with it. On the other hand, Pang's first experience of "marriage" had been a deeply traumatic one. Having tasted just days of freedom after years of abuse, and having come so close to home without having yet reached it, Pang was understandably reluctant to commit herself to another man.

According to the Hmong tradition of marriage by abduction, a man would take a girl to his family home and keep her there for three or four days while she decided whether or not to marry him. It's very possible that Ji had in fact "kidnapped" Pang – in a consensual, cultural way, but without notifying her family as he should have.

Ultimately, Pang's decision seems to have been made by the fact that she simply didn't find Ji appealing. In a culture where girls were raised to be submissive, and in the situation where Pang had already followed Ji into his home in an unknown location and allowed him to cut her off from any potential source of support, I imagine her refusal must have come as a shock to him.

I'm sure that many other Hmong girls would have buckled under the pressure – but Pang could be extremely strong-willed when she wanted to be. Otherwise, I doubt she ever would have made it home.

IF LOVE IS A RED DRESS
(HANG ME IN RAGS)

The Jinshuihe-Pa Nam Cum border crossing lay in a remote, eerily-quiet region between forested mountains. I later went there with Pang, and she confirmed that's where she'd re-entered Vietnam.

The official crossing was a low flag-lined bridge across a narrow, concrete-walled river – but that's not where Pang had crossed.

Pang had been afraid of having any more trouble with the authorities, and had wanted to find a way across the border without passing through the official checkpoints.

Ji had brought Pang to Jinshuihe, just as he'd promised. She'd given him eight hundred yuan (about $120) to thank him for his help – but then she'd had trouble getting rid of him.

Ji wanted to come all the way back to Sapa with Pang – not to help her through the journey, but because he hadn't given up hope of keeping her as a partner. Already fearing the judgement of the Sapa Hmong community, Pang knew that arriving there with a strange young man would only make her situation worse.

She tried to dissuade him, gently at first, by saying if he

entered Vietnam he'd be caught by the police. Ji said it was no problem – he'd fill out the necessary paperwork at the official border crossing then find some way to cross illegally with Pang, still carrying the papers.

I don't know when or where Pang had bought the clothes she was wearing when she returned home, but she'd put them on before she reached the border. While Ji was filling out the paperwork, Pang stood alone near the border crossing – a teenage girl all dolled up in a short, scarlet dress and high heels. She said many men there took an interest in her. They asked for her phone number and she gave it to some of them, but in the end there were so many she began turning them away.

While the experience gave Pang a great boost to her self-confidence at a time when she was feeling alone and insecure, I was disturbed by her naïveté and how little she seemed to have learned after all she'd been through.

When Ji returned with his paperwork, Pang tried to explain why it would cause problems for her if he came with her to Sapa. She told him that if he really wanted to go there, then she should go first, and he could come to visit her at a later date. Ji refused to listen and insisted on coming with her, so Pang told him it was simply impossible.

While Ji had been away, Pang had made contact with Bao and me. We were making arrangements to come and find her, but hadn't yet found a second rider. Pang told Ji, "My friend is coming to get me. We're already going to be three people on one motorbike, and there won't be space for you, so you can't come with us."

Ji was upset but finally relented, and left Pang alone at the border.

Pang spoke to some local women, and asked if there was some other way into Vietnam. They pointed to a trucking route that ran southwards from the official crossing, cutting across the face of the mountains and descending into a distant valley, where it followed the very line of the border.

The women told Pang that if she followed that road, it would eventually lead her to a small bridge where she could cross into Vietnam. It would take ninety minutes to reach it on foot, or twenty minutes by motorbike.

Pang paid a local man to take her on the back of his motorbike, then crossed the border on her own. She'd finally reached Vietnam – but she wasn't home yet. She was lost and alone, a young woman stumbling in high heels through a remote forest somewhere deep in the mountainous borderlands.

"I feel very scary," she told me.

Pang met three Tai men on motorbikes who had just taken some people across the border illegally, and were now returning to their homes in Vietnam. She learned they were from Lai Chau, a small city fifty kilometres from the border, and the men agreed to take her there.

As they rode away from China, the group was stopped by two Vietnamese police officers who wanted to know where they were going, and why they were using that route. The men lied, saying they'd just been visiting some friends who owned a banana plantation alongside the border.

The police wanted to know if they'd taken anyone across the border – and when the men said they hadn't, the police became angry with them. They demanded to see their identity cards and motorbike registration papers, and warned them never to use that road again. They asked who Pang was, and what they were doing with her.

Pang explained that she'd been tricked and sold in China almost four years ago. She'd finally found her way back to Vietnam, and was now trying to get back to Sapa. The police asked which ethnic group she was from, and which village.

They believed her story – but bizarrely, after making such a fuss about the men taking people across the border illegally, they didn't seem particularly interested in helping Pang.

Instead, they put the responsibility on Pang's driver, telling him to take Pang back to Sapa, and threatening him if he didn't. The driver protested, pointing out the fact that he wasn't from Sapa, he wasn't going there, and it would be an extra four-hour round trip from his home in Lai Chau. The police didn't care.

"You have to take her to Sapa," they said. "If we find out you didn't, we won't leave you alone."

Pang said she felt miserable, and wanted to cry. The man told the police he'd take her.

It took an hour and a half to reach Lai Chau – but instead of taking Pang to Sapa, the man took her to his home. He said only he'd take her to Sapa if she paid him, and wanted to know how much money she had.

After Pang had first been taken to China, she'd been reluctant to use Chinese currency because she didn't know how it worked – and now she didn't seem to have any idea of what it was worth in Vietnam. For the ride to Sapa, she gave the man the local equivalent of half a month's wages.

When the man realised Pang was utterly clueless about exchange rates, it seems he decided to take her for all she was worth, and "helped" her change the rest of her money.

Even if Pang had understood the value of Chinese currency, she was hardly in a position to bargain: she didn't know where she was, or how else she might get home. The fact that she'd suggested meeting us in Lao Cai, on the opposite side of Sapa, shows just how lost she was.

Knowing he'd be riding through the mountains at night, the man took a warm jacket for himself – but offered nothing to Pang, though she was clearly underdressed.

When they began riding again, Pang had no idea if the man was taking her to Sapa, and was scared that he might sell her again. It was only when she saw a distance marker with "Sapa" written on it that she knew she really was going home.

"Then I feel very happy!" Pang said, and became very excited as she finished her story. She said she'd whooped with joy when they'd passed the familiar Silver Waterfall, just twelve kilometres from town.

"I make very loud," she said. "He say, 'You happy, right?' I say, 'Yeah, very strange for me.' I think, 'Hi Sapa, I coming back!'"

And so Pang's long journey ended the same way it had begun, all those years ago: on the back of a stranger's motorbike.

The man gave Pang his number, and told her to call him if she ever wanted to go back to China again.

"We can be friends," he told her.

HOW A RESURRECTION REALLY FEELS

It seemed that Pang had left her "husband" on a Saturday morning, and she finally reached home the following Thursday night. As we sat there outside her village home that Friday morning, she told me she was "very happy about to see all my friends and my family, and very happy to wear my old dress" – meaning her traditional Hmong costume. (That particular costume was in fact being worn for the very first time.)

Curiously, when Pang and Ji had parted at the border, Pang had ended up with the paperwork he'd filled out there, with all of his personal details. I was interested to see it, to learn a little more about this strange young man and where exactly he was from. I also wanted to see Pang's bus tickets, to understand the route she'd taken across China – but when Pang had arrived home she'd tossed the papers aside, and they'd been used to light the fire that morning.

Ultimately, though, none of that really seemed to matter: Pang was home, and that simple fact was more than enough to delight us both. To Pang, home meant more than her village, her family, and her community – it was the certainty that she would never again feel as lost as she had over the past few years.

I watched as Pang came to terms with her new reality. When I asked how she felt about the man who'd bought her, Pang first began referring to him as her husband, as she always had – then she interrupted herself. He could no longer claim that role in her life, and was suddenly relegated to being "the Chinese boy", or "the boy before".

How did Pang feel when she thought back over the last few years of her life?

"Right now I have no feel," she told me. "Because I just… Oh, forgot already."

What about her baby?

"I do not feel I have baby," Pang said. The child belonged to "the Chinese boy", not her.

Pang had often feigned indifference towards her daughter, though I knew her true feelings were deeper and more complex. Their relationship was complicated by the fact that Pang's daughter had already been taken from her just one month after birth, and raised as a Chinese child whom Pang had rarely seen. I wasn't sure if she even recognised Pang as her mother.

Motherhood had been a traumatic experience for Pang. She'd also given birth to a second baby girl in China, who had died earlier that year.

I asked if Pang wanted another husband, boyfriend, or any more children – and to each question, her answer was an immediate and emphatic "No."

What would she do with her life?

"I can find some job for working, have money, go to travel. I don't want to marry anymore."

While I greatly admired Pang's courage, I was uncertain where it would leave her in relation to the local Hmong community. Pang's physical journey might have been over – but emotionally speaking, I had the sense that she still had a long road ahead of her.

After we finished talking, I took Pang back to Sapa, where she'd already become the subject of much gossip and speculation. Some of the locals had recognised her the evening before – including her friend and fellow survivor Vu, who'd performed an incredulous double-take when she'd seen Pang riding on the back of my motorbike.

Vu was the first person Pang visited in Sapa that morning, and the two girls sat together on the bed in Vu's simple rented room. Pang admitted that she didn't know what she was going to do now that she was home. Vu spoke about how difficult her own return home had been, and admired the high heels Pang had been wearing the night before. She said she'd also brought a pair of high heels back from China – blue ones – but they were now broken.

Afterwards, I went with Pang to the market. Local women flocked around her as if she were a celebrity, though Pang seemed to have mixed feelings about the attention being showered upon her.

The women clamoured for Pang's phone with their indigo-stained hands, to see some photos that May had recently sent of herself. They were thrilled to see how much weight May had gained since she'd disappeared. In a culture where so many went hungry, plumpness was a sign of relative wealth, and was often desirable.

"Oh my God! May is so fat," exclaimed one. "She has such a big belly and big boobs."

"She's fatter than you are," another told Pang.

"She's very beautiful," said a third.

As the chatter continued, I watched Pang's initially buoyant mood gradually deflate, as her joyous return became something very different. It was clear that none of the women had any interest in trying to understand what Pang had been through, what she was still going through. Her traumas were trivialised, even by May's sister Dinh.

Dinh took Pang by the arm and walked her up to the town square, where another group of women quickly gathered. Before long, there were about fifteen women encircling Pang, many with babies strapped to their backs.

"I thought Pang was dead," one remarked.

The women asked Pang about China, but didn't seem to listen to her answers. She stood there biting her lip and occasionally making an unconvincing attempt at laughter as they told her she'd made a terrible mistake.

"Ah, if I could, I would go [to China] too!" declared Dinh, laughing. "For sure! If you stay there for a long time, then you can speak Chinese and it's fine. Don't you need your baby anymore?"

"If I had a baby like you, I wouldn't have come back," said another.

"It's a baby girl, I'm sure you'll miss her," someone else chimed in.

"You'll miss her a lot."

Dinh was the only one of three sisters who hadn't been kidnapped and sold in China – and, behind her laughter, she genuinely seemed to wish that she had also been taken. That fact, more than any other, best illustrated the extraordinary attitude of the Sapa Hmong women and the community that Pang was now trying to reintegrate into.

The other women judged Pang harshly for leaving her child in China, without understanding the months of agony and indecision it had taken Pang to make that choice. They didn't understand that the life Pang had run away from in China had been even more painful to her than the loss of her little girl. They didn't understand, and they didn't want to understand: they simply dismissed Pang as a heartless and uncaring mother.

It was almost as if the women maintained a collective fantasy that China was a wonderful land of ease and luxury, and didn't want to hear anything to dispel that illusion. Or perhaps they simply couldn't imagine anything worse than their own lives in the villages around Sapa, therefore life in China could only be better.

For years, Pang had wanted nothing more than to return home to her own people – and within a matter of hours, she wanted my help to escape them. I took her for a walk by the lake, and she broke down and cried.

Pang seemed to realise that all of her relationships in Sapa had now changed, but was still trying to understand how, and what her new status there might be.

When Blue Dragon had brought Vu home from China, as well as taking care of her basic needs like ensuring she had somewhere safe to stay, they'd offered her a wide range of medical, psychological, and legal support options, plus education and vocational training possibilities, and help reintegrating with her community.

By choosing to return home unassisted, Pang had not only placed herself in far greater danger during her journey, but she wouldn't automatically receive that support after her return. She could still have Blue Dragon's help if she wanted it – but now that she was home, Pang just wanted to fit back into her community and forget about everything else.

Pang's family gave her their full moral support, but there was little else they could do for her. I quickly realised that the only other support Pang would receive was whatever I could arrange for her: a situation for which I was entirely unprepared and unqualified.

I wanted to do everything I could to help Pang rebuild her life – both for her own sake, and for May's. I felt that if Pang reintegrated successfully, then May would find the courage to return home and follow her example.

I'd carried my camera on that first day, and had filmed snippets of Pang's social interactions whenever it had seemed appropriate – but now I put my camera away, and only very rarely filmed Pang again in Sapa. As important as the 'Sisters for Sale' documentary was to me, Pang's reintegration now took precedence, and following her around with a camera wouldn't make that process any easier.

For that reason, few people know what happened to Pang after her return home – but the challenges she faced were to reveal the true complexity of Sapa's human trafficking crisis, and form what is perhaps the most crucial part of this entire story.

I could never have imagined just how quickly everything would spiral out of control, and how surreal life would soon become. Within weeks, a local man would be threatening to kidnap Pang and kill me, Pang would be threatening to kill herself, and May's family would be threatening to kill us both.

SHE MOVES IN HER OWN WAY

Upon my return to Sapa ten days earlier, one of the first people I'd met with was Chan.

During my investigation in Sapa earlier that year, Chan had been my main interpreter, my greatest ally, and one of my closest friends in Vietnam. We'd spent three months working closely together – and while it might not have been obvious to others, the moment I saw Chan I knew that something had changed.

There are two questions you should never ask a woman: but you can't spend your whole life playing by the rules, either. During my initial interview with Chan, I'd asked her how old she was – and I now asked her the other forbidden question.

"Chan, are you pregnant?"

She glanced quickly around, and placed a finger on her lips.

"Shh!" she said. "It's a secret. We didn't tell anybody yet."

"I won't tell anyone," I said, "but you won't be able to hide it much longer."

Of all the Sapa Hmong girls and women I knew, Chan was the one with the best grasp of Western ideas and attitudes – and, interestingly, was one of the very few who had chosen a local partner over a foreigner. Rather than taking her chance to escape the life she'd been born into, she'd not only chosen to remain in Sapa, but to return to her village.

In July 2011, May and Chan had planned to travel together to Hanoi, to attend a hospitality school there. May had delayed her departure, and was kidnapped the very next day – so Chan had gone to the school alone.

At that time, there was a Swedish man who had a romantic interest in Chan, despite the fact she was still in her mid-teens. Sapa Hmong girls are typically eager for such opportunities to escape the poverty of village life. While many of these marriages ultimately fail, they provide the girls with foreign citizenships and far greater possibilities in life.

Surprisingly, though, Chan had rejected the Swede in favour of remaining with her own community. At the school, she'd been charmed by a handsome young Hmong man named Sung, who came from the Muong Kuong border region north of Lao Cai.

With her friends May, Pang, and Cho all having been recently kidnapped, Chan had been acutely aware of the risks of socialising with an unknown young Hmong man – but a young Hmong woman has good reason to take such risks, for a chance to determine her own fate before she's pushed into an unwanted marriage. And sometimes, it's worth the gamble.

While I imagine that Chan had been more cautious than some of the other Hmong girls, she admitted to having been scared the first time Sung had taken her to visit his village, which lay within sight of a remote stretch of the Chinese border. It was more than a typical "meet the parents" nervousness – it was a fear that she'd be sold and would never see her home or family again.

Chan and Sung had now been together for three years. Sung was one of the kindest and most considerate Vietnamese Hmong men I'd met, one of the few who spoke passable English, and the only one I called a friend. Earlier in the year, he had also invited me to visit his village and meet his family.

Sung was a remarkable young man with a remarkable family. His mother was a shaman – and, after Sung's cousin had been kidnapped, it was Sung's father and his brother-in-law who had crossed the border, distributed her photo, evaded the traffickers' ransom demands, and brought the girl home safely. Among all the human trafficking stories I'd heard, theirs stood alone, demonstrating an exceptionally courageous, proactive attitude.

After I returned to Sapa and learned that Chan was pregnant, she only needed to hide her secret for another week or so: she and Sung were getting married.

Pang had come back from China on October the ninth. The tenth was her first day in Sapa, and the eleventh was Chan and Sung's wedding.

I was delighted to see Chan marrying the man she had chosen, and attaining the things she wanted in life. I had immense respect and admiration for all she'd achieved.

While Chan had chosen to marry a Hmong man, she was doing so on her own terms. A Hmong woman traditionally moved to the village of her husband. In this case, however, Sung was not only moving to Chan's village, he would be moving into Chan's own house.

From her work guiding tourists, Chan had saved enough money for the land and timber to build her own home near the centre of the village. For the sake of custom, she would briefly accompany Sung back to his village, then they'd return to Sapa together and begin construction.

Their planned return to Sapa was an acknowledgement of the power Chan held in their relationship, and the fact that she could earn more in Sapa than Sung could in his village. Chan had told Sung in no uncertain terms that if he misbehaved as so many other local men did – by drinking too much, becoming violent, or fooling around with other women – she'd throw him out of her house.

I wasn't sure how Chan's conditions might translate into reality, and I hoped she'd never have to test them, but the very fact of a Sapa Hmong woman attaching such conditions to her marriage was unprecedented. The fact that Chan had achieved so much by age nineteen was simply phenomenal: I had no doubt that she'd be an inspiration and role model for the next generation of Sapa Hmong women.

The fact that Sung had accepted Chan's terms and superior financial status with respect and humility was an excellent indicator of his own character, and would also be a positive example for the local men.

In many ways, Chan was the person I'd once hoped May would become – and in some ways, our friendship in Sapa had replaced the friendship May and I had once shared there.

A wedding is a popular ending to the stories we tell each other. If there was a happy ending anywhere in Sapa, perhaps it was Chan and Sung's – though I'm sure that anyone who has been married can tell you that a wedding isn't really an ending at all, merely a beginning.

WEDDING DAY

Chan had been sold into marriage for twenty million dong (about $950), twenty litres of rice wine, and an eighty-kilogram pig. Some girls' families asked only a third as much cash for their daughters; others, three times that amount.

Chan had already demonstrated a value to her family and community that was impossible to put on any price tag. The idea that such a phenomenal young woman (or any young woman, for that matter) could be traded for meat, alcohol, and a wad of banknotes was still incomprehensible to me. As Chan herself had pointed out, however, within her community the sale was still necessary to safeguard her reputation.

Pang and I met with Chan in Sapa in the morning, and we travelled out to the village together – but at the last moment, Pang had a change of heart and said she didn't want to go to the wedding. Chan went ahead with some of our friends while I sat with Pang nearby.

I'd thought Pang would be happy to see her friends again – but I could understand her reluctance, after the treatment she'd received in Sapa the day before. What's more, it seemed the last wedding she'd been to had been her own, which stood in stark contrast to Chan and Sung's loving union.

Eventually Pang came with me to Chan's family home, then baulked again, and when at last she did go inside she walked straight back out. I felt it was best to give her some time alone, and briefly joined the festivities.

When I'd first lived in Sapa four years earlier, I'd attended a Hmong wedding in the same village. Chan had tried to convince me it had been her sister's wedding – but I couldn't remember ever having met Chan in 2010, and very much doubted that I'd ever been to her home. Then I found myself sitting cross-legged in almost exactly the same place on the same floor in the same house, and with a startling sense of *déjà vu* I realised that Chan was right.

Four years earlier, I'd been sitting there surrounded by my Hmong friends – but now that group had changed dramatically.

Only three girls from the original group of ten were at the wedding. Chan was there, of course, though as the bride she sat at a table outside with Sung. May, who had always been at the centre of the group, was thousands of kilometres away in China. Vu hadn't come – nor had Little Chu, who was now married. Zao was there, and Chu had come from Lao Cai, where she was now studying.

Anemi was also a friend of Chan's. She'd come up from Hanoi for the wedding and was staying for five days. Having already arranged to interview me for an article during that time, the fact that her visit coincided with Pang's first days in Sapa gave Anemi an unexpected insight into the complexities of the local trafficking crisis.

Pang did eventually join us – but not for long. It was clear that she felt uncomfortable there, and I found myself in an awkward position.

I'd agreed to photograph Chan's wedding and had already taken a series of photos and videos for her. There was still much more I could have done – but I could see Pang spiralling into another crisis.

My experiences in French Canada had given me a far

deeper awareness of, and sense of empathy for, those who were suffering. Having accompanied Pang through her complex emotional journey since our reunion in China, I felt a powerful sense of responsibility for her.

In my support, it was clear that Pang had found the comfort she now needed. Even when surrounded by her childhood friends, I was the one she turned to – which felt especially strange given the fact that I'd never really considered Pang a close friend, as I did Chan.

Chan and Pang were both experiencing once-in-a-lifetime events. I would have loved to have stayed there to celebrate Chan's wedding, and felt terrible leaving without having taken more photos – but Pang was leaving, I could see how much she needed a friend, and I simply couldn't be there for them both.

In China, as I'd ventured ever-deeper into the shadowy world of human trafficking, I'd told myself I'd come back up into the light when my work was finished. I found myself beginning to wonder if my work would ever truly finish, if I could ever return to the carefree life I'd known. Perhaps I was wrong to think of it as work: perhaps this was simply my life now.

As I write this, seven years after the fact, Chan's secret is out – and proved to be a little girl, who is now attending primary school.

CAUGHT IN THE BRIARS

When she first arrived back in Sapa, Pang had no home of her own. She stayed either with her family in the village, or in the rented rooms of various unmarried girlfriends in Sapa – but she quickly realised that she had little in common with her former friends.

Some of Pang's friends were now married, and some were not. Like many traditional cultures, Hmong culture recognised only two types of women: married women, and unmarried virgins.

As a trafficking survivor, Pang herself fitted into neither category, and now felt a strange distance between herself and her friends on both sides. She no longer seemed to know where she belonged, and neither did anyone else.

As the weeks passed, Pang came to consider me not only as her best friend, but her only friend.

"Be careful," she warned me. "If you die, I have no friends. My friends before is very changed, so I have no friends."

It was young Hmong men who had originally profited by Pang's kidnapping – and it was young Hmong men who now tried to profit from her social isolation.

Immediately after her return, Pang began receiving a

great deal of persistent attention from local men who were interested not in marriage, but sex. Knowing that she was neither married nor a virgin, and was therefore a "bad girl" with few possibilities for marriage, they were eager to take advantage of her.

Pang denied any desire for marriage or even a boyfriend, and seemed repulsed by the idea of sex. At the same time, though, she wanted to find some way to restore her reputation and rejoin society, and marriage seemed the only way to do that.

Unfortunately, Pang was very susceptible to flattery, which helped to boost her battered self-esteem. The men who now surrounded her would tell her anything to get what they wanted, and Pang was desperate to believe them. She found herself struggling to find just one good man who might be sincere in his affections, who might help restore her honour rather than destroying it further.

Pang had been emotionally volatile even before she'd been trafficked. She then had years of unprocessed trauma from having been betrayed, kidnapped, held captive, sold, repeatedly raped, abused, forced to bear two children for a man she hated, losing both children in different ways, and being ostracised upon her return – and now these men had set her on a rollercoaster of soaring hope and inevitable crushing disappointment.

It wasn't an easy position for any young woman to be in. The trafficking survivors Pang knew had been similarly tempted – and, having found no way to restore their reputations, many had eventually succumbed to the pressure and temptation of the men who surrounded them.

Pang knew another trafficking survivor named Khu who shared a rented room with another unmarried girlfriend on the outskirts of Sapa. When Pang first returned to Sapa, Khu invited her to stay with them.

I went with Pang when she first visited the room, on the night of Chan's wedding. We were surprised to find that both girls had Hmong boyfriends in the room when we arrived. Khu's boyfriend was drunk, and a little surly at our intrusion. Pang clearly wasn't comfortable with the situation, but the two girls told their boyfriends to leave and insisted Pang stay, so she did.

Pang came to my hotel early the next morning, and she was furious. The boyfriends had come back later in the night with some other men. Pang had been sharing a single bed with Khu, whose boyfriend had drunkenly climbed into bed and started having sex with Khu while Pang had been trying to sleep. In the morning, while Pang was in the bathroom, someone had stolen the money from her purse.

Pang was disgusted, and scathing in her judgement of Khu – and yet, for either girl, the only hope of rejoining Hmong society was to find a man willing to redeem her by marriage, and that man was nowhere to be found.

This sexually-liberated behaviour was also revolutionary, in its own way. It was made possible only by the fact that Sapa Hmong girls had an independent source of income from tourism and could afford their own rooms, away from their families. Their behaviour would never have been tolerated within the confines of traditional Hmong society, where they would have quickly found themselves homeless and destitute as a result.

Under the circumstances, though, it seemed very short-sighted. The inevitable small-town rumours meant the girls' reputations suffered further – and with little awareness of or access to birth control, the girls would inevitably fall pregnant, which only made their situations even more desperate. They underwent risky and expensive abortions, while the men they slept with evaded all responsibility.

There were also unmarried, sexually-active young women in Sapa who had never been trafficked. It seemed that some had been abused in their villages as children, while others had been used and abandoned by tourists as teenagers. I didn't know if any had consciously chosen that way of life as adults, though it seemed unlikely.

These "bad girls" were most commonly referred to as the "bar girls", thanks to their habit of staying out late drinking and flirting in certain bars.

Several of these young women – including Khu – would ultimately bear a child out of wedlock, which in the eyes of the local community was perhaps the most shameful thing a woman could do.

I was concerned about Pang, knowing how fragile her self-confidence was, how susceptible she could be to compliments, and how short-sighted she could be.

It wasn't just the local men trying to tempt her into that way of life – Khu and some of the other "bad girls" seemed to consider it inevitable that Pang would eventually become one of them. They encouraged her to join them in the bars, and wanted to introduce her to the young men they knew.

I hoped that she'd be careful: if Pang went down that path, she would only be making a bad situation worse, and could easily lose any hope of leading a normal life.

Ultimately, though, Pang's life was now her own, and whatever she did was her own choice.

MAKE YOU FEEL BETTER

Pang was no longer a victim of human trafficking – she was a survivor, and I wanted to make sure she did more than merely survive.

I couldn't do everything for Pang, and it would have been foolish to try. My first priority was connecting her with other people who could help her in ways I couldn't.

I'd come to Vietnam on a three-month visa. I had just seven weeks left and no intention of returning, so I wanted to provide Pang with support that would last long after I was gone.

Pang chose to live in Sapa, rather than returning to her village. She moved in with an aunt while we tried to find her a room of her own.

Two of my friends owned and operated a high-end trekking agency, and they offered Pang a good job as a tour guide – but it would be several weeks before she could start. Local girls who took tourists trekking to their villages faced steep fines if caught without a licence, and the checks had become more frequent. Pang applied at the Sapa police station for an identity card, so that she could then begin the process to become an officially licenced guide.

But a successful reintegration would involve far more than just helping Pang find a job and a place to stay. Although Pang had carried little home with her from China, she bore the emotional baggage of her experiences there.

While Pang was a very emotional person, Hmong people rarely seemed to speak about their emotions, and she was no exception. She acted tough and assured me that she was okay, even when she was very clearly not okay.

With the possible exception of May, Pang had told me about her experiences in China in more detail than she'd told anyone – but there were certain subjects we'd skirted around and never spoke about. I'd never asked Pang about her second child, who had died earlier that year, and I'd never asked about the sexual abuse she'd suffered at the hands of her "husband".

These things were beyond the bounds of our friendship, and – if Pang wanted to speak about them at all – I knew I wasn't the right person for her to have those conversations with.

What Pang really needed was a specialised trauma counsellor – but the idea was completely alien to her. When I raised the idea of talking to a stranger about her experiences in China, she found the idea bizarre and incomprehensible, as if I'd suggested she take up acrobatics.

One of my friends in Sapa was a retired Dutch psychiatrist named Aart, who had worked as a rational emotive behaviour therapist and now lived with his Kinh wife in the town centre. Aart was aware of Pang's situation, and he'd very graciously offered his services at any time. I introduced him to Pang on her first day back in Sapa – not as a professional, but as an understanding friend at a time when Pang most needed friends around her.

Over the following weeks and months, during our countless walks around Sapa together, Pang and I would often see Aart sitting on his balcony. He'd invite us to come and sit with him in his living room – and once he and Pang were chatting comfortably, I'd find some excuse to slip outside, or to join

Aart's wife in the kitchen.

While I'm sure our unscheduled and often brief visits were far from ideal in terms of providing Pang with the psychological support she needed, they allowed Aart to build a rapport with her – and when Pang had emotional crises I didn't know how to help her with, I could bring her to him.

Aart worked in consultation with his professional network in Europe to do whatever he could for Pang. He was wonderfully patient and supportive, and I very much appreciated having him as an ally.

Vu's aunt, Big Zao, had also escaped a forced "marriage" in China and returned to Sapa by herself – all while six months' pregnant. It was now five years since Big Zao had come home. She had married a local man named Zhe, and they were raising their own children alongside her Chinese child.

Of all the trafficking survivors in Sapa, I felt that Big Zao was the friend and positive influence Pang needed at what was such an uncertain moment in her life. Pang and Big Zao were already on friendly terms – but, having married, Big Zao was now living outside Sapa in a region that was not easily accessible to Pang. They had few opportunities to meet, much less to speak privately about their experiences.

Big Zao and Zhe ran a small shop selling snacks and soft drinks. The shop fronted onto a narrow, broken road that snaked along the valley wall beyond Pang's village. If Pang and I were visiting her family in the village, I'd sometimes suggest a detour to visit Big Zao. We'd buy a couple of drinks – and, as with our visits to Aart, once Pang had settled into conversation with Big Zao, I'd go outside and sit with Zhe at the front of the shop.

BEEN CAUGHT STEALING

A week after Pang's return home, we had a particularly memorable visit to Big Zao's house.

Zhe had witnessed the theft of his neighbour's motorbike earlier in the day. Now, as he and I sat drinking tea outside his house, we saw the thief ride past on the stolen bike, and we immediately leapt on our own bikes to give chase.

It was a wild ride over a rough, unfamiliar road with fallen rocks scattered everywhere, motorbikes heading both ways, and the valley wall plunging steeply away on one side. The asphalt was broken and we rattled over the bare stony earth in places where it had come away entirely.

Of the three of us, Zhe was most familiar with the road, and I followed his line. He closed in on the thief and called for him to stop – but the thief kept riding. The chase only ended when Zhe pulled ahead and veered across the thief's only line of exit, forcing him either to stop, risk a collision, or take a bone-shattering tumble into the valley below. It was a hazardous manoeuvre, but it worked. I came in from behind to trap the stolen bike at the edge of the road.

The thief was just a sullen, pimple-faced teenager. He was unprepared to fight us both, and there was nowhere he could run to: the valley wall rose steeply on one side of the road, and dropped away on the other. As he began edging away, Zhe grabbed and held him by the scarf.

Our pursuit had attracted the attention of other passing villagers, who stopped and began to gather around. There was a brief interrogation: the thief was discovered to be from another village fifteen kilometres away, on the other side of Sapa. Calls were made, and the motorbike was confirmed as stolen.

Within minutes, the thief was encircled by seventeen men. The blood was still thrilling in my veins from our pursuit and I wasn't sure what would happen next, but wasn't particularly surprised when the first fist landed on the side of his face.

One of the men twisted the thief's scarf tightly around his throat while others punched and slapped his head, face, arms, chest, and stomach, or kicked at his legs. I'd never witnessed such an intensely cold fury so close at hand.

With their weight of numbers and the knowledge that the thief would never dare strike back, there was no urgency to the villagers' attack. It was a measured, clinical proceeding, like pulling the legs off a beetle.

Unable to defend himself against so many, the thief simply cringed away from the blows as he fought to keep his balance, keep his breath, and hold back his tears.

The motorbike's owner arrived, outraged, and launched his own fierce assault. I remembered what May's father had said when I'd told him I wanted to bring May's traffickers to justice. He'd said that when the time came, he would do that himself, in his own way. While I never imagined he'd actually do it, I now began to understand what he'd meant.

The thief twisted and turned in search of a way out, but there was none. When he asked his attackers to loosen the scarf, they tightened it. With a mouth full of blood, he pleaded for mercy nobody was prepared to give.

The thief turned his eyes to me, the only foreigner present, and twice appealed for my intervention with his only word of

English – "Hello" – but my sympathies lay with the villagers. I didn't share their anger but I understood it, and the only time I moved to intervene was when one of the villagers stooped to lift a rock in his fist.

I'd always hated any form of cruelty, and still do – but since Kashmir I could more easily understand the sense of frustration and powerlessness I now felt around me, and its potential to erupt into violence.

If I'd found myself in the same position four years earlier, during my first trip to Sapa, I would have tried to protect that thief from violence – but since then I'd heard far too many stories about young men just like this one, and lost too much faith in those who were paid to uphold the law.

Beyond the bright facade painted on for the sake of tourism, Sapa lay in a wild, corrupt region with few certainties for its inhabitants. Local police officers had a reputation for spending their work hours getting drunk, watching pornography, sleeping, or simply not coming to work – then demanding bribes from victims to perform their duties. If the authorities couldn't be relied upon to deliver justice, who was I to stop a victim from his own crude vengeance?

In any case, could I have stopped so many angry men even if I'd wanted to? I don't know. There were many questions raised by this story that I lost sleep over, but this was never one of them.

In that poverty-stricken valley, there were few possessions more highly prized than a motorbike or a buffalo. I'd seen what hardships the villagers would endure to obtain such things honestly, and this brutal form of deterrence was one of the few protections they had against theft.

The villagers were clothed simply, their hands rough and dirty from their labours in the fields. The thief stood at their centre in a clean new shirt and brand-name jacket, silver rings gleaming on his fingers. This was precisely the kind of young man I'd heard described in endless variations by victims of human trafficking.

In Sapa, a woman was merely another possession – and if this man was shameless enough to steal another man's motorcycle, then why not someone's daughter?

The Sapa Hmong girls generally didn't view the local Hmong men as very promising partners: far too many had a reputation for being habitually drunk, abusive, or unfaithful.

Instead of bettering themselves, many of the young men did just the opposite, turning to crime to acquire money and possessions to make themselves more attractive. They stood against their own communities, not for the sake of any greater good, but for their own selfish ends – and, sadly, it all too often worked.

In the struggling communities of the Sapa Hmong, financial security meant far more in a potential partner than it did in Western societies, where a certain standard of material comfort could often be assumed.

Like so many of us, the Hmong girls were dazzled by wealth, and rarely stopped to ask where it came from. Sadly, much of that wealth came from the sale of girls just like themselves – and each sale, of course, only brought more wealth, which made it even easier for these men to attract new victims.

The myriad abuses that May and her friends had endured had begun with poverty, a lack of education, the mistreatment of women – and callous young Hmong men like this one. These men played a leading role in countless horrific stories but were so often faceless, taking what they wanted and vanishing before anyone could comprehend how much damage they'd done.

If young men like this one didn't prey upon their own communities, May and her friends would never have been taken, and there would be no need for this story. There was a certain grim satisfaction in seeing just one of these thieves caught red-handed and cast upon the mercy of the villagers.

The thief's lips were swollen and encrusted with dried blood. He spat blood on the asphalt, and dribbled it over his scarf. His pants were scuffed with dirt from all the kicks he'd received, and his pockets had been turned out.

What little money he'd carried was counted out by the side of the road and handed over to the motorcycle's owner. Beneath the seat of the bike, they found an umbrella and a sheathed, straight-edged knife.

The thief was marched forcibly along the road to the village police station – but it was empty. By this time the crowd had grown to more than fifty villagers, including knots of women in traditional garb and gaggles of children in school uniforms.

Twenty-five minutes later, wearing a football jersey in place of a uniform, the police officer was the last to arrive.

NORTHWESTERN SKIES

It was clear that Pang's return to Sapa had been too much too soon, and that she was emotionally overwhelmed.

I'd taken her on various trips to the villages to visit her relatives and Big Zao, and I noticed that she really enjoyed being on the motorbike, away from everyone else.

I'd given Pang a pair of sunglasses – the first pair she'd ever owned – and she loved to wear them on the back of the bike. She hid herself behind the mirrored lenses, convinced that nobody could recognise her.

Sometimes I went riding alone in the mountains, just for the sake of riding, and now I began taking Pang with me. I rigged up a mighty little speaker on the bike so we could listen to rock as we rolled.

While I'd been having my own personal crisis in Quebec, one of my friends had taken me on a three-day roadtrip for a change of scenery, and it had really meant a lot to me. Pang had often mentioned her desire to travel – yet the only travelling she'd ever done outside Sapa was when she'd been trafficked.

I'd been thinking about making a motorbike trip to Dien Bien Phu, a provincial capital near the Laotian border, and I asked Pang if she wanted to join me. She bought herself some new jeans, a Mickey Mouse hoodie, and some sneakers, and away we went.

Our five-day, seven-hundred-kilometre circuit took us through Son La, Dien Bien, and Lai Chau, three provinces that were even more remote and poverty-stricken than the region around Sapa.

Here, smoke from black mounds of burning vegetation mingled with low-hanging clouds, colossal clumps of bamboo seemed to hang in the air, and simple wooden huts clung to hillsides overshadowed by thickly-forested mountains. In places, I half-expected great prehistoric beasts to come crashing through the darkly-massed trees.

Some valleys lay drowned behind dam walls, while others were divided into innumerable small plots where buffaloes gnawed at the yellow stubble of rice stalks. Women wore Vietnam's iconic conical hats, and public notices embellished with skeletons warned of the dangers of contracting HIV from intravenous drug use.

A cluster of giant bronze warriors commemorating victory over the French stood guard over the heart of Dien Bien Phu itself. Pang and I spent Sunday morning at a beautiful and entirely untouristed small-town market bustling with Red and White Hmong and Black Dao people.

As we wound our way through the mountains, it was a privilege and a delight to see Pang truly come back to life, rising like a phoenix from the ashes. We sang, laughed, danced, explored new places, and made new friends. Pang decided I was a "number one" tour guide – and that wasn't all she said, either. She was chattering constantly for five days.

"Me, I talk too much," she said.

"Your nose very long, like elephant," she told me.

We passed a pregnant sow, and she told me my girlfriend got too big. We passed a group of buffaloes wallowing in the mud, and she told me my friends were so smelly.

"Don't make me laugh too much," she said. "Or I get too hungry."

For the first two days, the roads and weather were highly variable. Within ten minutes of the first major cloudburst, I was soaked to the skin through five layers of clothing, including a brand new rainjacket that was so useless it might just as well have been made of tissue paper.

With the wind chill factor that came from riding, I was frozen stiff, and we stopped in a little place to wait out the rain. Unfortunately, those five layers were most of the clothing I'd brought for the trip, and I had nothing warm to change into.

Pang, who had been riding in my rainshadow in a cheap plastic poncho, was almost completely dry. Seeing me shaking with the cold, she immediately offered me her prized new Mickey Mouse hoodie – and while Pang and I have very different body shapes, I accepted it gratefully.

I was clearly stretching it in every direction and we could both hear the stitches popping – but Pang only grinned at the way it looked on me, and was happy to have helped.

I remembered how I'd felt after my experiences in Quebec: despite having my material needs fulfilled, I'd lacked a sense of meaning and purpose in my life. I'd been deeply grateful to those who had helped me, and wanted to do what little I could to help others. I now saw the same attitude in Pang, as she began to reveal a more thoughtful, selfless side to herself.

On arrival in Dien Bien Phu we were approached by a pair of Belgian touring cyclists, Joeri and Ingeborg. Joeri had stepped on a piece of steel reinforcing and could barely walk – but hadn't found anyone at the local hospital who could speak English.

Pang and I accompanied the Belgians back to the hospital. Pang translated so that Joeri could get the medical attention he needed, then they treated us both to dinner.

Pang's self-esteem soared at being acknowledged as a useful and appreciated member of society. I saw what a confident, high-spirited young woman she would have been in Sapa if only her community had been more supportive of her return from China.

"Look at me!" she said. "I nice people too, okay!"

As we sat talking after dinner that evening, Pang again found herself called upon to act as an interpreter – but under very different circumstances. A middle-aged Jordanian man was trying to arrange a prostitute in the garish karaoke bar next door, and was deeply disappointed to learn it was an establishment only for drinking and singing.

AFTER MIDNIGHT

After Pang's return, she began having unusually vivid dreams which she'd often describe to me.

On one occasion, Pang dreamt that May had already returned home. They'd been eating together at Sapa's market, and May had been smiling and crying at the same time.

Another night, Pang had dreamt of her father, who had died before her abduction. He told Pang that he had been with her in China and was with her still, and she awoke in tears.

After months of insomnia and nightmares, I found myself sleeping more soundly and had some of the most joyous dreams of my life. On several occasions I actually woke myself up with laughter before slipping comfortably back into sleep.

During our roadtrip – thanks to the long days riding through the mountains, and time away from my laptop – I slept longer and more deeply than I had in many months.

After our first day of riding – through pouring rain and blazing sun – I'd found myself utterly exhausted. I was glad to find a small hotel just as the daylight, and the last of my energy, faded.

There were two rooms available at the hotel, and Pang and I planned to take one each – but we quickly discovered that one was inhabited by an untenable stench. It overpowered us both from the doorway, and there was no chance that either of us would spend a night in there.

We were in a remote area, I didn't have the energy to keep riding through the dark in search of another hotel, and Pang didn't mind sharing a room – so we did. It was barely seven o'clock when I fell into bed and into a deep slumber.

At two o'clock in the morning I awoke with a ferocious hunger, and – with as little light and noise as possible, so as not to wake Pang – began devouring a pear. Pang woke anyway, and found it hilarious that I was eating in the middle of the night: the concept of having a midnight snack was entirely unfamiliar to her.

"You're crazy for sure!" she declared – then she joined me.

By then we were both fully awake, so Pang took out her phone and began showing me her photos from China. In the peaceful silence of those early-morning hours, our conversation took a deeper turn, and Pang began sharing all kinds of things she'd never told me about her time in Guangdong.

One odd aspect to May and Pang's emotional journeys was that both girls were certain their "husbands" had been sleeping with other women. While the girls were thankful that it relieved some of the sexual pressure on them, each had felt a jarring mix of emotions at being rejected by a man she'd never wanted in the first place.

May had already told me that while her "husband" rarely allowed her to leave the house, he himself now returned only out of necessity. He no longer came home for lunch, would return in the evenings only long enough to change into his "handsome" clothes, and often had his phone switched off. While May had never enjoyed her "husband's" presence, she now found herself more alone than ever.

When May had first been kidnapped, she'd been held captive in her middleman's home with several other trafficked girls. On the day that May's "husband"-to-be had come in search of a "bride", one of the other girls had found him attractive. She and May had both been disappointed when he'd bought May instead.

May was still in contact with that girl by phone. On hearing that May was going home to Vietnam, the girl had joked, "If you gonna go back, I gonna find your husband!"

May had replied, "If you want, you can find him right now!"

Even more surprising was the story Pang now told me. She said that while looking through May's phone, May's "husband" had been impressed by a photo of Pang, and had secretly begun calling her. He told her that May was stupid, and that he wanted to come and visit Pang in Guangdong. Pang had been angry with him, eventually threatening to call the police if he didn't stop calling her.

"Why you calling to me, stupid boy?" she said. "You have nothing to do in the daytime? If you want to die, just come!"

Pang still had her Chinese SIM card, and someone from China was still calling her. Though she never picked up, she believed it was May's "husband".

As with many of the stories Pang told during this time, I wasn't sure exactly how much of this story was true – but it seemed like a very odd thing to invent.

Our conversations rambled in every direction. Pang recounted a conversation she'd had with another trafficking survivor in China, who had been married three times – once in Vietnam before her abduction, then the Chinese man she'd been forced to marry, and finally a Chinese Hmong man she'd married by choice after her escape. The girl had wanted to know why Pang was going home to Vietnam, when it was so easy to find a husband or boyfriend in China.

"Why you people always talking about husband?" Pang demanded. "I don't have husband, I'm not gonna die. I have no husband I can go wherever I want, it's easy!"

Pang spoke of her frustration at being judged in Sapa: "You look my face, you look my body, you think I'm very stupid people – but you don't know what is in my heart."

Eventually, Pang and I fell back asleep – and spent another two hours talking when we woke in the morning.

I saw how happy Pang was to unburden herself of the things she'd carried for so long. As much as she loved the roadtrip itself, having a safe space and a friend to talk to seemed to mean much more to her.

I couldn't provide the targeted therapy that Aart could – but Pang spoke more freely with me, for much longer periods of time. While it wasn't an arrangement I would have otherwise considered, after that first night Pang and I agreed to share rooms for the remainder of the journey, and our late-night conversations continued.

Just to be perfectly clear, this arrangement was made with the explicit understanding that Pang and I were nothing more than friends, we were always fully clothed in each other's presence, and there was no hint of any romantic or sexual interest from either side.

Others might have assumed we were having a sexual relationship, but something more surprising was happening behind those closed doors. For the first time, after all the time we'd known each other and all we'd been through together, Pang and I were forming a genuine friendship.

I'd never expected any kind of reward in return for the help I'd offered Pang – but in its own way, this felt like one.

On our return journey from Dien Bien Phu, the sun beamed down from clear blue skies, the road surface improved, and the ride was simply stunning. On our last day, we almost ran over a two-metre snake, I gave Pang her first lesson in riding a motorbike, and she showed me the road she'd used to cross back into Vietnam.

Pang mentioned that she hadn't been swimming in years, so we stopped for an hour and a half by a quiet stretch of river. The mountain water was too cold for me, so I sat out in the sunshine listening to Pang, in her shirt and shorts, delightedly splashing and chuckling to herself.

"Me, I so happy," she said. "All my life, I never happy like this."

It had certainly been a long time since I'd laughed so much. Pang said she'd have many stories to tell when we got back to Sapa, like when she saw two crazy people wake up in the middle of the night to eat something.

It was easy to see why Pang's hopes for the future centred around travelling, and it wasn't simply the influence of foreign tourists in Sapa. Away from the pressure of her community to marry and conform, Pang had the freedom to be herself and take control of her life.

I knew it would take more than a roadtrip to solve Pang's problems, and I didn't know if her newfound happiness would survive the caustic atmosphere of Sapa – but even though life would never be perfect for her, it seemed like she'd be okay, and maybe that was enough.

BUT I FEEL GOOD

Pang and I had taken a long, meandering route back from Dien Bien Phu, and had crossed paths several times with the Belgian cyclists, Joeri and Ingeborg. The Belgians arrived in Sapa the same afternoon we did, and the four of us arranged to meet for a drink at a local *bia hoi* that evening.

I'd never drunk alcohol with Pang. She drank very rarely, and – not surprisingly, given her experiences – seemed to associate drinking with being taken advantage of. She'd told me about a twenty-five-year-old American tourist who had gotten her drunk and kissed her when she was just fifteen.

"I too small," she said. "I not really understand about this."

The same year, Pang's traffickers had pressured her into getting very drunk, and had kidnapped her early the next morning while she'd still been under the influence of the alcohol.

Pang had been drinking once in China with her work colleagues. She'd felt lonely thinking of all her friends in Sapa, had become terribly drunk, and said she was "very, very shy" the next day.

In her state of exhilaration following our roadtrip, Pang decided to drink beer with Joeri, Ingeborg, and me. She pointed out that she was an adult now and could drink if she wanted to. She drank two or three glasses – and while she wasn't drunk, she was tipsy.

A group of young Hmong men at the next table saw her there, and began coming over to drink with her. One took a particularly keen interest in her.

One of the few Sapa Hmong men who spoke passable English, he introduced himself by the somewhat ludicrous name of Lucky Charm, told us he worked at a nearby hotel, then spent the rest of the evening speaking with Pang in her own language.

Lucky Charm was about twenty years old. He told Pang that his girlfriend – who supposedly bore a striking resemblance to Pang – had run away to China two years earlier. When he'd first laid eyes on Pang, he believed his long-lost love had finally returned – and even after he realised his mistake, Lucky Charm continued to profess his love for Pang.

At the end of the evening, I offered to walk Pang back to a friend's room where she was to stay that night, and Lucky Charm tagged along. As we passed my hotel, I was surprised by Pang's announcement that she'd be fine to walk back alone with her new friend.

Until that moment, Pang had been very vocal about her distaste for Hmong men, and I didn't see Lucky Charm as a particularly honest or trustworthy example.

I'd felt responsible for and protective of Pang since her return from China, and never in my life had I felt more like a concerned parent than in that moment. As with Isabela in Kashmir, and May's decision to wait for Sebastien in China, I felt sure Pang was making a poor and potentially dangerous decision – but it was still her decision, not mine.

While Pang was tipsy, she seemed affected less by the alcohol than by a reckless exuberance at finally feeling in control of her life once more. She'd regained her freedom, just as I'd hoped – and it would be beyond hypocrisy for me to try to take it away from her now.

I didn't know if Pang planned to get romantically or sexually involved with Lucky Charm, but the stakes were high for Hmong women, and there was no coming back from some decisions.

I knew that, and so did Pang – but her newfound freedom included the freedom to make her own mistakes. She assured me she'd be perfectly fine with Lucky Charm – and while I wasn't convinced, I let her go.

I don't know exactly what happened between Pang and Lucky Charm that night, though it quickly became clear that he was about as lucky as breaking a mirror over a black cat beneath a ladder. I'd thought he might be trouble, but I never could have imagined just how much trouble he'd be.

Pang told me he'd tried to come inside her friend's room, but Pang wouldn't let him. When she shut him out he refused to leave, lingering on the doorstep for another six hours, until five o'clock in the morning.

The next day, Lucky Charm had been searching for Pang in Sapa, asking her friends where she was – and when he found her, he began grabbing at her in the streets. He threatened to kill himself if she wouldn't marry him, and threatened to kill any other man he saw her with – by which he meant me.

LUCKY MAN

Pang, who dismissed other Hmong men as "stupid boys", considered Lucky Charm to be genuinely dangerous.

I began making enquiries around town, and the reality was worse than I'd feared. I was surprised that I'd never been aware of Lucky Charm before, as many of the locals seemed to know him by sight, if not by name.

Earlier that year, a charitable centre had opened just outside Sapa, offering shelter to street kids. Lucky Charm had worked there for a time, and that's where he'd learned to speak English. We spoke to the manager, who told us Lucky Charm had been thrown out for his constant fighting and extreme unpredictability, and he wasn't welcome back.

From everything else I heard about Lucky Charm, I wasn't at all surprised he'd been thrown out: I was only surprised they'd let him stay long enough to learn as much English as he had.

Others described Lucky Charm as "an animal" – notoriously aggressive, somewhat psychotic, known to tear off his shirt at the slightest provocation. He loved to brawl, carried a knife, and wasn't afraid to use it. His gang – presumably the group of young men we'd seen at the *bia hoi* – would often join him in his violence.

It seemed that declarations of love paired with threats of violence were standard behaviour for Lucky Charm, with the only real variable being the target. He was said to have a history of sexual violence, and those who knew him advised simply to avoid him, even to avoid eye contact. It wasn't hard to imagine why his ex-girlfriend had fled the country, if that's what she'd done.

A friend who worked with the local Hmong community warned that "angry Hmong boys have nothing to lose – they can be really, really stupid". He advised bringing Pang's elder brother to Sapa, so that he might speak with Lucky Charm's father in an attempt to resolve the situation without any loss of face.

Lucky Charm, however, was rumoured to have beaten up his father, and by all reports was beyond the influence of his family, which ruled out any hope of a diplomatic solution. I was told that he was part of a local "mafia", and while I wasn't sure exactly what that meant in the context of Sapa, it was clear that he could make plenty of trouble if he wanted to.

One surprising but seemingly true rumour I heard about Lucky Charm was that an American man had taken him travelling three times to Cambodia. I wondered if Lucky Charm had become involved with some kind of smuggling, or if he himself had been preyed upon.

While I'd been making my enquiries, Lucky Charm had been making a few of his own. He wanted to know who I was and what my relationship was to Pang, and he was trying to get at her via her friends and family.

Lucky Charm began following Pang around – and if she spoke to anyone, he'd want to speak to them, too. One of Pang's friends had tried to reason with him, explaining Pang's current situation, and telling him that if he truly loved her, as he claimed to, then he should stop scaring her. Needless to say, the effort was wasted.

The situation escalated quickly. Lucky Charm openly

declared his intention to kidnap Pang – which was perfectly acceptable within Hmong culture, and could happen at any moment. Once he had Pang in his hands and home, he could do anything to her.

It was all too much for Pang, who had only just found her way back to a better place emotionally. Her protective shell shattered completely, and Aart did his best to hold her together.

"I feel very scary and hate him very much, but he can do anything what he wants," Pang said. "Make me think too much. All night, cannot sleep."

Yet Pang stubbornly refused to remove herself from danger. Mutual friends had offered her an excellent place to stay on the fringes of Sapa where she could be both comfortable and safe from harm, and I'd accompanied her there.

Aware of the risk, and against all reason, Pang returned to town, and still went after dark to places Lucky Charm had already followed her. I could give Pang support and advice – but I couldn't give her both protection and freedom.

At my insistence, Pang reported Lucky Charm's threats to the police. They were already well aware of Lucky Charm, following an incident in which he'd attacked a man who he'd claimed had stolen one of his girlfriends. The police were supposedly already trying to catch him – but they clearly weren't trying very hard, as he still walked openly on the streets of Sapa. They didn't even bother pretending to do anything to help Pang.

Pang thought the best solution was to pose as my girlfriend – which was really no solution at all, as it did nothing to protect her while only giving Lucky Charm more reason to lash out at me.

Her only other plan was a far more horrific one.

"If people take me go, I just kill myself," she told me – and she meant it, too.

I hated the game of whispers, of hearing everything secondhand and waiting for Lucky Charm to make his move.

He was one of very few Sapa Hmong men who spoke enough English for us to communicate directly. I wanted to find him, and to find out how much truth lay behind the rumours. I preferred to take my chances with Lucky Charm than live in fear of him.

While it might not have seemed particularly intelligent to seek out a volatile, knife-wielding psychopath who'd made explicit threats against my life, I'd just spent four long, agonising months sitting helplessly by while disaster had threatened and occasionally struck my friends. Now, at least, there was something I could do, no matter how mad it might have seemed. I wasn't going to be intimidated by a kid who shared his name with a breakfast cereal.

The dangers I'd faced until now had generally been abstract – but this one had a face, a name, and a physical presence. I'm not a fighter by any means, nor am I built like one, and it was the only time in my adult life I've walked willingly into what seemed very likely to become a physical altercation.

There was a sense of wanting to protect Pang, as I'd failed to do for Isabela, but I felt none of the anger I'd felt in Kashmir. All I felt was an overwhelming sense of frustration, knowing all that Pang had been through to regain her freedom and happiness, and seeing it all being torn so senselessly away.

I had neither a plan nor a weapon: I had no interest in escalating the situation further. All I had were "ifs" – if a fight broke out, and if it remained between just the two of us, and if I could find some way to get rid of the knife, then I felt confident I could hold my own. Lucky Charm was more solidly built and clearly had more fighting experience – but like most Hmong men, he stood a full head shorter than me, and I had much greater reach.

The only place I knew where to find Lucky Charm was also the place he seemed least likely to slice me open: the hotel where he worked. If he was away from his gang and risked his job by attacking me, then I imagined he'd be less enthusiastic to do so.

I knew the hotel: coincidentally, it was the same hotel that May and I had been standing outside when we'd said our goodbyes four years earlier, the last time I'd seen her in Sapa.

Hotels in Sapa tended to provide meals and sleeping quarters for their staff, so I went to Lucky Charm's hotel in the early evening when I felt sure he'd be there – but he wasn't.

The front desk staff told me that Lucky Charm had worked only three or four days as a trial waiter and bartender. He'd been sleeping there, and had been expected to work that evening – but he'd disappeared twenty-four hours earlier, and nobody knew where he was. The staff said that if he came back, he'd be fired.

When I stepped back outside, the night air felt a little colder. Pang and I were exposed, while Lucky Charm remained hidden behind an absurd pseudonym and a host of chilling rumours. He knew who we were, where we lived, and the places we regularly went.

On that first night, I hadn't paid Lucky Charm enough attention to remember his face, and he could have been any one of the young Hmong men on the streets. He was out there somewhere – an unhinged young man with a weapon, a gang, and a lust for violence. By all accounts, he wouldn't hesitate to carry out the threats he'd made against us.

Lucky Charm suffused our lives with a weird creepy feeling that was hard to shake. I'd walk Pang home each evening then return alone through the dark and twisting laneways of Sapa. It felt good to get back to the Yellow Dragon and shut the door. When I'd wake up the next morning, it felt so distant and dreamlike – only to begin all over again.

Our best hope was a horrible one: that the impulsiveness that had drawn Lucky Charm to Pang would draw him on to some other unlucky soul before he acted.

SEMI-CHARMED LIFE

The menace of Lucky Charm lasted for five long, nerve-wracking days before taking a surprisingly comic turn.

On 1st November, Lucky Charm was riding his motorbike through the mountains. One of the other young men who'd spoken with Pang at the *bia hoi* was riding as his passenger. They'd gone riding out to the Love Waterfall beneath Fansipan, and were on their way back to Sapa. In the course of conversation, Lucky Charm learned that his friend was also interested in Pang and intended to pursue her.

Lucky Charm was notorious for his explosive bursts of aggression. He told his friend to back off, because Pang was his. They argued, Lucky Charm crashed the bike, and both of them were injured. Lucky Charm was hospitalised with a badly damaged leg, which was said to be broken.

On hearing the news, Pang and I were both underwhelmed by grief, and high-fived our way through our utter lack of sorrow.

At least for the moment, Lucky Charm had rendered himself harmless – and without a physical presence, he was no longer frightening, merely ridiculous. Unfortunately, his pursuit of Pang was far from over.

We soon discovered that Khu's drunken, surly boyfriend was one of Lucky Charm's friends. Khu was convinced that this boyfriend would soon marry her, and thought it was a great idea that Pang marry Lucky Charm, even suggesting a double wedding.

Without bothering to ask how Pang felt or what she wanted, Khu had given Pang's phone number to Lucky Charm. It was an incredibly stupid thing to do, and Pang was understandably furious. Lucky Charm began calling and messaging Pang from two different numbers at all hours of the day and night with the frequency you might expect of a bed-ridden obsessive.

Pang said she'd change her number, but she didn't. At first we just let her phone ring and then I picked it up a few times. For a while my foreign, male voice had the desired effect of scaring Lucky Charm off, and he'd hang up immediately. Finally he mustered the courage to ask me if I was Pang's boyfriend.

"Pang doesn't have a boyfriend. I'm her friend. You're not, and she doesn't want to talk to you."

Click.

Khu also began calling and messaging constantly, trying to convince Pang that "Lacky Chang" was really a nice guy – and when Pang still refused to speak to him, Khu became abusive.

"F*ck you," she said. "He really loves you."

Eventually, Pang snapped. She began answering Lucky Charm's calls and teasing him as a vent for her frustration.

"Of course I'll marry you," she laughed. "When there are two suns in the sky, and roosters lay eggs!"

During our roadtrip to Dien Bien Phu, we'd met a small boy dressed in a mock police officer's uniform. When Pang had kept telling me how cute he'd looked, I'd begun referring to him as her "little policeman boyfriend". It had become a running joke between us – and Pang now began expanding on the fiction, infuriating Lucky Charm with fanciful descriptions of the police officer she was supposedly dating.

While it didn't seem wise to provoke a character like Lucky

Charm, it was Pang's way of claiming her power back – and for someone who wasn't comfortable sharing her emotions, laughter and anger were the only outlets she had.

In the same way, Pang had deliberately provoked her "husband" in China with false claims that she had waiting for her a "very, very special boyfriend in Vietnam".

"Shut up your mouth," said Pang, when Lucky Charm tried to threaten her. "Your leg's broken enough already. If you follow me, I'll carry the big knife and cut your leg off."

Lucky Charm warned her to think before she spoke. Pang told him she'd been thinking already, and would be very happy to see him die. Lucky Charm said that because he was in hospital and couldn't do it himself, he was now paying someone else to follow her. Singing to the tune of a then-popular Hmong song, Pang began improvising lyrics about wishing Lucky Charm dead and taking all his chickens after he was gone.

Two days later, Lucky Charm's mother called to say her son had come home from the hospital, but all he did was cry all day and wouldn't eat anything. She, too, had decided that the only solution was for Lucky Charm to marry Pang.

"Me, I never see people stupid like this," said Pang.

I remembered the story Pang had told me of the night she'd locked her "husband" out of their apartment. At first he'd tried threatening and intimidating Pang – and when that hadn't worked, he'd called his mother for help. For all the power he had to terrorise Pang, behind his bravado Lucky Charm was equally pathetic.

Just when it seemed as though the situation couldn't get any more absurd, Lucky Charm rang Pang to ask if she could buy him some more credit for his phone – so that he could continue to harass her. When she predictably refused, he asked if she'd call him back. Pang and I were gobsmacked – but he was serious.

Lucky Charm's friends and relatives then began calling, and Pang abused them all in turn.

"He don't care if you like him or not," said one of Lucky Charm's friends. "He just care he love you very much."

Lucky Charm was clearly using a definition of love I wasn't familiar with. Pang's mother Bao was worried that Lucky Charm's friends and relatives would kidnap Pang on his behalf, but Pang refused to consider the danger.

I couldn't understand how, in a close-knit society where a young Hmong woman could be irredeemably shamed for actions that harmed nobody, a violent and emotionally unstable young man like Lucky Charm could be left entirely unchecked. It was disgusting that local law enforcement knowingly allowed him to terrorise girls and women with complete impunity – and it was beyond belief that the only members of the local community willing to intervene in the situation were those who encouraged and supported his behaviour.

As we soon learned, Lucky Charm's leg wasn't actually broken – and as it got better, the situation only got worse for Pang.

IT'S TOO LATE

There was an unexpectedly poignant moment one evening as Pang and I were laughing and joking by Sapa's main square. Pang stopped suddenly, pointing at a lamppost with a flowerpot hanging on either side.

"Like me and May," she declared. "Me, I'm like this," she said, pointing at the first flowerpot, bursting with tiny pink blossoms. Then she pointed at the second plant, which hung dark and withered from its pot: "She stay in China, like this."

I was beginning to feel the same way.

Almost immediately after Pang's return home, May had stopped working at the restaurant. Her "husband" seemed to have learned that Pang had run away and, fearing May would do the same, he'd taken her back home. She was again spending long days alone there with her baby girl – which meant she had plenty of time to talk.

From Pang's first days in Sapa, she and I had been calling May regularly via my laptop. After saying hello, I'd often step outside so that May and Pang could speak freely in their own language.

I felt that Pang could help May, in the same way that Aart and Big Zao had helped Pang, and I wanted to keep them connected.

During my search for May and Pang in China, May had been the most eager to return home – but she was also a more reflective, less impulsive person than Pang. Over the months, she'd become overwhelmed with myriad fears about the future of her daughter and herself, and had lost her resolve to escape her "husband".

Pang could understand May's position better than anyone and she was the most vocal advocate of May's return. Pang had also been mired in endless uncertainties of the future that awaited her in Vietnam, and now knew how wonderful it felt to have regained her freedom. Despite the judgement she'd received in Sapa and the terror of Lucky Charm, Pang had no regrets about having escaped her "husband" and come home.

A few months earlier, I'd hoped that May's planned return home would inspire Pang to follow. Now the situation was reversed, and I hoped Pang would inspire May. If nothing else, Pang could give May a clearer understanding of what she could expect on arrival in Sapa, so that she could make a more informed decision.

May had indeed been inspired by Pang's homecoming – but in the worst possible way. Rather than allowing Blue Dragon to bring her back safely and legally, May was now determined to come home by herself, just as Pang had.

May was afraid that if she was caught trying to escape with anyone else, her "husband's" family would prevent her from leaving – or else they'd prevent her from ever returning to see her daughter again.

"I want to go back for sure, but I want to go back myself," May said. "I don't want someone come to take me go there."

May didn't know the way home, and would have to cross immense distances to reach Vietnam. She would almost certainly be caught by the Chinese authorities in the borderlands, if not before – and without a Chinese identity card, she wouldn't be able to escape them as Pang had.

Pang had come to realise just how risky her return had

been, and how fortunate she was to have reached Sapa at all. Regardless of anything Pang and I said, though, and without any convincing reasons of her own, May was determined to do it her own way.

May said she argued with her "husband" every day, and was constantly telling us how desperately she wanted to come home to Sapa. Now that she'd stopped work, the fear of a second pregnancy had returned to give a renewed sense of urgency to her escape – and yet, for all her talk, May did nothing. At times she fell into despair, saying it was "too late" for her – and then she let pass every opportunity to leave.

May's words and actions just didn't add up: once again, there seemed to be something she wasn't telling us.

There was no assurance or assistance we could offer May that we hadn't offered already. As the weeks passed, Pang lost patience with May's inaction, and spoke to her with less frequency, less insistence, and less hope.

Almost a month after Pang's return, her mother Bao came from the village to spend a rare evening with us in Sapa. Pang, her mother, her aunt, and I met for a simple dinner at the market.

It was a beautiful evening. The two elder women told me how much they appreciated all I'd done to find Pang in China, having both believed that they'd die without ever seeing Pang again. They'd keep me in their hearts forever, they said.

Bao had thought it impossible to find any of the trafficked girls in China. She told me her "heart was happy" to see Pang come home, and said she'd never let her go again.

Bao had brought some unexpected news from her village where, a few days earlier, she'd met with May's mother Dung and eldest sister Dinh. Bao had encouraged Dung to trust me, telling her I was a good man and only wanted to help. Dung said she didn't want my help: May was fine in China, she said, and I should leave her alone.

There was nothing surprising in Dung's comments – the real surprise came from Dinh, who told Bao that May had fallen pregnant once more, and was expecting her second child in six months' time.

If Dinh's claim was true, it would not only explain May's strange behaviour, but it also seemed to give a hard limit to her potential return home. I was convinced that whichever country May gave birth in would be the country in which she'd spend the rest of her life.

STUCK IN A MOMENT
YOU CAN'T GET OUT OF

I'd learned not to trust everything I heard in Sapa, no matter how reliable the source might seem. When I called May and asked her directly if she was having another child, she denied it.

"I have my girl holiday right now!" she declared – using a phrase that suggested that in May's experience, sex was an even less pleasant process than menstruation.

But if May wasn't pregnant, then why was she still in China?

May said her father Lung was "crazy a lot" and would be "not very happy to see [her]" back in Vietnam. He'd made it clear that May wouldn't be welcome home if she returned without the permission of her Chinese "husband" – and so May was again seeking that permission.

May's "husband" gladly took advantage of this power she'd given him and used it to control her, baiting her with false hopes – just as Pang's "husband" had done when Pang had hoped to return home with his permission.

May was waiting for a moment that would never arrive. She constantly assured us of her imminent return to Vietnam, but her date of departure was always pushed back and remained ever out of reach. May swore that she was coming home in August, then December, then January, then February, then May, then June, and then the following August.

Her "husband" had proven to be a violently possessive and endlessly manipulative man who promised May things he had no intention of delivering. He had no interest in allowing May to leave, and Pang and I were certain he'd never let her go.

Some of the things May's "husband" had promised her were extremely implausible. He said that he'd accompany May to the border and let her cross back into Vietnam with their baby while he simply waited on the other side of the border for several weeks. At other times he promised May that he'd accompany her back home for a full month, perhaps even two – but only if she waited until next year, or the year after.

As each promised date approached, of course, May's "husband" simply invented a new one.

"Her husband is like some crazy guy," Pang told me. "Today say 'Okay,' tomorrow say, 'No.' After tomorrow say, 'Okay,' after tomorrow again say, 'No.'"

But this strategy wasn't crazy at all: it was working. May herself had told me many times what a liar her "husband" was, yet she kept believing him. It was incredibly frustrating to see how, after the devastation of each broken promise, she continued to swallow his lies.

"Chinese people not very good, every day liar," May said. "In China, you marry China boy, they liar to you. My husband, everything is liar. Last year he say if I have a baby he bring me back to Kunming. Now I have a baby, I say, 'I want to to Kunming.' He say, 'No, after Happy New Year.' He liar to me. I think, whole my life he do not bring me go to Vietnam."

(Kunming was the capital of China's Yunnan province, which bordered Vietnam – but May used the term to refer to the entire province.)

Lung's refusal to welcome his daughter home was based on two false beliefs: firstly, that she would become an unmarriageable burden, and secondly, that May's "husband" was a wealthy man who treated her well.

There didn't seem to be much I could do about the first belief – but if I could help Lung understand the truth of May's situation in China, then perhaps he'd allow her to come home without the permission of her "husband".

Since I'd first made contact with May in China, my actions had been guided by what she wanted. May had specifically asked me to conceal the reality of her situation from her family – but now it was time to tell them the truth. It was horrific that she should continue to suffer just to make her parents feel better at a time when she most needed their support.

Pang supported my decision and wanted to help me, so we rode out to May's family home in the village. May's parents weren't there, so we spoke to her second brother Tzu.

Tzu said his parents now spoke to May very rarely, and received most of their news via May's second sister Cho. Cho had assured them that May was very happy in China, loved her "husband" very much, and didn't really want to come home.

I told Tzu what I'd seen and heard of May's "husband" and home life in China. Pang verified my statements to the extent of her own experiences, and explained how horrible it had been to have been forced into "marriage" and motherhood so far from home.

We wanted May's family to understand the facts so that we could all work together to support May and she could make her decision free of any misguided family pressure – but Tzu refused to believe a word we said. He remained convinced that May's "husband" was a good man and a wealthy one.

Tzu and I had radically different definitions of what it meant to be wealthy, and even of what it meant to be good. In a culture where even the behaviour of a violent, unpredictable young man like Lucky Charm was not only accepted but encouraged by those around him, the criteria for being considered a good man were remarkably low.

May's "husband" was emotionally, physically, and sexually

abusive – yet he and his family had always provided food and shelter for May. Perhaps Tzu and I were both right about May's "husband", according to our own definitions.

Even as Pang and I were trying to bring us all closer together, May's family seemed determined to push us further apart. Bizarrely, they became upset at Pang for supposedly starting the rumour of May's pregnancy, though I'd been there when Pang had first heard it as news from Bao.

Bao was the sweetest and purest soul in Sapa. I had no doubt whatsoever that she'd told us the truth, and she'd brought the news directly from May's family. It seemed that May's sister Dinh had invented the story on the spur of the moment to get rid of Bao, and now May's family were angry that Pang's family had repeated it.

A rift opened between the two families. It was a frustrating, needless small-town drama at a time when we all had far more important issues to focus on. I felt as though we were turning in circles, and that none of us were getting anywhere – least of all May.

YOU KEEP ME HANGIN' ON

I knew that the decision May faced was an enormously complex one – even so, knowing May, I was surprised she hadn't taken more decisive action. I'd thought she would have taken her chances and made the best of them, rather than defaulting through indecision to a life she hated.

Pang blamed May for the situation she was now in, and thought she was foolish for having told different stories to different people – missing the obvious irony that Pang herself had done exactly the same thing before her own return.

A new distance had grown between May and Pang that was more than just geographical. No longer able to understand each other's situations, they'd begun drifting apart, just as Pang had drifted away from her other friends in Sapa.

Sebastien was also deeply confused and frustrated by May's behaviour. He said the only chance he'd have to visit Asia was during his holidays for Christmas and the New Year. He tried to set an end date on May's decision by telling her he wanted to meet her in Sapa for the New Year – but even that failed to move her.

"I need to stay in China for New Year," May said. "After New Year I come for sure! I come by myself."

Nor did Sebastien seem to realise that when he and May talked about the New Year they were talking about two different things: he meant the beginning of January, and she meant the Lunar New Year in mid-February.

I felt a sense of great responsibility for May, and had seen her as the central figure of our documentary – but now I also began detaching emotionally from whatever might happen to her.

It wasn't that I didn't care about May anymore, but – for the sake of my own mental wellbeing – I simply couldn't maintain that level of emotional investment. I'd been on that rollercoaster for too long, and now it seemed as though May would be stuck there, going around and around forever. I couldn't keep hanging on, waiting for May to make what seemed like the right decision: I had to start letting go.

Like many people, I could be slow to learn, and even slower to change. After witnessing a series of ill-advised decisions made by people I cared about, however, I was gradually coming to realise that their choices were beyond my control. Having already shared my thoughts and offered my advice, all I could do was accept their decisions, even when I was certain they were misguided and even dangerous.

As much as I would have loved to have been in Sapa when May returned, there was no saying if or when it would ever occur. Pang told me that if I was only prolonging my stay in Asia for May's sake, then I was wasting my time. If she'd been in my position, Pang said, she would have given up on May a long time ago.

"If [it was] me, I go far away already, not here anymore!" she said. "Very important is yourself. You have to think about this."

While Pang was the last person I would have expected to be giving advice on emotional self-care, she was right.

Pang and I had been pouring what time and energy we had into giving May the support she needed – but we both had our own lives to go on with, and we simply couldn't wait forever.

For seven or eight months, May had been telling me how desperately she wanted to escape China. What worried me most was that if she couldn't muster the courage to come home while she had our full support, then I was certain she never would.

The moment was already passing: I'd soon be leaving Sapa, and Pang had little patience left for May's inaction, especially while she herself was under attack from May's family.

The longer May's indecision lasted, the less moral support she'd receive. Soon, the only voices left in May's life would be those of her "husband", her family, and the other trafficked women who had already resigned themselves to forced "marriages" in China – all of whom were telling May to stay where she was.

After having taken great pains to remain impartial, I now wondered if I should have been more forceful in my opinions, to counteract those voices. If May expected the men in her life to tell her what to do, perhaps I'd only confused her by offering her so little guidance and merely creating space for her to find her own way. By remaining a neutral presence, it seemed I'd let the negative forces in May's life swamp her in paralysing doubt.

Worse still: since my time in India, I'd had doubts of my own about May, and was no longer sure if I could believe what she told me.

When I spoke to May, she seemed determined to return home – but when they spoke in their own language, Pang said that May still didn't really know what she wanted, and even now could change her mind from one moment to the next.

May had recently told Pang she was waiting for Sebastien to rescue her from China – an idea so absurd I didn't know whether to laugh or cry. A moment later, May had said she'd come home in August the following year, after her daughter's second birthday.

If May wasn't being honest with me – if I couldn't believe the things she told me – then our conversations felt pointless.

It seemed I'd become just one more man in May's life who she was trying to please by telling me what I wanted to hear: a painful realisation after all we'd been through together.

May had once told me she was afraid she'd be stuck in China forever and eventually die there, because her "husband" would never make up his mind. I began to believe she was right – not because of her "husband's" indecision, but her own.

WE THE PEOPLE WHO ARE
DARKER THAN BLUE

After weeks of searching, Pang finally found a room of her own – in fact, she'd been remarkably lucky.

The room had been rented by another young Hmong woman who was now leaving the country to be with her French husband. In the expectation of an eventual return, the woman was leaving all her furniture and many of her belongings behind, and would continue to pay rent on the room.

The woman knew Pang, was aware of her situation, and offered her the use of the room – and so rather than moving into a typically bare concrete room, Pang found herself living in relative comfort. The pink-and-white wallpapered room came with a bed, a small vinyl couch, and plastic shelving, plus all the bedding and kitchenware Pang would need.

The room was nestled in a complex of similar rooms, most of which were rented by other young women from the villages. Pang had very few belongings of her own to move in, and was soon settled comfortably.

Unfortunately, she hadn't yet been able to start work. Pang, and my friends' agency which had offered her good work as a trekking guide, wanted her to be legally licensed to avoid getting fined.

When Pang had applied for her identity card at Sapa's main police station, she'd been told it would be ready in a week and would cost 20,000 dong (about a dollar). She revisited the police station regularly in the hopes that her card would be ready.

After two weeks, Pang was told that the card would take at least two more weeks, maybe a month – or she could have it immediately if she was willing to pay a special processing fee of 350,000 dong (about sixteen dollars).

It became clear that the police were holding Pang's identity card and wouldn't give it to her unless she paid the "fee" – and so she did. If you wanted the police to do anything, she said, you had to give them "money for the drinking".

With her identity card in hand, Pang could then begin the application for her tour guide licence. I was a little concerned about this as it seemed to involve a written test and Pang was barely literate.

I had a Kinh friend who worked at Sapa's tourist information centre. He'd arranged an appointment for me to meet his boss so I could learn exactly what was needed for the licence, and to see how Pang might best be supported through that process.

When I arrived for the appointment, the boss was drunk and clearly had no interest in helping me. I didn't bother rescheduling.

Then – less than two weeks after Pang had finally paid the extra "fee" to receive her identity card – the police raided her housing complex in the night, banging on doors and demanding to see rental papers. They knew, of course, that most of the tenants were illiterate and that no such papers existed: it was simply an excuse to seize the identity cards of everyone in the complex.

The tenants were told to reclaim their cards at the police station the next day – and when Pang tried to, the police demanded a payment of 400,000 dong (about eighteen dollars).

While these might not seem exorbitant sums, by local standards Pang had already paid half a week's average wages to get her identity card. Now she'd have to pay even more than that to get it back – though she didn't have any income, because her lack of identity card prevented her from working legally.

Pang anticipated more frustration and exploitation during the process to obtain her guide licence. Sick and tired of giving all her money to greedy officials, she gave up on the identity card, and on her hopes of becoming a licensed trekking guide.

I'd wanted to find a way of giving Pang money without just giving her money. I also wanted to find some way to thank my family for the support they'd given me over the past year, and thought about buying them some of the Hmong costumes on sale at Sapa's market.

A woman's Black Hmong costume includes two jackets, a highly decorative belt, culottes, and leg warmers. While the last two items could be bought new at the market for just a few dollars, the creation of the jackets and belt took an enormous investment of time and energy.

Hemp fibre was spun, handwoven, and dyed – up to a dozen times, depending on the strength of the solution – in a barrel of indigo; narrow strips of red and white material were stitched around the sleeves; broad bands of intricate, richly-coloured embroidery were added to the belt, sleeves, and collar; and a rounded stone was used to polish the outer jacket to a sheen.

Each costume was unique, and carried great personal value – the belt alone could take eight months to produce. The newness of a woman's costume was measured by how few times it had been washed, as it would lose a little colour with each wash.

Pang came with me to look at the costumes at the market, but wasn't very impressed. She told me that her own costumes were newer and more beautiful, and half-jokingly told me I could buy those instead. I told her I would, if she was willing to sell them to me.

Pang called her mother Bao, who said she wouldn't have wanted anyone else to buy the costumes, but she'd be happy for Pang to sell them to me. Curiously, this was one decision that didn't seem to require male approval: it seemed the women had ownership of their own clothes, if nothing else. I let Pang and Bao set whatever price they liked, and soon found myself in possession of three of Pang's costumes.

One was a costume that Bao had made, intending it as a gift for Pang's newly-married sister – but when Pang had first made contact from China, Bao hoped she'd one day come home, and had promised to keep the costume for her return. This was the brand-new costume that Pang had worn on her first day back in Sapa.

The other two costumes featured the belts and jackets embroidered by Pang herself in the two years before her abduction. The most beautiful belt was the one Pang had been working on when I'd first lived in Sapa in 2010. She'd completed it and had planned to wear it for the first time at the 2011 New Year celebrations – but had been abducted immediately beforehand, and so it had sat untouched for years.

I sent the three costumes as gifts to my mother, father, and brother Nick. Pang still had two costumes of her own to wear in Sapa, and she and her family wouldn't have to worry about money for a long time. It was a simple yet elegant solution for both of us.

In her gratitude, Pang used some of the money to buy gifts of her own for my mother and sister.

IF I LAUGH

Aart had been wonderful in giving Pang whatever emotional support he could, especially in times of crisis – but Pang never formed the habit of visiting him regularly, as I'd hoped she would.

During our roadtrip, I'd seen how much it meant to Pang to have a safe space and a friend to talk to, and I'd told her she was welcome to come and visit me anytime at the Yellow Dragon. This had been especially valuable for Pang when Lucky Charm was still at large and the streets of Sapa were unsafe for her.

In early November, Pang started work at a local café. The café was owned by a European man and his Hmong wife, and Pang alternated between morning and evening shifts there.

It was great to see Pang living independently, working, and saving her money, just as she'd hoped to do. I found myself with more free time, which I spent in the restaurant or my room at the Yellow Dragon, working on the 'Sisters for Sale' documentary.

The Yellow Dragon lay on the most direct route between Pang's room and the café, and she'd often visit before or after her shifts. I was happy to make time for her whenever she wanted to talk or just needed a friend.

We'd often go walking through town to see Aart, visit the market, or get ice creams. Sometimes in the evening we'd meet with some of the other Hmong girls and walk around the lake or kick a feathered shuttlecock between us in the square.

On other days Pang and I would just hang around the hotel: we'd call May, video chat with my family, or watch films like Wes Anderson's 'Fantastic Mr Fox', which quickly became our favourite.

Pang had decided to embroider a headband for me, using fluorescent colours and a geometric design of her own invention. Sometimes she'd just sit quietly and stitch while I worked on my laptop, glad to have some company rather than sitting alone in her room.

Because the Yellow Dragon was my home, sometimes Pang would surprise me in the middle of domestic tasks, which led to some amusing scenes. Once she appeared while I was handwashing some of my laundry – and, insisting that boys didn't know how to wash clothes, told me she'd do it for me. I said no, but told her she could stand there and watch me, and I'd show her that some boys did in fact know how to wash clothes. Pang watched me like a hawk and after I'd finished, begrudgingly conceded the point. She demanded to know who'd taught me, not believing that a "boy" could have worked it out all by himself.

Another time, Pang found me experimentally stitching some beautiful strips of Red Hmong embroidery onto my favourite pants, which were wearing thin at the knees. This time, we both quickly realised that Pang's needlework was far superior to my own, and she showed me a better technique.

Pang was so impressed by the resulting fusion of Eastern and Western styles that she surprised me a few days later with a gift: a new pair of pants she'd bought at the market, with bands of local embroidery she'd bought separately and stitched around the knees. I wore them proudly.

As so many of the Hmong girls in Sapa shared the same

names, there were often adjectives added to distinguish them – like "Big Zao", "Little Chu", or "Crazy Shu". I now found myself with a local nickname of my own: "Crazy Pants Ben".

The exuberant joy that Pang had felt on our roadtrip had been rapidly dispelled by the menace of Lucky Charm and the realities of life in Sapa – but, as the pieces of her life began falling into place, she developed a new sense of quietly-growing optimism.

At the Yellow Dragon, Pang found a self-confidence she could carry with her back out into the streets of Sapa, knowing she had a safe place to replenish it whenever she needed to.

When she was in a good mood, Pang was hilarious, and we had plenty of fun together. She had a habit of making loud and incredibly inappropriate comments in public, knowing it would be a struggle for me not to break out in shocked laughter.

One day at the markets we found ourselves standing near a Kinh woman wearing heavily-applied cosmetics, and Pang couldn't help herself.

"Oi, monster!" she blurted. "Look at the lady's make-up, like monster! I feel scary when I see that!"

On seeing middle-aged Western men with young local women, Pang would declare, "So many sugar daddy, oh! Old buffalo eat the young food!"

One morning Pang led me on with a long and elaborate story about an unnamed twenty-eight-year-old Sapa Kinh divorcée with two children who supposedly had a crush on me. I was mystified and couldn't imagine who Pang might be referring to, when her story suddenly ended with, "Only joking! Nobody likes you!" and she exploded in laughter.

Pang's constant comment on witnessing the incomprehensible behaviour of other human beings was, "Some people, huh?" – a phrase often accompanied by a disbelieving shake of the head, which soon became my own habitual response to any oddities I witnessed. It was one of several phrases I adopted from my time in Sapa and carried with me around the world.

Pang described me as "eat-too-much, talk-too-much Ben".

"Lucky boy!" she exclaimed, meaning me.

"Lucky boy? Why?"

"Because you is my friend!"

I told Pang I was happy she'd come home.

"Don't need you happy, I happy myself!" she declared.

I'd begun editing a new video for the project's website, in which I introduced myself and my reasons for returning to Asia. Pang, of course, immediately began poking fun at it.

"My name is Ben Longnose, I come back to Vietnam to eat!"

"Always think eat!" she told me. "Your mouth is very itchy, huh? You see something, you just want to eat, itchy mouth!"

Whenever we ate together, Pang always took too much chilli. I often reminded her – but she never listened, and never learned. She'd wipe her mouth with a flourish, as if finishing a magic trick – and then sit there as if overcome with emotion, clearly suffering, often crying, and completely unable to speak. I joked that it was the only moment's peace I ever had.

During my time in China, to ease the jealousy of May's "husband", I'd enlisted the help of a Californian woman, Michelle, who had posed as my partner. After talking about Michelle constantly for a week with both May and Pang, I'd never mentioned her again, and it was clear that she no longer played a role in my life.

Pang also knew that I'd lived and travelled extensively with my former partner, Dominique, without ever marrying her. On that basis, Pang had decided I was "very play" with women.

"You is my friend, it's okay," she told me. "But if you is my boyfriend, you die very long times ago!"

When I held the door for Pang, saying, "Ladies first," she took it as an insult.

"I is not lady, okay? I is only nineteen years old, don't call me lady!"

Pang had a hilarious obsession with her unshaven legs and

spoke about them often. She said her lengthy "leg beard" was considered very lucky in Hmong culture, and ensured that she'd either be rich or find a good husband. As she had no interest in finding any kind of husband, she was convinced that she'd soon be "rich for sure".

One thing that horrified me in Sapa was seeing the married, middle-aged Hmong couples who came to town from the villages. Rather than walking side by side on the footpaths, the man would stride ahead and his wife would follow several paces behind, like an obedient cow being led to market.

It was a clear illustration of the deep inequality between Hmong men and women, and a literal demonstration of the concept that men lead and women follow. It deprived the women not only of any decision-making power, but of their very dignity as human beings.

If Pang and I were walking in the street together and I glanced away for a moment, I'd often turn back to find she'd vanished. After a moment of confusion I'd realise that she had, yet again, paused and slipped into step behind me. I'd turn around to find her hunched over and plodding along with a vacant look on her face, in her best imitation of an older village woman.

I don't know how many times Pang pulled the same trick, but she got me every time – which was every bit as hilarious as it was infuriating.

Some people, huh?

After such a long and challenging year, it felt wonderful to take life slowly and feel at home again, with good friends around. Those weeks became a magical time in my life, just as my first stay in Sapa had been, with the stars often aligning in strange and unexpected ways.

I'd step outside in the morning and find that the street outside the Yellow Dragon was full of my friends, who just happened to be converging from all directions at that particular moment. I'd enter a café and realise the tables were all filled with people I knew. Without any prior arrangement, Pang and

I would both happen to leave our rooms at the same time and bump into each other at the same tiny intersection in the back laneways – then do exactly the same thing again the next day.

The pieces of my life just seemed to fall into place by themselves. I was no longer pushing against the world but flowing with it, and the only thing that was required of me was to be present and open to the experience.

NOT YOUR LOVER

Having a close personal connection with such a recent survivor of human trafficking gave me the rare privilege of witnessing each twist and turn of Pang's emotional recovery.

Before long, however, I realised that I'd become too close, and Pang was beginning to think of me as more than just a friend. I couldn't tell if it was merely a schoolgirl crush or the more sober realisation that a relationship with a foreigner like myself could help save Pang from her own culture. It was likely a mixture of both – and in any case, the result was the same.

There were many things I was willing to do to help solve Pang's problems, but there was no chance of our ever becoming involved romantically. The longer she held that hope, the more awkward the situation became – and, like Sebastien, it was a situation I'd made worse with my carelessness and naïveté.

I'd learned that May's sister Cho had returned to Sapa, and she agreed to speak with me. I'd unthinkingly asked Pang if she'd interpret our conversation – but on reflection, I doubted that she had the necessary skills or emotional distance, and tried to replace her with my usual interpreter, Chan.

Pang took that as a personal rejection from the one friend she'd felt she could rely upon, and it triggered an emotional crisis in her. To salvage the situation, not only did I let Pang interpret for Cho's interview, I agreed to wear Hmong costume that Sunday.

Sunday was Sapa's market day, and had traditionally been one of the best opportunities for young men and women to interact and potentially meet a partner. By promoting it as a spectacle – the "love market" – and encouraging tourists to invade the safe space which made those interactions possible, tourism agencies had tarnished the very thing they were trying to sell.

Even so, Sunday remained the most social day of the week, with many villagers gathering in their best traditional costumes and promenading between the square and lake.

I didn't have a Hmong costume and had never had any interest in wearing one, but Pang said she'd borrow one for me, and it seemed like a harmless bit of fun. It was only when she and I were walking through town in our costumes that I realised how we must have looked together: like a couple.

From what I've seen on my travels around the world, the cultures that make no allowance for platonic friendships between men and women seem to be those with the most destructive relationships between the sexes, where men too often view women as objects and don't know how to interact with them as human beings.

In Hmong culture, which permitted no public displays of affection, the mere fact that Pang and I were a man and woman spending time together – especially in traditional costume – was taken as proof of romance.

It took me so long to become aware of Pang's affections because I simply didn't think of her in those terms, and any romance between us was never within the realm of possibility. To my mind there was an insurmountable distance between us, as between family members, or between a teacher and a student.

I was in my early thirties, while Pang was not only a very recent survivor of human trafficking, but a barely-literate teenager from a radically different cultural and economic background. I still thought of her as a girl, though of course she was now a woman who had experienced things I could barely imagine.

When Pang told me, as she often did, that she wanted to remain single, I took that at face value. In hindsight, her affections seem obvious, but so do most things.

There was another Hmong girl in Sapa named Zy who had lingered on the fringes of May's group of friends without ever really being part of it. Zy was a sly gossip-monger who delighted in provoking people with lies she'd claim to have heard elsewhere. I'd never particularly liked her, had fallen out with her when I'd first lived in Sapa, and found that she hadn't improved since then.

Zy was one of Sapa's "bad girls", though her reputation had been somewhat salvaged by a long-term relationship with a European boyfriend whom she hoped to marry. Pang had now begun spending more time with Zy, and seemed to be pinning her hopes on having a similar relationship with me.

I hadn't told anyone that Pang and I had shared rooms on our roadtrip. Now I realised that Pang had told Zy, who had interpreted that fact in the most obvious way and shared it around Sapa.

Zy began hinting continually, in her obvious and irritating way, that Pang was in love with me, and referred constantly to Lucky Charm in an absurdly misguided attempt to make me jealous. I had no patience for her, and was glad when Pang also got sick of her.

Rumours quickly began to emerge that Pang and I were in a romantic relationship – not only from the Hmong community, but also from my Kinh friends, who knew Pang came to visit me at the Yellow Dragon almost every day.

"Ben fall in love with Hmong girl," they told me.

I prefer the clarity of direct conversation to suggestions and subtleties of behaviour. When I tried to address the issue openly, Pang assured me that we were just friends, and maintained her earlier statements that she didn't want a boyfriend or husband.

Pang was getting too close, while May was drifting ever further away – and I was no longer sure I could believe what either of them told me. I knew I had to begin stepping away – but I also knew that Pang had nobody else to give her the emotional support she needed. If I stepped away too quickly she'd spiral into another crisis.

I needed to dissuade Pang gently, without hurting her more than she already had been. I found myself in the awkward position of trying to maintain a presence while also keeping my distance. It was a delicate balancing act that left me feeling guilty of being there for Pang both too much and too little.

That was how things stood between Pang and me when Lucky Charm reappeared in our lives.

On 10th November – nine days after his accident – Lucky Charm called Pang in the early morning to say he could walk again and would marry her this year whether or not she wanted to. Over the following days, Pang and I began hearing rumours that Lucky Charm was making arrangements with his friends and family to kidnap her.

On 15th November, we learned from Lucky Charm's uncle that Pang was to be kidnapped the following day. He tried to convince Pang that it would be better if she simply gave in and married Lucky Charm. Pang's bravado cracked, and she became genuinely scared.

Since returning from our roadtrip, Pang and I had occasionally visited the local *bia hoi* together, and we did so again that evening. Pang rarely drank much – but this time she drank destructively, gulping down each glass and going back for more while I was still only halfway through mine.

Flush with the cash I'd given her for her Hmong costumes, Pang invited others to join us, and we soon found ourselves sitting with a circle of other Hmong and Red Dao people. Pang pushed us all to drink more and more, and showed no signs of stopping herself. When I encouraged her to slow down, she told me she was an adult now, and could do whatever she wanted. Every time she looked away I emptied her glass across the pavement, and she was too drunk to notice.

"Ben, sorry, huh? I little bit crazy tonight. My eyes turn around right now. Ben, do you eyes turn around already? For sure, I not gonna walking tonight."

When Pang finally agreed to leave, she could barely stand. As we moved slowly down Cau May Street, with Pang leaning heavily against me and my arm around her for support, I realised I'd become the suspicious older Western man walking the young drunk Asian woman home late at night.

While Pang herself would never have made the first move, she seemed to be hoping that something would now happen between us. That might have helped solve her problems with Lucky Charm, but it was something I'd simply never do.

At times Pang would stop and hug me and refuse to go anywhere – which was extremely awkward not just socially but physically, because she'd lost all sense of balance and it was all I could do to keep us from falling down in the street together.

Close to Pang's room – where our path was complicated by stairs and steeply-sloping concrete – we met with Zy. For the only time in my life I was glad to see her, and she helped me half-carry Pang the rest of the way home.

At last we put Pang to bed with a bucket and a bottle of water. Like many trafficking survivors, she preferred to sleep with a light switched on.

Pang was angry with me as I was leaving, reminding me that I'd promised to look after her. I told her I already had.

"No friend with you," she said, as I pulled the door shut behind me. While I couldn't lock the door from outside, I felt sure that even Lucky Charm wouldn't be brazen enough to kidnap a girl from her own bed.

RECKLESS

The next day was a Sunday – Sapa's market day.

I awoke early, deeply worried about the abduction Lucky Charm had organised. A marriage by abduction could be brutally violent even under ordinary circumstances, and I hated to think what it might become in the hands of a man who was already notorious for needless aggression.

I knew there was nothing I could do to protect Pang against a gang of men determined to kidnap her. If Lucky Charm found her today, he would take her – and if he didn't, it seemed certain he'd keep trying until he did.

I took Pang some breakfast from the market. She said she was "very shy" after being so drunk, and was worried about what she might have said. When I said she told me she wasn't my friend anymore, she said that was impossible.

Pang had first been kidnapped in a moment of weakness while she'd been hungover. I now wondered if history was to repeat itself: despite her weakened state and Lucky Charm's clear intent to abduct her, Pang was still determined to go to the "love market". There was nothing I could say to dissuade her, and so – with a terrible sense of foreboding – I accompanied her. Zy joined us.

Sapa was famed for its mists and fogs, and the three of us waded through the murky soup that smothered the town. The park above the square and the paths around the lake were filled with packs of young Hmong men who materialised, loomed suddenly, and vanished close at hand.

Nine months earlier, during the Lunar New Year festivities, I'd spent days walking back and forth over these same pathways – around the lake and back through the park to the square – in the strange hope of filming an abduction for marriage to include in our documentary. This phenomenon had seemed so impersonal then, but now it had become something very different.

I felt tired and seedy, and my nerves were jangling. I'd seen how swift and merciless an abduction for marriage could be. Aware that Pang could be seized at any moment, I paid the men more attention than usual, and was disturbed by how lecherous and predatory they seemed.

Groups of men passed us staring intently at Pang and Zy. One young man circled the lake on his motorcycle, pulling up alongside every girl he saw, wanting to know if she had a boyfriend. When Pang told him she was already married, he moved on to the group of girls immediately ahead of us. Another man, somewhat drunk, demanded Pang's phone number, and told her that he wanted to marry her.

Were these the best marriage prospects Sapa could offer a young Hmong woman?

There was no doubt at all that if Pang stayed out in public that day, Lucky Charm would kidnap her. It was only a matter of time – but defiance had become a matter of pride for Pang. She looked forward to the "love market" each week, and refused to let Lucky Charm take that away from her. I knew that she was scared – yet Pang refused to stay hidden, and brushed off my suggestions to go elsewhere. Perhaps she felt she deserved a few moments of her life free from the fear of men.

Help came in an unexpected form. Zy began inventing

stories about how horribly I'd treated Pang the night before, and claimed that I'd been swearing at Pang when she'd been too drunk to remember. Pang was soon sick of her nonsense, and agreed to come back to the Yellow Dragon with me to call May.

Afterwards, I walked Pang to work, and she thanked me for watching out for her – not seeming to realise how little I could do to protect her against Lucky Charm and his friends.

"I'm so happy I have very good friend," Pang told me. "I don't have to be scary walking."

We later learned that Lucky Charm and his friends had indeed been out hunting for Pang that day, and the only thing that had saved her was being hidden by the heavy fog. Pang had been lucky, but it was clear that Lucky Charm wouldn't give up so easily.

Pang had the next day off work, and said she'd come to the Yellow Dragon first thing in the morning – but she didn't, and when I went to her room, there was no sign of her. Nobody there could tell me if she'd returned from work the night before: she usually finished around ten or eleven and walked home alone. One of the girls had been trying to call her, and couldn't reach her.

Several nerve-wracking hours passed before we learned that Pang was safe, and had simply been asked to work an extra shift that morning.

That afternoon, Lucky Charm found Pang and grabbed her in the street – but he'd been drinking, and without his friends to help him, Pang managed to get away. She said he was now walking almost normally, without any brace, cast, or crutch.

The ongoing threat Lucky Charm presented was taking a severe emotional toll on Pang. She was left in a strange, unusually silent mood – and when Lucky Charm called her, she literally screamed at him over the phone.

I didn't know what to do. The danger Lucky Charm posed was a deeply distressing one. It seemed almost certain that within a matter of days, he and his friends would drag Pang off – to rape, suicide, or an abusive marriage. I couldn't just sit around and watch that happen: but there was nothing I could do to stop it, either.

Pang had consistently responded to Lucky Charm's threats by refusing to back down and knowingly placing herself in danger – and while I admired her courage, under the circumstances it wasn't a wise approach, and it was only by chance that she hadn't been taken already.

I couldn't stop Lucky Charm from kidnapping Pang – and once he did, he'd have the full support of the local culture. The police wouldn't intervene, and there would be nothing I could do by myself.

Again – as with Isabela, and with May – I felt a sickening sense of helpless frustration as I watched this new tragedy unfold around me. I couldn't help protect Pang if she refused to take even the most basic steps to protect herself.

I'd worked hard to give Pang control of her own life. She now had as much control as she ever would, and what she chose to do with that life was up to her. I could only accept her choices.

In any case, my Vietnamese visa was expiring in just two weeks, and I would be leaving Sapa – perhaps forever. Pang's affections for me had made it clear that I needed to disentangle myself, but I wasn't sure how to do that when she was still so emotionally reliant on me.

As I worried about the problem, the solution presented itself. A Western friend and his local wife invited me to dinner one evening. Just as we were leaving the Yellow Dragon, Pang walked past – but she was in a strange mood, and wouldn't even acknowledge us when we spoke to her.

Pang appeared the next day while I was eating noodle soup at the market. She was still behaving oddly and didn't say anything: she just stood there. I asked why she hadn't spoken to me the day before. Pang said something had happened which had made her very angry. She'd come to the Yellow

Dragon to talk to me about it, but then saw me leaving with my other friends.

Later that day she broke down and cried, but still wouldn't tell me what had upset her so badly, and never did. She seemed to consider it a personal betrayal that I wasn't available to her when she most needed me, even if I'd been completely unaware of the situation. Deciding that I was an unreliable friend, she began closing herself to me.

Perhaps it was a self-protection mechanism: perhaps Pang felt abandoned, knowing that I would soon be leaving Sapa.

Under other circumstances, I would have reassured Pang and worked to repair the damage between us – but now I just let her go. While I knew it wasn't easy for her, I also felt it was for the best.

I'd done all I could for Pang: the time was rapidly approaching for me to leave Sapa and see what remained of my own life.

WINNING A BATTLE,
LOSING THE WAR

Since I'd first returned to Sapa nine months earlier, I'd been careful to keep my work there a secret, even from many of my closest friends. It was a necessary precaution in an area that was home to highly-active criminal networks.

My secret was already at risk when I'd brought back photos and videos of May and Pang from China, and it proved impossible to keep when it arrived in the form of a human being.

Pang told many different versions of the story of her return home. My own role in that story was highly variable, depending on Pang's mood on any given day. On some days Pang claimed her return had been inevitable since her first day in China, and my part was negligible. On other days, I was said to have been an instrumental part of the process.

For reasons I never quite understood, Pang often told people that I'd rescued her – and while that wasn't true, it quickly became common knowledge that I was working to help trafficked girls. Pang told me I'd become "very famous" both in Sapa and in her village as someone who could bring back girls from China.

Having my secret shared increased the danger to Pang,

May, and myself – but in a way, it was also a relief. I'd felt uncomfortable concealing my true purpose from my friends, including many who had inadvertently helped me, and I was now finally able to speak openly with them.

For months, I'd been working in secrecy, seeking out stories of human trafficking. Now those stories began converging on me from all quarters, confronting me with the true magnitude of the local trafficking crisis.

I'd had no doubt that human trafficking was a monstrous issue in Sapa. Seeing the pain on the faces of so many family members left behind, though, struck me in a way that nothing else had.

Desperate strangers began approaching me at all hours of the day, or calling my name from street corners. Almost everyone, it seemed, had lost a sister, daughter, cousin, or close friend to human trafficking.

After two years immersed in the horrors of human trafficking, I thought I was finally becoming numb to it – but I found that these stories still had the power to shock me.

In one example, a girl had been forced into "marriage" with a Chinese man and had given birth to his child. When the baby had fallen ill and died, the girl's "husband" had become furious, accused her of killing it, and had somehow succeeded in having her convicted of the supposed crime. As a foreigner who spoke little Chinese and had no resources of her own, there was little the girl could do to defend herself. Following a long chain of deeply traumatic events – betrayal, trafficking, sale, rape, and the death of her child – the girl now found herself languishing in a Chinese prison.

The women who approached me – and they were all women – had nowhere else to turn, and many had been waiting years for someone who might help them.

"You go to China, you find my sister," one implored me.

"You very good friend," another said. "If I have friend like you, I happy all my life."

Unfortunately, I wasn't the friend they so desperately

wanted, and I didn't have the solutions they needed. When it seemed appropriate, I'd refer the women on to Blue Dragon. For the most part, though, the girls in question had disappeared years earlier, had never made contact, and I knew there was nothing that Blue Dragon or anyone else could do to find them.

No doubt there were thousands of women across Vietnam's northern mountains who had the same stories: Sapa certainly wasn't the only or even the worst-affected location. For every girl like Pang who succeeded in returning home, there were too many who simply vanished and were never heard of again.

Blue Dragon's staff were doing all they could with the resources they had available, but Michael acknowledged that their best efforts still represented merely "a drop in the ocean".

"We're rescuing ten or twenty girls a year," he told me. "Hundreds, if not thousands, are being taken across that border."

With the exceptions of May and Pang, Blue Dragon had always brought home the girls they'd gone to rescue from China. Sometimes, though, Blue Dragon never got that far. There were other victims who reached out only to vanish before a rescue could be arranged, and whose fates remained unknown.

Michael and Georges from Alliance Anti-Trafic both agreed that ultimately, the most impactful work was not assisting individual girls, but catching and imprisoning their traffickers.

"The real goal is not to save one girl," Georges said. "She's already a victim. The goal is to prevent other victims."

Both organisations were working to further develop Vietnamese anti-trafficking laws, and both offered legal support to survivors. Blue Dragon tried to ensure that trials were held as close as possible to the villages where the girls had been taken – as a means of spreading awareness, and as a warning to other potential traffickers.

After sixteen years spent fighting human trafficking in

Vietnam, Blue Dragon compiled the data they'd gathered. Incredibly, despite forming just one and a half percent of the total Vietnamese population, Hmong people represented one-third of both victims and traffickers. Poverty and a lack of education both played major roles, as did personal cross-border connections.

The girls trafficked from Sapa were taken almost entirely by young Vietnamese Hmong men who were poorly-educated, several years older than their victims, and operating in their own local areas. Most were in their twenties; some were already married and had children of their own. Whether from greed or desperation each had chosen to prey upon his own community as a means of getting ahead in life, just like the motorcycle thief I'd encountered outside Sapa.

On average, it seemed the kidnappers were paid around $1,500 per girl, or eighty percent of the local annual income. However, this figure could vary wildly: one convicted trafficker had received ten times this amount for one girl, while others had received just a few dollars or nothing at all, having been deceived themselves by the middlemen.

According to the girls' own stories, two local men had been involved with trafficking Pang into China, three with Vu, and four with May. I spoke at length with the girls – and by comparing descriptions, they confirmed that they'd all been trafficked by the same gang of Vietnamese Hmong men.

I'd hoped that we could gather enough evidence to find and prosecute the men, but soon realised that was unnecessary. In 2012 – the year after May and Pang were trafficked, and perhaps six months after Vu was taken – the gang had been caught trafficking another girl across the border.

Before Pang's abduction, two of the men had brazenly visited her home in the village, where they'd met her mother Bao. Bao had attended the trial in Lao Cai and confirmed they'd been the same men who'd trafficked her daughter.

The gang came from northern Bac Ha district, and the man who had kidnapped Pang from Sapa was found to be the ringleader. He received a lengthy prison sentence after confessing to trafficking four girls – but this figure didn't seem to include May or Vu, and the true number of his victims remains unknown. The other three members of his gang were also convicted, and received lesser sentences.

Bao was my only source of information on the trial – but she'd forgotten many of the details, and I couldn't find anything online.

Curiously, Blue Dragon believed that Vu's primary trafficker remained at large, having slipped across the border to evade an arrest warrant. Perhaps only part of the gang had been caught after all.

In any case, it was clear that the deterrent of prison was all too often outweighed by the greed or desperation of local men. Teenage girls were still being kidnapped in ever-increasing numbers, and far too many were never seen or heard from again.

MIDDLEMAN

Once across the border, the Vietnamese Hmong kidnappers had sold the girls to Chinese Hmong middlemen.

The fact that May and Pang had been put in phone contact with each other in China suggested that they'd been sold by the same middlemen. Though it seemed less likely, it was possible that Vu had also been sold by the same family.

Of all the people who had abused her over the past three years, May hated her middlemen with a special passion. She hated them more than the kidnapper who'd betrayed and sold her, and more than the "husband" who'd forced her to bear his child.

It was the middlemen who seemed to have scarred and traumatised May the most deeply, stripping her of her clothing, money, jewelry, and her last tokens of home, aggressively breaking down her resistance with threats of murder. The middlemen had also profited most by May's sale, taking the bride price that would otherwise have been paid to her family. May told me how she'd seen her middlemen sell "very small girls" to men as old as sixty.

I was taking a closer look at May's wedding DVD, wading through the tedious segments I'd previously skipped over, when I noticed something incredible: there was a middle-aged couple in the video who seemed to be playing the part of May's parents. Were these the middlemen who had sold May to her "husband", caught on camera?

A squat bulldog of a woman with short black hair, a hard-set jaw, and a bright red jacket was shown sitting beside a thin, large-featured man with close-cropped grey hair and simple dark clothing.

Before the "groom" appeared, the woman fed May boiled dumplings, then combed her hair; May, in turn, massaged the shoulders of both the woman and the man, and the three of them posed together, their eyes flickering nervously. Presumably, these rituals were to symbolise that the "bride" had been well taken care of by her supposed parents, and that she paid them all due respect.

The "groom" then came to take possession of his "bride", and together they bowed to May's supposed parents, who sat largely expressionless, saying and doing only what was necessary. At one point, though, the woman smiled – and in that moment, it was easy to believe that she and May were indeed related. In fact, she shared a stronger resemblance with May than May's own mother Dung. May and her supposed father, on the other hand, could not have been more different in face and build.

Did May's "husband" even realise he was buying a trafficked girl, or did he believe he was just paying a bride price to her family?

May, Pang, and Vu all confirmed that their "husbands" had been tricked by the middlemen, who had passed the girls off as their own daughters or nieces, and made excuses as to why they couldn't speak Chinese. Much later, when May and Pang finally learned to speak the language, they confronted their "husbands" with the truth – but by then it was too late.

Pang recounted the conversation she'd had with her "husband", about seven months after their "marriage":

"'Okay, I tell you the truth'," she said. "'I is not Chinese people. I is Vietnamese people. Hmong girl living in Vietnam. Understand?' I say that to he, and he say, 'Wha-wha-wha-what?' I say, 'I is not Chinese people, I is Vietnamese people.' He say, 'Oh, you is Vietnamese people?' I think, 'Yes.' Then maybe he feel very strange. He just looking, looking, looking. I think, 'Looking for what? You never see me before or what?' And then we just blah blah blah. After maybe twenty or thirty minutes he say, 'I don't care, you is Vietnamese people or Chinese people – now you is my wife!'"

Pang told her "husband" that he'd never actually married her because he'd never met her family or given them any money. He said he'd met her cousins and given a lot of money to her aunt. Pang explained that he'd been tricked, and her real family had never received anything from him.

Pang's "husband" – who didn't sound particularly intelligent – demanded to know why Pang had lied to him by pretending to be Chinese when they'd been "married". Pang pointed out what should have been obvious: that she hadn't lied to him because she hadn't been able to speak a word of his language. He was the one who'd chosen to "marry" a girl he couldn't communicate with.

The supposed aunt who had sold Pang had claimed that Pang was from China but couldn't speak Chinese because she'd just returned from studying abroad.

Pang's "husband" was supposed to believe that this illiterate village girl had spent years receiving a foreign education yet understood nothing at all of the predominant language of her own country. At the same time, he accepted the fact that he'd have to buy Pang an entire wardrobe because she possessed no clothes but those which she was wearing at the time, and that she owned no other belongings whatsoever.

The lies seemed so ludicrously transparent – yet Pang's "husband"-to-be had apparently accepted all this without question. He was so overwhelmingly ignorant it seemed almost wilful, and when Pang finally told him the truth – that she'd been trafficked from Vietnam – he was still determined to believe that it was Pang herself, not her traffickers, who had lied to him. Ultimately, though, he didn't really seem to care one way or the other.

May had a similar experience with her own "husband". When she told him the middlemen were not her parents, he flatly refused to believe her, only relenting when she lost her temper and began screaming it at him.

In any case, it seemed to make little difference to May's "husband". He seemed upset only that he'd been tricked into paying so much money – twenty thousand yuan ($3,000) – to the wrong family.

I would have assumed that it would be a matter of some importance for a man to realise that his "wife", and the mother of his child, had arrived in his country, his life, and his bed entirely against her will. The fact that it really didn't matter to May and Pang's "husbands" helps illustrate how these girls were viewed: not as human beings with their own thoughts and feelings but as interchangeable baby-making machines.

Vu hadn't told her "husband" she was from Vietnam: he'd found out when he'd received a phone bill with hundreds of dollars' worth of international calls she'd made using his phone.

Vu's middlemen had told her "husband" they were her brothers, and I realised that one of them also appeared in her wedding DVD. They'd arranged a Chinese identity card for Vu, with her new Chinese name on it. Vu's "husband" had only learned her real name months after they'd been "married", when he'd seen her typing an email.

"He say, 'What is that?' 'Oh, that is my family name and name.' 'So what about the name your brother telling us?' 'That is not the real one. They is not my brother. My brother and my family stay far away – they stay in Vietnam, not in here.'"

The "husbands" weren't innocent – but they were deeply ignorant. I wondered how many "weddings" these middlemen faked their way through, passing off kidnapped girls as their own daughters, nieces, and sisters.

While most "husbands" only ever bought one girl, and the kidnappers typically handled only one girl at a time, the middlemen dealt in larger numbers, and could have as many as a dozen girls held captive at any given moment.

As the name suggests, it was the middlemen who stood at the centre of the supply chain, as the crucial link between the kidnappers and the customers. To break the networks, they were the ones who had to be stopped.

May had long fantasised about someday revenging herself upon her middlemen – but how? Of all the traffickers, the middlemen were often the hardest to locate, and some of the hardest to prosecute.

May's wedding DVD proved nothing: we needed a name, an address, and statements to the Chinese police. We had none of those things.

May, as a witness, was still under the control of her "husband", and I couldn't even get into China to help her. I didn't know where to begin – but then we received some unexpectedly good news.

Earlier that year, after I'd met with May in China, the Chinese police had tried to arrest May's middlemen. The wife had been caught but the husband was in hospital at the time, and the police had failed to find him there. On hearing that his wife had been taken, he'd gone into hiding – and that was the last I'd heard of him.

When I re-established contact with May in October, she told me that the husband had now also been caught, and – though she had no further details – she believed that he and his wife had both been imprisoned.

I WANT YOU BACK

The middlemen had sold May, Pang, and Vu on to their Chinese "husbands", whose homes were scattered across eastern China.

The vast trafficking networks that stretched from Vietnam in every direction across China existed only for the sake of these "husbands", and was sustained by the money they poured into it.

While the kidnappers and middlemen had physically played only brief roles in the girls' lives – spanning weeks, days, or sometimes only hours – May, Pang, and Vu had been tied to their "husbands" in much more intimate and longer-lasting ways.

To my mind, the fact that these "husbands" had been ignorant of where the girls came from didn't make them any less guilty – and as much as it outraged my sense of justice, it quickly became apparent that these men would never face justice for their crimes.

The border between Vietnam and China, and the lack of concrete evidence, presented seemingly insurmountable legal difficulties. With scant evidence, the victims would have to return to China and, as foreigners, testify against Chinese nationals under a legal system known to be strongly biased towards locals – or else they'd have to attempt extradition, which seemed equally futile.

Ultimately, though, the greatest obstacle to justice was the girls themselves, who didn't want their "husbands" punished, for a variety of reasons.

On hearing May and Pang's stories, some people assume that part of their reluctance to leave China or to prosecute their "husbands" was a result of Stockholm syndrome, by which a victim forms an emotional attachment to her captor. While I never saw any indication of this, the girls had certainly become attached to their "husbands" in other ways.

In Pang's absence, her "husband's" family was taking care of her child. The last thing she'd ever want would be to give them any reason to neglect or abuse her little girl.

May's "husband" was also providing for May's daughter, and – unless she could make up her mind to leave him – for May herself.

The strangest and most surprising situation, however, was Vu's.

Of the three girls, Vu was the one I would have least suspected of having feelings for her "husband". She'd fled from him at the first opportunity, and wished she'd done it sooner.

Two years after her dramatic escape, however, I was amazed to learn that Vu was still in contact with her Chinese "husband", and was actually considering going back to him.

"I don't know do I gonna going back or not," she told me. "Right now he not marry yet. He still wait for me."

Vu's "husband" still called her sometimes. She'd call him, too – though not very often or for very long, because it was "very expensive" to call China. After having spent only six months in China, two years earlier, I was surprised that Vu still spoke enough Chinese to converse with her "husband" at all.

The biggest question, though, was not how Vu still spoke to her "husband", but why?

Vu said she was happy with her life in Vietnam – but she

knew she'd have to marry before long, and after two years she still hadn't found a "good husband" in Sapa. She didn't want to marry a Hmong man: too many were drunk, violent, and made their wives do all the work, she said.

It would be better to be married to anyone but a Hmong man, Vu thought – even her lazy, neglectful, significantly older, and remarkably unattractive Chinese "husband" who lived thousands of kilometres from her home and family.

Vu had grown into an attractive young woman with a delightful smile who spoke English well and worked with Western tourists. While I was very conscious of the prejudice within the Hmong community against survivors of human trafficking, I found it both startling and tragic that she still hadn't met a better man than the one who'd bought and abused her. If Vu felt the need to get married and was looking outside her own community, she seemed to have an excellent chance of finding a foreign husband – but that hadn't happened.

When they'd been living together in China, Vu said she'd been constantly angry or bored with her "husband", and had fought with him every day. Like May and Pang, Vu also felt certain that her "husband" had been sleeping with other women, and told me how furious she'd been when he'd once come home with a love bite.

After she'd returned to Sapa, though, Vu had missed her "husband".

"When I coming here, I crying a lot about him," she told me. Two years later, she said she still missed her "husband" sometimes, but only when she was bored. If she returned to him, it wouldn't be for emotional reasons, but for purely practical reasons.

In any case, Vu felt her "husband" still held a valid claim to her, having already paid a substantial bride price for her. Even though the money had been taken by her Chinese Hmong middlemen and Vu's own family had been completely unaware of the arrangement, Vu's "husband" still considered it binding – and, surprisingly, Vu felt his claim was legitimate.

While Vu was willing to return to her "husband" in China, she made it clear that she wouldn't go back on the same terms. Curiously, she was now dictating her own conditions to the man who had bought and controlled every aspect of her life – and whether or not she returned to China was entirely in his hands.

Vu said she'd only go back with her "husband" if he came to Vietnam first and completed the paperwork to marry her legally. This was where they had reached an impasse: Vu's "husband" wanted her back, but – perhaps suspecting a trap – he wasn't willing to risk his own freedom by crossing the border to claim her.

"If he coming here, we can make the papers for marry," Vu said. "If not, I not going back."

I was disoriented by Vu's revelation, and disappointed that the girls' "husbands" would never face justice. I took consolation in the fact that, unlike the kidnappers and middlemen who could keep taking girls continuously, the "husbands" typically bought only one girl each.

In that sense, while the "husbands" collectively drove the trade in girls, they were individually the least harmful members of the network.

Vu kept waiting for her Chinese "husband" – but he never came to get her. She remained in Vietnam, eventually giving in and marrying a Hmong man.

LOVE AND TRUST

It seemed that the men who had kidnapped May, and the middlemen who had sold her to her "husband", had now all been stopped. But there was one more link in the chain, the very first: the insider who had betrayed May and her friends to the kidnappers.

The insider wasn't a stranger from somewhere else: she was someone the girls had known and trusted in Sapa. With five girls having been kidnapped from May's group of ten friends, I'd realised that someone very close had been betraying them to the traffickers... But who was it?

When I'd first lived in Sapa, I'd been friends with May's cousin and closest friend Zao, a particularly intelligent girl. It was Zao who had first alerted both me and May's family to May's abduction, and it was clear that she knew the most about it. She'd been the last person in Sapa to speak with May, was said to have been in direct contact with May's kidnapper, and was later known to have been in secret communication with May and Pang in China. During my three-month investigation in Sapa earlier that year, Zao had behaved in very strange and suspicious ways.

When I'd met with Zao that January, she'd brought her

boyfriend, a sullen young Hmong man – and when I told her I was gathering information about May and Pang's abductions in an attempt to help the girls, Zao and her boyfriend had both simply walked off.

After our meeting, Zao's story changed and began falling apart. She stopped speaking to me, refused to speak to anyone else about me, and wouldn't say anything more about May's disappearance, even to her closest friends.

Several months later, during my search for May and Pang in China, I'd received an unexpected message from Zao asking if I could help find another friend of hers who had recently been kidnapped. While there wasn't enough information to help, I was glad that Zao had re-established contact.

At the beginning of October, within a day or two of my return to Sapa, Zao's boyfriend had died suddenly. When I heard the news, I went to visit Zao and offer my condolences. I still didn't know if she could be trusted, or how she might receive me – but she'd invited me in for a chat and seemed glad to renew our friendship.

Zao and I saw each other several times over the following weeks, though she was often withdrawn into grief. After leaving Chan and Sung's wedding, I'd passed Zao's brother's house in the village. Zao had been sitting alone inside, rewatching a video of her boyfriend's funeral.

Two weeks before my departure from Sapa, while walking through the complex of rented rooms that surrounded Pang's room, a voice had called me from a darkened doorway. It was Zao. She asked if I could help her put together a slideshow tribute of her boyfriend, and I told her I'd be happy to.

Zao and I spent a few hours making the slideshow on my laptop at the Yellow Dragon, and then we called May together. Afterwards, I asked Zao if she was willing to share her story with me.

It had been ten months since I'd first approached Zao for an interview, and had long since given up all hope of getting one – but at last, she agreed to speak with me on camera.

I could hardly believe it was finally happening, and without any preparation we began recording immediately in her rented room.

For all of my previous interviews in Sapa, Marinho had operated both cameras while I'd asked the questions. Now I had only a single camera and had to perform both roles. While the resulting footage was unimpressive and the information was no longer necessary to find May or her traffickers, the seventy-minute interview was fascinating and answered many lingering questions I'd had.

"I see a lot of boys, they come here, want to try to steal my friends," said Zao. "Even they try to steal me also."

Several years earlier, Zao had been at the market with Pang and another friend when three young men began following them and speaking with them. The men were "very sweet" and "very nice" to the girls.

On Sapa's lake were a number of swan-shaped pedal-boats built for two. Each of the men quickly singled out one of the girls, and offered to take her for a ride on a swan.

Pang and the other friend were flattered, and would have happily gone with the men – but Zao felt it was all too good to be true, and flatly refused.

"I used to be very bossy," Zao told me. "I no speak nice to them, because I think they're no good boys. I scary if they follow me or if they steal me to sell in China."

May had once avoided me for several days after I'd jokingly called her "bossy", and it amused me to hear Zao describe herself the same way.

Zao had a theory that people who trafficked girls looked and spoke differently from those who could be trusted. Without understanding the specifics, I wasn't sure if there was any real basis to her theory, or if it was simply another superstition in a community already riddled with irrational beliefs.

In either case, Zao's instincts seemed to have served her well. She convinced her two friends they were in danger, and began yelling at the men.

"I say, 'I hate people who is coming here and stealing the girls to sell in China! I wish I can kill all of them!'"

The man who had been courting Pang became furious, but he and his friends realised they'd lost their advantage and quickly left.

Zao never again saw the other two men in Sapa – but the "boy Pang liked" returned many times. She'd often see him in the square, and warned her friends about him. Zao said the man had tried to take her own sister before finally taking Shu.

At the time, Shu had been working as a trekking guide. She'd been spending a lot of time outside Sapa, and hadn't heard Zao's warnings. Shu was a Catholic and the man had claimed to share her faith, accompanying her to church before he'd kidnapped her and sold her to a Chinese brothel.

Zao's description of the man's behaviour reminded me of an arcade claw machine, where the player uses a descending metal claw to try to grab any one of a variety of plush toys that lie waiting beneath. After failing the first time, he simply tried again, and again, until he won his prize.

It was two years before anyone saw Shu again, and she was never the same.

HARD-HEADED WOMAN

It seemed that Zao had a talent for identifying traffickers, and her role had been that of a Cassandra: someone who had seen the signs, but whose warnings had all too often been ignored by her friends, including both May and Pang.

"I say to Pang, 'You don't scary this boy?' She say, 'No, I don't scary. I don't care.' Pang she say, '*I don't care.*'"

Pang's stubborn refusal to take seriously the possibility of being kidnapped was unsurprising: she was now reacting in a similar way to the threat posed by Lucky Charm. It was sad to see how little Pang seemed to have learned from her earlier experiences, and I had the sense of history repeating.

Before her own abduction, May had had a boyfriend named Chinh in Sapa – but Zao knew she'd also been spending time with another young man whom she worried would take May and sell her in China.

"I tell her many times. I think, 'You'd better to stop to talk to this boy, you have very good boyfriend here, just don't talk to he.' May say, 'I don't talk to he, but he keep calling me.' I say, 'You can just change your number, don't talk to he.' But I think at this time, May already get very crazy for he. May say, 'This boy is very handsome.' I say, 'Yes, he's handsome, but if he's not a good boy, you better stop talking to him.' May don't listen to me."

May had invited Zao to come with her on the day she'd been abducted – but Zao had been very tired, and spent much of the day sleeping instead. She hadn't realised who May was spending the day with.

On awakening in the early evening, Zao wanted to have dinner with May, so she called her and asked where she was. When May said her friend had taken her from Sapa, Zao misunderstood the situation. She knew that Chinh wanted to marry May, and believed that he'd now kidnapped her for marriage.

(As Catholics, Chinh's family shunned the practice of marriage by abduction, but Zao didn't realise this at the time.)

When May said she wasn't with her boyfriend but her other "friend", Zao became worried.

"I say, 'Okay, so coming back, you don't scary you go to China?' She say, 'No.' I say to her, 'You should come back, because this boy – I don't think they are good boy.'"

Zao couldn't have guessed that this phonecall would be the last time anyone in Sapa would hear May's voice for two and a half years.

As darkness fell and May still didn't reappear, Zao called Chinh to confirm that he hadn't kidnapped May for marriage. He said he hadn't, but Zao didn't know what to believe. She went to the hotel where Chinh said he was working to make sure he was really there.

Chinh hadn't mentioned Zao in his own account of that evening, but it sounded like it had been a very confused and chaotic time. Chinh, Zao, and May's other friends all frantically began calling May and each other, desperate for any news.

"We call May, we try to speak with her, but the boy take her phone already. Not only me – there is many friends try to call May. Some of them say, 'I think this boy take May's phone and we cannot call her anymore.' After that we call to her family and we tell them. And after they call to the police."

After seeing so many of her friends vanish from Sapa, Zao had little faith in the local police.

"There is many girls stealing to sell in China," she said. "They call the police, but the police do nothing, we don't see they get any back."

Zao knew that May's kidnapper had a cousin who lived and worked in Sapa. After May's disappearance, Zao found and spoke with the cousin, in the hopes of uncovering information she could pass to May's family – but her inquiries led nowhere.

"I feel very bad," she told me. "Bad, and sometimes very angry if you think why the police don't do nothing. We are local, we can't do anything."

A year after Pang's abduction and about seven months after May had disappeared, the same gang of men had kidnapped Vu.

The group of ten friends had now been whittled down to half its original size. The remaining girls began comparing descriptions, and Zao realised it was the same men preying upon them.

Just a month after Vu was taken, one of the men had called Zao, hoping to claim yet another victim from the same group of friends – but Zao understood who he was, and she wasn't to be caught so easily.

"Before you take my friends, now you want to take me too?" she demanded. She'd kept the man talking, trying to learn what his gang had done with her friends – but she learned nothing useful, and the man hadn't called again.

Zao told me how much she'd missed her friends after they'd vanished.

"Sometimes I go on Facebook to see Pang and May's picture," she said. "I just write down their name on Facebook, I see their picture, I feel miss them a lot. When I saw Pang come back, I feel very happy. Now we see almost every day."

With just a few metres between their rented rooms, Zao and Pang were now neighbours.

Rather than eulogising life in China, Zao was one of the few women in Sapa who seemed to truly grasp the horrors that trafficked girls endured and who supported their return home. She hoped that May would also return home soon.

"I think it's much better she's coming back," said Zao. "The [Chinese] culture, everything is totally different from here. It's better for her to come back here, to live with her family."

Immediately before our interview, Zao and I had phoned May via my laptop, and the two girls had spoken for half an hour in their own language. May had told Zao she wanted to come home but was reluctant to leave her baby and fearful of being judged in Sapa.

"She say to me, 'If I coming back, people will say something very bad to me.' I say, 'That's not important! Of course you go to China and come back, people say something bad! But just come, don't care what other people say to you. You have friends to help you.'"

BETTER MAN

Zao didn't know who had introduced May and Pang to the men who'd kidnapped them. She'd become very worried, though, by a new tactic that had recently emerged in Sapa and had already claimed numerous victims.

There were now young women in Sapa who were not just acting as insiders, introducing victims to their kidnappers, but who had actually begun kidnapping other girls directly.

Zao told me of one young woman who'd come to live in Sapa – not from one of the local villages, but somewhere further afield. She'd been selling handicrafts on the streets, where she'd befriended several local girls. In their free time, she invited them to come and visit her village.

By that time, the girls had learned to be wary of men who came from outside Sapa, but had no reason to suspect a woman. One at a time, they'd gone with her and never returned. When the other girls realised what was happening and began to talk, the woman left town and never came back.

"That's why now we better not be friend with people who is not from here," Zao told me, before admitting that locals also trafficked girls to China.

In a village very close to May and Pang's, Zao said there

was another girl who had convinced five or six of her friends to come shopping with her in Lao Cai. A driver had taken them in a hired minivan. Some of the girls had later escaped and returned home, but most had never been seen again.

"We cannot trust anybody," Zao said. "Cousins steal cousins to sell in China."

I believed everything Zao had told me. She didn't seem to have anything to hide – so why had she spent so long hiding from me?

When I'd seen the photographs Zao wanted to use for her slideshow tribute, I realised the boyfriend who'd died was not the boyfriend I'd seen with Zao in January. Gradually, she began telling me her own story, and at last I understood why she'd treated me so coldly during my investigation.

The reason for Zao's silence was painfully simple, and one I never would have guessed. For all her efforts to protect herself and her friends against being trafficked, Zao had been unable to protect herself in other ways.

She told me the boyfriend I'd met in January had been a jealous, controlling, and violent man who had often beaten her. Zao had wanted to help me but her boyfriend had refused to let her speak with me, and she knew better than to argue with him.

While I knew, logically, that even the most intelligent people could find themselves trapped in patterns of abuse, I still struggled to comprehend how someone as clever as Zao could find herself controlled by such a brute, and was deeply sorry for the part I'd unwittingly played.

Zao had been living with the daily threat of violence – and with my persistent enquiries, I'd made that threat, if not that violence, worse for her. By trying to help one friend, I'd unknowingly hurt another. I tried to remind myself that it was her boyfriend's fault, not mine, but that didn't make me feel any better about it.

For months, Zao had been controlled and abused in ways that had been invisible even to her closest friends. We all knew that she'd been behaving strangely but hadn't known why, and might never have known.

We were right there, but Zao had been too terrified to reach out for help – or perhaps her situation had developed so gradually that even she hadn't yet realised its full horror. If it could happen to such a perceptive, street-smart young woman, I felt sure it could happen to anyone.

Until the day that Zao's boyfriend had finally pushed her too far, the violence had all occurred behind closed doors.

One day, after I'd left Sapa, Zao's boyfriend had begun beating her in public on the popular Dragon's Jaw mountain above Sapa. The incident had been a wake-up call to Zao, helping her realise just how dreadful her life had become, and she mustered the courage to leave her abuser – an incredibly brave and difficult thing to do in a small town like Sapa.

Over the past two years, Zao had occasionally been contacted by another young Hmong man named Veej who had studied in Hanoi before taking a good job with the military.

Zao was very wary of young Hmong men from outside Sapa, especially if they seemed too good to be true. Veej came from a region east of Muong Kuong, very close to the Chinese border, and very close to where May, Pang, and Vu's traffickers had come from. Zao hadn't wanted to speak with him, and had ignored his friend request on Facebook.

But then Veej had come to Sapa with one of Zao's cousins who had studied at the same school in Hanoi. When Zao met Veej in person, she felt sure she could trust him. They began dating, and he treated her far better than her previous boyfriend.

Zao loved Veej, and had hoped to marry him – until his sudden, tragic death at the beginning of October. Away from the discipline of his barracks, he'd died instantly in a drunken motorcycle accident.

I helped Zao assemble a three-minute tribute video which we later uploaded to YouTube. There were photographs of Veej in his military uniform, in an FC Barcelona shirt, in a waistcoat playing a guitar, and of he and Zao together, with their arms around each other. The final three photos were a long Flower Hmong funeral procession, a simple wooden coffin being lowered into the earth, and a large shield of white roses Zao had placed over the grave.

I showed Zao how to overlay text on the video.

"You're the only one I've ever missed," she wrote. "You'll stay in my heart for the rest of my life."

HOME AGAIN

Most trafficking victims are deceived and betrayed by someone they know personally. In Blue Dragon's report on traffickers, only one in twenty convictions involved a victim who had been betrayed by a blood relation – yet the report acknowledged that these numbers were likely skewed, as victims were often reluctant to speak out against relatives.

I'd suspected May's middle sister Cho of betraying May and her friends to their kidnappers.

Taller, leaner, and two years older than May, Cho was the first of the group to have been trafficked – and then she'd come back. Not even her closest friends could say what had happened to Cho in China, or how she'd returned: she hadn't told anyone.

Nobody could agree how long Cho had been gone – some said months, others said days. It was almost comical how wildly divergent the stories about Cho were, but there was one point everyone could agree on. After May and Pang had been kidnapped, Cho had returned to China of her own volition, seemingly to join her traffickers.

According to Blue Dragon, it was a popular misconception that traffickers were often former victims. In their experience, this occurred in less than two percent of cases in Vietnam – yet from the stories I'd heard, it seemed to be more common in Sapa.

Cho now came and went between China and Vietnam as she pleased. She'd chosen to marry a Chinese Hmong man in the mountains near Nanxi, just across the border. They had two children together – a two-year-old boy, and a baby girl who'd been born during my time in China five months earlier.

Cho had now become the conduit through which May's family received most of their news of May. Cho's potential involvement with the traffickers could also help explain the family's distorted understanding of, and lack of sympathy for, May's current situation in China.

I'd tried twice to arrange a meeting with Cho in China earlier that year. Cho had been willing to meet me, but her husband had become furious and forbidden it, seizing her phone so that we couldn't even speak to each other.

My suspicions had begun shifting from Cho to her husband when he'd craftily interfered with my attempts to meet May in China. I'd discovered that May's "husband", Pang's "husband", and May and Cho's father were all connected, and Cho's husband stood at the centre of that network. How was he connected to Cho's traffickers – or was he one of them?

One of the first people I'd met upon my return to Sapa in early October was Chan. Chan had plenty of surprises for me: not only had I learned of her own pregnancy and imminent marriage, as well as the very recent death of Zao's boyfriend, I also learned that after three years in China, Cho had also run away from her husband and returned to Vietnam.

The news was soon confirmed in a phonecall with May.

"Cho, she going back to Vietnam already," May told me. "She at my parents' house right now, maybe she not coming back [to China] anymore."

I asked May how long Cho had already been back in Vietnam – and in a wonderful example of the vague grasp of time Sapa Hmong people had, she replied, "Maybe already twenty days, two weeks, or one month."

After a particularly vicious attack by her abusive husband, Cho had taken her baby girl and fled back across the border, planning to remain in Vietnam permanently.

Cho was staying with her brother and parents in their home outside Sapa. As with Zao, I'd long since given up any hope of interviewing Cho – and while she was now away from the influence of her husband, she was back under the influence of her father Lung.

Shortly before speaking with Chan, I'd spent an hour or two sitting with Cho's mother Dung and elder sister Dinh, sharing the photos and videos of May I'd brought back from China. While Dinh spoke little English, she spoke enough to be able to tell me that Cho had returned from China, and she knew that I would have wanted to know – but she'd never said a word.

It struck me as very typical of Sapa, that the answer was right there in front of me yet I would never have known without asking the right question in the right way. Even then, the truth might have been hidden from me: May's family remained as incomprehensible to me as ever.

I knew that Lung had already lied to conceal the truth about Cho, but I still didn't know what that truth might be, and didn't know if I'd ever have a chance to find out.

I was told that Cho was spending almost all of her time at the family home in the village. I didn't have any way of contacting her without going through her family, and it seemed they didn't want me to know she was there.

I did hear, however, that Cho had occasionally been seen at the Sapa market, and asked my friends to keep watch for her.

Two weeks later, it was the recently-returned Pang who spotted Cho at the Sunday markets. Instead of approaching her directly, Pang came to get me – and by the time we returned, Cho was gone. Pang and I began scouring the streets of Sapa, hoping that she hadn't already left town.

Pang finally found Cho again in the town square, and I'm

not sure I would have recognised her without help. I'd met Cho four years earlier – but she'd been a girl then, and was now a tired-eyed young mother with a baby on her hip. Of the three sisters, Cho bore the greatest physical resemblance to her father Lung.

I really didn't know what to expect from Cho: even if she herself wasn't against me, her father certainly was, and he was now the most powerful influence upon her.

Surprisingly, Cho agreed to tell me her story on camera. I realised I'd have to record the interview as soon as possible, before Lung learned I'd made contact with her and ordered her not to tell me anything more, just as he had with Dinh. Cho would be returning to the village – and her father – within just a few hours, so the interview would have to take place that same day.

After almost four years in China, though, Cho had forgotten most of her English. I would have normally had Chan or Chu to interpret for me – but I was unable to retract the offer I'd unthinkingly made to Pang.

When the interview began – in one of the rooms at the Yellow Dragon – it quickly became evident that Pang didn't bring the same level of energy and enthusiasm to the role. Despite having been one of the main focuses of my work, Pang took little interest in its broader purpose of raising awareness, and didn't much care what Cho's story might be.

As I'd guessed, it was the only opportunity I ever had to interview Cho. Incredibly, she told me things she'd never told anyone – but Pang didn't bother interpreting most of it. Much later, when the footage was fully translated, many fascinating details emerged – and a few moments of hair-tearing frustration when Cho had been partway through telling me something fascinating, but Pang had become impatient and told her to skip it.

"You don't have to say so much," Pang said in Hmong, interrupting Cho's explanation of her captivity in China. "He asks too many questions."

It seemed bizarre that Pang would be so reluctant to interpret for me after having just fought for that very role. I'd realised she wouldn't be a great interpreter, but I'd never have guessed that she'd actively undermine my work.

It was my fault for having thoughtlessly offered her the role in the first place – yet, as frustrating as her behaviour was, Pang's presence added intriguing new insights to Cho's interview.

The very fact that Cho had agreed to speak with me, especially in Pang's presence, strongly suggested that she wasn't the insider who had betrayed her friends to the traffickers. As I quickly realised, though, I had so much more to learn from her. At long last, I had enough information to piece together Cho's story, and it was an extremely unusual one.

BREAK ON THROUGH
(TO THE OTHER SIDE)

In early 2011, Cho had been living in Sapa. She had a job cleaning rooms at a nearby hotel and was sharing a room with May, who was selling handicrafts on the street.

Cho met two young Chinese Hmong men who'd come to visit Sapa. She showed them the hotel where she worked and the room she rented with May, and she introduced them to May. The two men invited Cho and May to eat with them.

"We went to where they barbecue meat near the church," Cho told me. "We'd only eaten a piece of bread and two bananas, then I can't remember anything else. When I awoke, I was already in China. I didn't go so far – just to the square!"

Cho told the story as if she herself could hardly believe it. After finishing the bananas and bread, Cho said she felt very sleepy, and wasn't conscious of what was happening around her.

"It was crazy," she said. "When I awoke, I didn't know where I was, or where Vietnam was."

It wasn't clear how May's part in that story was supposed to have ended: surely she hadn't sat there and watched her unconscious sister being carried away on the back of a young man's motorbike? As with so many of these stories I heard, I assumed that Cho had in fact gone willingly with her trafficker, and her claim of having been drugged was a fiction to help protect her reputation in Sapa.

Cho's kidnapper had taken her to Wenshan, a city about sixty kilometres from the border. He took her to a market and bought new clothes and shoes for her to wear.

Holding her tightly by the hand so she couldn't get away, the kidnapper then led Cho to a tall apartment block where they met some Chinese Hmong people – a middleman, his "wife", and an older woman.

Cho's kidnapper had told Cho that he'd kidnapped her for marriage, and the others now maintained the charade. They claimed to be the kidnapper's elder brother, sister-in-law, and mother, respectively.

Cho later learned that the middleman's "wife" had also been trafficked from Vietnam. She cooked lunch for them, and they all ate together as a "family": the traffickers and two of their victims.

After lunch, the family spoke of making preparations for the wedding, which was traditionally negotiated between the bride and groom's families.

The older woman told Cho, "Daughter-in-law, you stay here, [the supposed husband-to-be] and I will go to the market and buy some meat and rice wine, then we'll come back and take you home."

Cho sat waiting all afternoon – but when evening fell and her supposed husband-to-be still hadn't returned, she began to cry.

"I cried and cried, and said, 'Oh my God, why are they gone such a long time?' The [middleman] said, 'Don't cry, they already sold you to me. Now they have their money and they've gone home. So what are you crying for?' Before he told me, I was crying just a little. Now I cried a lot, and very loudly."

When the others had left, the middleman had taken a small black bag and hurried after them. Cho now realised he'd been paying the kidnapper, whom she never saw again. It's not clear who the older woman was, or what role she'd played: it seems likely she was an intermediary between the kidnapper and the middleman.

There was a separate, windowless apartment upstairs in the same building where the middleman kept his trafficked girls. Cho thought she was the only one he'd bought, but when he took her inside, she saw it was full of girls of various ethnicities who had all been taken from Vietnam.

"He grabbed my hand, dragged me inside, and locked the door. I couldn't go outside anymore. The man in the house bought us, to sell us again to the Chinese."

There were ten girls in the apartment, and Cho remained locked up there with them for six or seven days. One day, a group of five men had brought four more trafficked girls there, while the other girls were gradually sold off as "brides" to Chinese men.

Cho now understood the true reason why her kidnapper had bought her new clothes and shoes – "to make me look beautiful for the Chinese men who came to see me."

For the first three days and nights, Cho said that all she did was cry, knowing that she, too, could be sold at any time. Men had been coming and examining her as a potential purchase from the very first day.

The middleman was often there watching the girls – and when he wasn't, the only door was always locked with two heavy padlocks, each with a shackle as thick as your finger. There was no other way in or out of the apartment.

By her final day in the middleman's apartment, most of the girls had already been sold. "Two fat Chinese men" came to look at the five remaining girls and considered Cho before selecting a girl of Vietnam's Tai minority. The Tai girl cried a lot, while the Chinese men went to get the money to pay for her.

The middleman stayed there watching the girls – but soon after, his wife called him to say their young son was missing.

The middleman went downstairs to help look for the boy – and Cho saw her opportunity.

The girls were required to do their own cooking, and the middleman brought them kitchen implements as necessary – including a cleaver. Cho took it and smashed a hole in the wooden panelling of the door. She made a hole "only large enough for a child", but the girls were able to squeeze through.

No doubt the girls had been threatened against attempting to escape, and each suddenly faced the decision to risk running away or to remain behind. For the Tai girl who had just been sold, there was no question. She squirmed through the hole, followed by a Red Dao girl, and they both ran away. The two other girls were too afraid to leave, so Cho was the last to wriggle out through the hole she'd made.

Cho found herself alone: the Tai and Red Dao girls had disappeared without waiting for her. When she ran downstairs, the middleman reappeared and tried to stop her, but he'd been drinking. Cho slipped past him and ran out of the building.

A woman's Black Hmong costume includes a pair of leg warmers. These are typically tapered strips of cheap black velvet over two metres long, which are wrapped and tied around the leg just below the knee.

I'd heard another story in which two girls had used a crude rope made of their unrolled leg warmers to descend from an upper-storey window – but I'd never heard of anyone who'd escaped their middlemen quite as dramatically as Cho had.

Cho was crying, and didn't know where she was going. She ran and ran until she found a small market, where she saw a married couple "collecting rubbish to sell". Cho recognised them as Hmong by the design of the woman's skirt.

"Aunty! Are you also Hmong?" she called.

The woman said they were, and asked why she was crying. Cho explained that she was from Vietnam but had been kidnapped and didn't know how to get home. The couple took her back to their own home and called the police.

The police soon located the other two escaped girls,

brought them all back to the border, and handed them over to the Vietnamese police in Lao Cai.

Cho's family had no idea what had happened to her – and when the police told them that their daughter had been trafficked, had escaped, and was now in Lao Cai, they refused to believe it. The police had to send them a photo of Cho before they sent their sons to collect her.

"Friday, the Hmong man kidnapped me from Sapa to China," Cho told me. "The next Friday I arrived back in Sapa again."

TODAY I MET THE BOY
I'M GONNA MARRY

After she'd come back from China, it seemed that Cho's parents had been very angry with her, blaming her for her own abduction. They wouldn't allow her to remain in Sapa, and had taken her back to live with them in the village.

When I'd first spoken to Cho's parents, they'd told me how devastated they'd been by her disappearance. Not knowing what to do, they said they'd cried almost every day and night. They were overjoyed when she'd come home safely, and were terrified that she'd be taken again: that's why they'd kept her at home with them.

Which of these stories was true? I'm sure they both were. When those who rarely express their emotions experience a sudden loss of control, fear can very easily manifest as anger lashing out at any available target.

Hmong girls usually only moved back to the villages when they were married. After life in Sapa, village life must have seemed dull and restrictive for Cho, and going back to unpaid labour in the fields must have been a rude shock after she'd been paid for easier work in Sapa. Occasionally, Cho still went to Sapa to sell handicrafts – but, at her father's insistence, made the long journey back to stay in the village at night.

What I most wanted to know was how Cho had met her Chinese Hmong husband: I was sure that would give me the key to their relationship, and help me understand what kind of man he was.

Cho said she'd remained in the village for about eight months – "until about October, the season when we dry the cardamom." By that time, Pang and May had both been kidnapped.

There was a fifty-year-old Hmong man in Cho's village who had developed contacts among the Chinese Hmong community after his own daughter had married across the border.

This man had developed an unusual method of trafficking girls. Rather than kidnapping girls for unknown buyers in China, he cut out the middleman by bringing Chinese Hmong men to Sapa to select their own brides. He and the prospective "husband" would then traffic the girl together.

This method further muddied the waters between crime and culture. While it still involved trafficking a girl across an international border, the "husbands"-to-be were all Hmong and the process more closely resembled that of a traditional marriage by abduction.

In that context, it seemed that the man from Cho's village held the strange dual roles of both trafficker and matchmaker. Perhaps the best term to describe him is "broker".

As with the traditional abductions for marriage, under these circumstances it was more difficult to understand how willing or unwilling these girls were to go with their traffickers – and with my own interpreter actively interfering with the interview, it was often impossible to grasp the finer details of Cho's story.

Cho knew of three local girls who had already been taken by this broker. In October 2011, he'd brought another Chinese Hmong customer to the Sunday market in Sapa to scout for potential targets. That's where they'd seen Cho, and the customer had selected her as his "bride"-to-be.

The two men took Cho across the border the same day. I had the impression that Cho – who already bore the stigma of having been trafficked, and was stifling under her family's control in the village – was not entirely unwilling to go with them. This possibility also somewhat blurred the line between human trafficking (where someone was taken against their will) and people smuggling (where they went willingly).

Cho imagined that life would become easier for her in China. She'd heard that one of the local girls who had already been taken by the same broker was now happy there with her Chinese Hmong husband.

In a traditional marriage by abduction, a girl would be held captive for three or four days while she decided whether or not to marry her abductor. During this time, she would theoretically be kept safe by his female relatives from any sexual advances. Her abductor would then take her back to her own family – either to release her, or to negotiate her sale price.

In this new corruption of the tradition, however, it seemed that Cho and the customer had slept together that very night. Having already paid the broker, he presumably felt entitled to her.

While Cho's father didn't know what had happened to Cho and hadn't given his permission for her to marry, and though there had been no wedding celebration with either family, Cho now thought of the customer as her husband.

Cho had already described the rest of her story in broad strokes, but Pang became restless and derailed the interview before I could fully understand what had happened next. Fortunately, I was now able to use Cho's account as a key for sorting through earlier versions I'd heard of her story, to understand which of them held the truth and to unearth further details from them.

It seemed that Cho's family had learned that the broker was responsible for their daughter's disappearance. They'd found him in the village and scared him with threats of the police and prison if he didn't bring Cho back. They wanted to meet Cho's supposed husband: if they liked him, they'd approve the marriage; otherwise they'd cancel it, and Cho would have to come home.

Cho and her husband had come from China with three other Hmong men, bringing chickens and rice wine for Cho's family. It was raining hard, and they were all drenched. Rather than wearing the Black Hmong costume of her birth family, Cho wore the Flower Hmong costume of her husband's family to signify that she was now married.

Traditionally, the family of the prospective groom would pour rice wine from a buffalo's horn for the girl's father. If the father agreed to the marriage, he would drink the rice wine. If not, he would set it aside.

Cho's husband didn't have a father to negotiate or pay a bride price, and he had little money to pay it himself. Cho's father, whose pride had already been deeply wounded by the defiance Cho had shown in accepting her husband without waiting for his own permission, was now insulted by the pitiful price he was offered for his daughter. It seems he wasn't impressed by Cho's husband as a person, either. He refused to recognise the marriage, refused to drink the rice wine, and refused to let Cho return to China, sending her supposed husband away without her.

Cho, who had believed herself married, now found herself separated from her husband by an angry father and a national border. She and her new husband had no way even to speak with each other. Once again, Cho felt trapped in the village, a captive of her own father.

Like any other Vietnamese Hmong woman, Cho was expected to be subservient to a man. In this case, though, it wasn't clear which man. Cho's husband had already claimed ownership by sleeping with her – but he'd never paid for her, and Cho's father hadn't conceded possession of her.

Culturally speaking, Cho's father held the moral high ground – but the deed had already been done. Cho now had the taint of being trafficked twice, and would be considered damaged goods by her community. If she didn't go with this husband, she might not be able to find another.

Unwilling to give up on his new bride, Cho's husband had returned to the family home at a later date with more money and more gifts – but nobody was home on that particular day.

Thick sections of bamboo had been used in the construction of Cho's family home, with each length of bamboo segmented into a series of hollow compartments.

According to one version of the story, Cho's husband had entered the family compound and found or made a hole so he could hide a phone within a bamboo hollow in a wall of the house itself. He'd then described the phone's location to the broker, who'd managed to pass the information to Cho.

Cho and her husband had begun speaking in secret. When she wasn't using the phone, she'd switch it off and keep it hidden.

Soon enough, Cho decided that she liked her husband enough to run away from her father and family home. When Cho's husband offered to come and collect her from Sapa, she agreed. Cho told her family she was going into town to sell handicrafts – then she vanished from their lives once more.

To Cho's mind, it was only logical that she would return to China.

"We were already husband and wife," she explained.

At last, I understood why Cho and her father had both concealed the truth of her story for so long: Cho's defiance was a source of great and lasting shame for them both.

Zao had given me a photograph she'd taken of Cho, who sat staring expressionless at the camera in the park by the lake in Sapa. Zao told me it was the last photograph taken of Cho before she ran away to join her husband in China. The date given on the file was 23rd October 2011.

YOU NEVER GIVE ME YOUR MONEY

In that year – 2011 – there had been a sharp increase in the number of girls being trafficked from Sapa, and the local community was reeling from their loss. Cho's second disappearance came as a cruel blow to her parents, especially after May's recent kidnapping.

Cho's parents didn't know if Cho was dead or alive, if she was in Vietnam or China, if she'd returned to her supposed husband or if she'd fallen prey to other traffickers. After making their own enquiries locally and reporting Cho's disappearance to the village police, they felt there was nothing more they could do.

It took Cho almost a year to overcome her shame and call her father Lung in Vietnam. She told him not to worry about her, she was still alive and living in China with her husband.

Lung had told me that Cho called perhaps only once a year after that – but he also believed she'd only been gone for a year and a half, which made no sense. When Cho called, no number appeared on Lung's phone, so the family was unable to call her back.

Lung claimed that the family had waited another year for Cho's second phonecall, though it was more likely to have been just a matter of months. The second time Cho called, she'd just given birth to her first child, a baby boy. She invited her parents to visit her in China and help name the baby.

Cho's husband had helped them cross the border illegally, and had brought them to his home outside Nanxi. Lung said Cho's new home and its surrounding mountains were almost identical to where the family lived in Vietnam, only Cho's husband grew more corn than rice.

Lung had been angry with Cho's husband, as he still hadn't received any payment for his daughter.

In Vietnam, a typical bride price ranged from around six to sixty million dong ($285 to $2,850). In China, with its dearth of marriageable women, the minimum bride price was said to be far higher – around sixteen thousand yuan ($2,400).

Again, Cho's husband offered Lung a pitifully low price for Cho – just two thousand yuan ($300) – promising more later. For Lung, such a humiliatingly low bride price only added insult to injury, and he was furious.

Lung had demanded that Cho return to Vietnam with him immediately. Cho had refused, remaining defiant even when he'd told her that she'd never be welcome back in the family home.

Regardless of whether or not Lung acknowledged her husband, Cho considered herself a married woman, and as such had already left her father's family. Ultimately, it seemed that Lung had no choice but to accept what little money he'd been offered.

Cho's husband had essentially offered to buy Cho on instalment, but it seemed that he'd failed to make any further payments, and bad blood remained between the two men.

Lung wasn't the only one who got less than he'd hoped for. Without her family nearby to support her, life for Cho in China was even more difficult than it had been in Vietnam, and the man she'd married with such high hopes had proved to be abusive.

Cho's family had ultimately visited her in China two or

three times, including for the Lunar New Year just three weeks before I'd first met them. Cho's father had declined to visit after the birth of Cho's baby girl.

Cho herself had returned to Vietnam three times. She'd stayed two or three nights after her elder brother Pao had committed suicide, and had stayed for four nights for the Lunar New Year in 2013. Now, however, she'd been back with her family for about six weeks, and had no intention of returning to her husband in China.

Despite his earlier threat, Lung had accepted Cho back into the family home. He seemed to be motivated less by a concern for his daughter than by the opportunity to spite her husband.

Because Cho's husband had only partially paid for her, Lung seemed to have no qualms about taking his daughter back.

This struck me as odd, given his behaviour towards May's "marriage". Lung had never received any money at all from May's "husband," and the two men had never spoken directly or made any kind of agreement. And yet, because May's "husband" had paid her traffickers – and perhaps because May kept secret from her family the ways that her "husband" abused her – Lung seemed to consider May's "marriage" more legitimate than Cho's.

Ultimately, though, it seemed to be a matter of pride rather than money. As I'd learned the hard way, Lung was a very proud man who would not easily forgive a perceived slight, and Cho's husband had offended him deeply.

While I'd been in China, Cho's husband had interfered with my search for May and tried to prevent our meeting. That fact had been surprising enough in itself, but Cho's husband had taken an oddly roundabout approach. Rather than simply calling May's "husband" directly – as he could have easily done – he'd instead told Lung, who had then warned May off meeting me.

I now wondered if Cho's husband had chosen that

approach in a failed attempt to redeem himself in Lung's eyes. Perhaps he'd wanted to show that he was acting in the family's best interests, and was willing to unite with them against a common enemy – me.

When asked about her life in China, Cho told me it was "no good". It was better living in Vietnam, she said, and much better never to get married. I didn't ask what her husband had done to her, but she remained angry with him.

Cho's husband was still calling her, crying on the phone, threatening to kill himself if she didn't return, saying their son was very upset without her.

"I say to my husband, 'I don't come back later. I stay with my mother, [and] my daddy,'" Cho said. Her use of the word "daddy" seemed more a reflection of Cho's low level of English, rather than any particular affection towards her father.

While I'd finally unravelled the mystery that surrounded Cho, her husband remained an enigma. The way in which he'd taken Cho from Sapa (not just once, but twice) showed that he was more than willing to overstep even the brutal customs of his own culture. Was he more deeply involved in the local trade in women, or was he simply an abusive husband? I didn't know.

Lung said he'd only allow May to return home from China on the condition that she found a new husband within two months, as he wouldn't allow her to stay in the family home any longer than that. Had Lung imposed the same condition on Cho? He'd made it clear that he considered his daughters to be burdens, and the last thing he needed was two more mouths to feed. Had he already begun pressuring Cho to remarry or return to her husband?

I wasn't sure, and it was too late to find out: the interview was already falling apart, and all of these questions remained unanswered.

SOME PEOPLE

As storytellers, we tend to shape our stories to what we believe our audiences most want to hear – and, as audience members, we tend to take from stories what we most want to hear.

We take the parts that conform with our own beliefs and reassure us we're on the right path, while discarding anything conflicting or awkwardly complex. We each seek out stories that fit comfortably within the larger story of our own life and cultural understandings.

As Cho's story unfolded, Pang and I each heard what we wanted to hear in it. We stripped away the story's complexity and broke it down into something small and simple we could each carry away with us.

To my mind, Cho's story was an understated tale of courage and defiance, defined by a series of daring escapes from the men who sought to control her: the middleman, her father, her husband.

While I stood in admiration of Cho's strength, I felt that her story was ultimately a tragic one. Like some small panicked creature smashing itself to pieces, it didn't matter which way she turned – she could never escape the culture that confined her, making her flight a futile one.

It seemed to make little difference whether Cho was in Vietnam with her father, in the borderlands with her husband, or even being sold to some stranger somewhere much deeper in China: the only true moments of freedom she would ever experience were those brief flights from one man's dominion to the next.

As Pang listened to Cho's story, however, she heard only a sinner's confession of shameful disobedience, and she couldn't have cared less about any further details Cho wanted to add.

While both of these interpretations were valid, neither reflected the whole truth. As with so many truths we cling to in life, each interpretation reflected just one aspect of a reality that was more complex than could be understood in the time we were willing to give it.

Cho had done incredible things, as well as committing deeply shameful acts within the bounds of her culture, but her story was much more than just the sum of these ill-fitting parts.

Partway through our interview, I noticed something strange happening between Pang and Cho. I saw that Cho was getting nervous but I didn't know why. I was aware that Pang wasn't doing a great job but would never have guessed she was actively shutting down the interview.

It was only much later when the interview footage was fully translated that I finally understood what had happened.

When Pang and I had found Cho in Sapa's main square earlier that day, I'd explained my work to Cho as best I could. I'd told her that I wanted to hear her story and use it to help other girls in danger of being trafficked.

In hindsight, it's not clear how much of that message Cho had understood. Pang had translated for me, but I don't know how well, and during our interview I realised that Cho often claimed to understand my English when she didn't.

During the interview, Pang had been impatient and pushed Cho to skip over the details of her story. When Cho insisted on telling her story properly, Pang began scaring her off with the thought of how she'd be judged by others in Sapa when they learned what she'd done. Pang wasn't trying to protect Cho: she was trying to upset her.

Pang interrupted Cho in the middle of her story, declaring that I was going to put my footage of Cho "in the computer" so that everyone could see it – which certainly wasn't true in the sense that Cho understood it.

While I felt the stories I'd gathered could have great impact in Sapa, I'd also come to realise they included many sensitive details shared by girls who were easily recognisable there. As such, my documentary remained targeted towards a Western audience, who had the power to support organisations fighting trafficking in that region.

None of my footage of Cho has ever been shared publicly in Sapa, and the documentary has been made freely available there only to the people who were involved in its production.

I didn't know how to explain any of that when the only interpreter I had available had very little interest in interpreting. Cho asked Pang if it was true I'd be sharing the footage "in the computer", and Pang assured her it was. Cho was no doubt imagining the local girls and women watching her confession on their phones or in the Internet cafés, judging her mercilessly.

"Nobody wants to be in the computer," Cho told Pang, in Hmong. "There are many people who don't like the girls who come back from China. They'll think, 'How can I come back from China and still have the shamelessness to speak in the computer?'"

While I didn't understand its source, I saw Cho's sudden nervousness and tried to reassure her.

"I don't want you to be uncomfortable," I said. "I'm just trying to understand the story. So if I ask something and you don't want to answer, it's okay."

Cho nodded, smiled, and assured me it was okay – then turned back to Pang and continued speaking in Hmong.

"I don't like to do this," she said. "People will speak badly of me."

"If you don't like it, tell him," said Pang, without telling me anything herself.

"They'll speak about the kind of girl that comes back from China and still has the nerve to go around and speak without shame," Cho said.

"Because you went by yourself," Pang told her, drawing a clear line between herself and Cho. "Me, I was kidnapped, so I speak without shame."

Of all the footage Marinho and I had gathered for the documentary, there are a few moments which affect me no matter how many times I see them – like seeing May sitting beside a teddy bear on the morning of her "wedding", Vu looking terrified in her own bridal dress, and the little moments of conflicting emotions that surround Pang's return home.

Some of this footage is dramatic, like the teenage girl being abducted from the streets of Sapa, while other moments are easily missed, like the look of sheer exhaustion in the eyes of a young Hmong mother.

Perhaps the moment that hits me hardest, though, is the moment that follows Pang's comment. Cho is sitting with her back against the wall at the Yellow Dragon, having finally shared the secrets she'd been keeping for years, as Pang declares her unworthy of the support of their community.

I'd tried to create a safe, non-judgemental space for Cho – and now she felt as if she'd been betrayed. Her eyes twitch involuntarily and she glances back and forth between Pang and me, no longer knowing who she can trust.

It was heartbreaking that even fellow survivors tore each other down when they most needed each other's support. Part of the reason why that moment touches me so deeply is the knowledge of what happened next.

Pang's restless behaviour throughout Cho's interview wasn't just a matter of boredom. She seemed to disapprove of my showing empathy and understanding towards someone who she felt deserved none. Pang wanted to make it clear that while she and Cho were both survivors of human trafficking, they belonged in two very different categories.

I hadn't forgotten that, until very recently, I too had judged Cho unfairly – but I'd done so privately, and was more than willing to listen to her own version of events.

Perhaps Pang was also shamed by Cho's story. Perhaps Pang had the sense that, with a little more courage, she too could have escaped her middleman and returned home in a matter of days rather than years. Perhaps she was resentful that Cho had so narrowly escaped all the terrible things that Pang herself had endured in China.

In listening to Cho's story, it seemed that Pang had wanted only to confirm her suspicion that Cho had returned to China of her own volition. To her, that was the only fact that mattered, and the rest of the story was irrelevant.

In the same way, when the other Hmong women of Sapa had heard Pang's own story, the only fact that mattered was that she had left her baby girl in China.

These were the facts that made Cho and Pang nonentities within the local community, denied any extenuating circumstances, deserving of any and all misfortunes that befell them.

In every story of every survivor, the local women could always find one fact to mark her as an outcast – and, perhaps, to convince themselves that their own superior behaviour would protect them against similar dangers.

A survivor's only alternative to sharing her story was to keep it forever locked up in silence, secret from even her closest friends, as Shu had done – but even then, the community would simply assume the worst.

It was easy to see how the Sapa Hmong women were held down and controlled by men through every stage of their lives. In this situation, however, it was primarily the women using what little power they had to torment each other.

Every day, in countless ways, these women had been taught

to feel inferior – and they seemed to respond by seeking moral superiority over each other, judging each other mercilessly, holding each other to impossible standards.

This, perhaps, was the most effective mechanism in the trap that held them all and left them so easily controlled by the men in their lives.

By putting Cho down, Pang seemed to feel she could raise herself up just a little, and find a point of solidarity with the rest of the community that would perhaps help them forget her own supposed wrongs.

Many human trafficking victims spent years trying to get home, only to realise they weren't welcome there anymore. The only place they were still wanted was with the men who'd bought and abused them, in the country they'd spent so long trying to escape.

There was so much more I'd wanted to ask Cho: about her husband, and her father's attitude towards her return. But Cho said she had a headache, her answers became vague, and the interview began falling apart. For a time I retreated to safer subjects, but I'd already lost the connection I'd shared with Cho.

After our interview, Cho returned to her father's house in the village, and I never saw her again. Just two weeks later, Cho's husband came to find her, demanding that she return with him to China – and she did.

Had Lung merely used his daughter as a pawn, a means of reclaiming some measure of pride and power from Cho's husband? Having proven his point, and unwilling to support Cho any further, it seemed he'd given her up with little fuss.

Cho – a strong young woman who'd been through so much, and had fought so hard to determine her own fate – no longer had any place in her own community. She'd returned to a country she didn't like and a man she didn't want to be with, because she didn't have anywhere else to go.

She remains there today.

WHO SOLD HER OUT

It was clear that neither Zao nor Cho was the insider who had betrayed her friends to the traffickers – but it was also clear that someone had.

Of May's group of ten friends, I felt certain it was none of the girls who had been trafficked – May, Pang, Vu, Cho, or Shu. I was equally sure it was none of their five friends who had remained behind in Sapa – Zao, Chan, Chu, Little Chu, or Ha. So who was it?

May, Pang, and Vu identified the insider as another girl their own age named Gom. Like Zy, Gom had been close to May's group of friends without ever really being part of it.

The girls had known Gom all their lives: she'd grown up with them in the village, lived with them in Sapa, and – one by one – had betrayed them to their traffickers.

I'd been vaguely aware of Gom without ever actually knowing her. I'd first heard rumours about her during my earlier investigation in Sapa, just as I'd heard rumours about Zao and Cho.

At that time, there were simply too many unknowns. I didn't know if the rumours were true, how many abductions Gom might have facilitated, if she'd been working alone, or if other girls in the same circle had also been involved. My suspicions of Zao and Cho had lingered until I'd had a chance to speak with them in person.

I'd eventually made contact with Pang in China – and when we met in person, she'd been furious with Gom.

"One day, if I go back, I will make Gom go in the jail," she told me. "She's not very nice, she's so shit girl. When I go back I will fight her. When she sell me she have a lot of money, she go to travel to Hanoi, [and] Halong Bay, I know already."

Pang's desire to have Gom imprisoned for her crimes was a major part of the reason why she'd wanted to return to Sapa. It had helped sustain her in China, just as May had been sustained by a desire to revenge herself on her middlemen. Neither girl wanted to spend her life feeling as though she'd been defeated by such horrible, immoral people.

Pang told me how she'd first met the men who would later kidnap her. She'd been guiding a trekking group outside Sapa one day when she'd received a call from Gom, asking where she was.

"I say, 'Right now, I'm trekking.' She say, 'Quick, come back faster, I'll introduce you to a guy.' I say, 'Who is it? I don't want to.'"

Gom had then given Pang's number to two young men who'd begun calling her directly.

"I don't know them, but they just call me, say, 'Come, we go to eat together.' I say, 'No, I don't know who are you guys.' They say, 'We are friends of Gom. Come, we go to eat.' He just call, call, call, call. Then I just close my phone, I think, 'Ooh, shoo!'"

When Pang had returned to Sapa, she'd agreed to meet Gom in the market to eat noodle soup, and Gom had brought the two men with her.

"If I don't know the guy, I will not talk to them, right? But Gom she says, 'You can talk to them, it's no problem.'"

With Gom's assurance that the two men were trustworthy, Pang felt it was safe to become friends with them. She never imagined that Gom and the men had something very different in mind.

On her final evening in Sapa, Pang had just showered after returning from a trek. When she stepped outside her room she found Gom and the two young men already there waiting for her.

"They say, 'Okay, we stay here waiting for you long time ago, you go to eat with us.' I think, 'No,' but Gom she just take my hand. She say, 'Okay, we go to eat in my room.' They buy many rice wine, many buffalo meat, then we go to Gom's room. They say, 'Okay, tonight we very happy, we can drink happy water together.' I think, 'No, I could not drink, because I still very young. I cannot drink.'"

Gom and the men had pressured Pang to drink, and together they'd finished a 1.5-litre bottle of rice wine.

"They just give a lot, a lot of rice wine, I drink, I don't know anything. So then I drunk. I don't know who bring me go to my room, and go to change my clothes, go to let me sleep in my bed."

Pang had woken up the next morning in the rented room she shared with her cousin. She'd vomited in the night, and now found herself wearing another pair of pants and one of Gom's jackets. One of the men was sleeping in her cousin's bed, and her cousin was nowhere to be seen.

"I wake up and say, 'Ooh, who is that?' Then I feel scary. I look my clothes, changed already."

Pang had called Gom to ask what had happened – and when she learned that Gom had allowed one of the young men to help change her clothing, she'd become so furious that Gom had hung up on her.

Pang had described the events that followed when I'd met with her in China – but when we spoke again in Vietnam, many new details emerged. This time, Pang made no mention of the "medicine" her kidnapper had supposedly drugged her with.

When the young man in her room had woken up, he'd told

Pang to follow him. Gom called to tell Pang that the two men would rent some motorbikes, and the four of them would go together to Bac Ha market.

Pang was supposed to be trekking again that day – but she was suffering her first hangover, and had little strength to resist their combined pressure.

"I feel very tired, I don't know what to do. I feel like my head is very, very heavy, so I cannot move my head."

The man had walked her up to the church, where he suggested they take a taxi to Lao Cai. Pang didn't want to, but he'd taken her hand and led her inside the vehicle. Gom called to reassure Pang, saying that she herself would come soon and meet them in Lao Cai.

Pang's friends and family soon noticed her absence. They began calling her – and when they realised she was in Lao Cai with a strange man, they became frightened for her safety and told her to come back immediately.

The man had spoken directly to Pang's sister, telling her he was going to marry Pang. When she didn't believe him, he hung up on her, and told Pang they were going by motorbike to Bac Ha.

Pang wanted to wait for Gom, but the man said Gom would soon be following them. He'd taken Pang's hand and put her on the motorbike. At first they'd driven towards Bac Ha, but then he said they'd go to his house first, and had taken a smaller road towards the border. Pang could hardly see anything in the rain and fog.

Pang's kidnapper had taken her across the border to the middleman's house, telling her they could wait there for Gom, who would be coming shortly.

Gom, of course, never came – interestingly, though, she did eventually call.

Pang's phone had been taken from her when she'd first arrived in China. Over the following weeks, she'd been very uncooperative and had made life difficult for her middleman. Not knowing what else to do, they seemed to have turned back to Pang's traffickers for help calming her.

When Pang had been in China for about two weeks, it seems that Gom had called directly to the middleman's phone, and had spoken with Pang.

"She say, 'You stay there, don't go anywhere, just stay here with the guy. In two or three days I'll come and see you.' I say, 'Where are you now? You can bring me back to Sapa?' Gom says, 'Right now, don't say anything, just stay there. Two or three days, I'll come and bring you back to Sapa.' Then Gom say, 'I'll call you soon.' That's all."

That was the last time Pang and Gom had spoken.

By that time Pang was well aware that her kidnapper had deceived her – but even then, she didn't realise that Gom had betrayed her, and still considered her a friend. It was only later that she understood what had really happened.

The following year, Pang's mother Bao had helped identify Pang's kidnappers at their trial. One of the kidnappers had acknowledged Gom's role in Pang's abduction, saying she'd received the same amount of money that he and his accomplice had.

Pang had been sold to her "husband" for eighteen thousand yuan ($2,700) – an unusually high bride price for Vietnam and an unusually low one for China, but ultimately a pitiful price for someone's life.

Pang's middlemen had taken almost two-thirds of that money for themselves. They'd claimed to have paid a total of twenty million dong ($950) to Pang's kidnappers, and it seemed that Gom had received a third of that sum – a little over three hundred dollars – in exchange for her betrayal of a lifelong friend.

Gom had taken her payment – and now Pang wanted her to pay for her crimes.

CASH MONEY

Gom was believed to have been involved in the abductions of three or four other girls, including May and Vu. There didn't seem to have been any insiders involved in the disappearances of Cho or Shu, who had been drawn into entirely different trafficking networks.

During her time in Sapa, May had shared rooms with several girls there – including her sister Cho, Zao, and their friend Little Chu, with whom she seems to have stayed the longest.

In mid-2011, however, Little Chu's mother learned that May had begun socialising with young men in their shared room. She was scandalised, and refused to let Little Chu stay with May any longer.

Little Chu took another room closer to the town centre, and May found a new roommate: Gom. A month later, May was kidnapped by a young man Gom had introduced her to.

That winter, Gom had invited Vu back to her rented room to watch TV. A young man from out of town was there with her, and another had arrived soon after – the man who would soon kidnap her.

Vu had been sitting on Gom's bed sewing and half-watching

TV, with her phone on the bed beside her. While she'd been distracted, it seemed that Vu's kidnapper had taken her phone and dialled himself, so that he had her number.

The two young men had left town soon after, but Vu's kidnapper-to-be began calling her constantly. At first she wasn't sure who he was, but he explained that he was Gom's friend whom she'd recently met. The man began sweet-talking her, she agreed to meet him when he returned to Sapa, and she disappeared the same day.

The girls who remained behind in Sapa had diverse opinions of Gom. One believed Gom was very friendly and considerate, while admitting that she didn't really know Gom well and had been warned off spending time with her.

"Most people say, 'Just don't go with her, never go with her.'"

Others considered her deceptive: "She a bit liar. When she say something, it's not very true."

Little Chu, who didn't like to speak badly of others, preferred not to comment when I asked her what kind of person Gom was. It was the only question in our hour-long interview she chose not to answer.

Some of the girls had already begun to suspect that Gom had been somehow involved in their friends' disappearances, but none of them knew for certain.

"No one sees, so no one can say anything – but they think she meet all the people that sell to China, maybe she earn some money with this."

During my investigation earlier that year, Gom had been sharing a room with her sister Ny in Sapa. By the time I returned to Vietnam in September, Gom had moved to Hanoi, where she'd taken a job at a travel agency. As part of her job, Gom moved back and forth regularly between Hanoi and Sapa.

Even before Pang's return home, I'd begun gathering information on Gom, including the name, address, and website of the travel agency. While I knew people who were close to Gom, I wasn't sure how to get her home address in Hanoi without raising suspicions.

Curiously, I'd found a Facebook account Gom kept under a false name. Rather than Sapa, she claimed her hometown was in Yen Bai, a province on the flatlands halfway to Hanoi. She'd shared plenty of photographs of herself, occasionally in traditional costume but mostly wearing Western-style clothing.

More interesting was the profile of the man Gom was listed as being "in a relationship with" – a young tattooed man who posed shirtless with swords, guns, and two fists filled with great fans of high-denomination banknotes. His other photos showed dirt tracks through the mountains, thick wads of Vietnamese banknotes piled in heaps, and a gang wielding various weapons.

Gom's boyfriend had photos showing dozens of weapons laid out on tiled floors: swords, machetes, lengths of piping, guns, a hand grenade, and what seemed to be extendable, broad-tipped spears. Beneath one of these photos he'd commented that the weapons were for his "ex lovers".

"Motherf*cker, I hate you," he wrote. "Love is full of lies and pain."

Like Lucky Charm, Gom's boyfriend portrayed himself as both a violent, vengeful menace and a tender romantic, which struck me as an odd mix. He complained that nobody understood him, and encouraged anyone to contact him if they wanted "a sincere love" or "a shoulder to relax upon".

He'd shared numerous selfies taken by several young Vietnamese women. The teenage girl who appeared most frequently was listed at various times as both his girlfriend and his sister. In one photo, she'd posed with far more cash than I'd ever seen in anyone's possession.

Each of the banknotes in the broad mound on the table before her was worth almost five days' average wages, and there seemed to be thousands of them. The way they were piled, though, made it very difficult to see just how many there were.

When I passed the photo to several people who had experience counting Vietnamese cash, they gave wildly-varying estimates representing anywhere between one and twenty-five years' worth of average annual wages. How a teenager would have access to such quantities of money remained a mystery.

She was a well-dressed, neatly-presented young woman who listed her hometown as Lao Cai, while the young man said he was also from Yen Bai.

Like Gom, they both used multiple names. Bizarrely, the man had used the other woman's name as the URL on his account, while the woman's URL was a completely different, seemingly Chinese name.

While there was nothing there to incriminate Gom, it was clear that she'd made some interesting friends.

One evening a week before Pang's return home, I was at the *bia hoi* in Sapa discussing Gom with a Western friend. One of the mysteries surrounding Gom was whether or not her family had also been involved with trafficking girls: we'd each heard various rumours.

Gom was said to have shared some of the money she'd received from trafficking with her family, and particularly with her sister Ny. The two sisters were said to have gone travelling together, spending Gom's money. When asked, Gom claimed the money had been sent to her by an older, wealthy Australian man who fancied her.

While I was speaking with my friend, I had the strange sensation of being observed. Glancing around, I felt a sudden shock at the realisation that Gom's near-identical sister Ny was sitting at the very next table watching me. With a sinking feeling in my stomach, I was reminded again just how small Sapa was.

I felt certain that we'd been caught out. A moment later the scene took a more surreal turn when Ny, one of Sapa's notorious "bad girls", began batting her eyelashes at me. Had she heard our conversation, or was she too busy thinking about other things?

SHE'S CRAFTY

Until Pang returned, there was little that could be done about Gom: we couldn't prove the crime without the victim.

I'd learned of a Hmong girl named Ling who had grown up in Pang's village and had been working as a cleaner in one of Sapa's hotels.

Soon after Pang had been trafficked, Gom and her father had offered to take Ling on a shopping trip to Lao Cai. Instead, they'd given her to the same gang of men who'd trafficked May, Pang, and Vu, who had then sold her across the border in China.

Ling had escaped China eight months later. Rather than Ling making a statement against Gom and her father, it was rumoured that Ling's family had been paid by Gom's family to maintain their silence.

Pang thought that was stupid – she'd much rather see Gom imprisoned than receive any amount of money.

"She in the jail, me happy for all my life," she said.

Now that Pang was home, she finally had the chance she'd long been waiting for, to see Gom imprisoned for the things she'd done.

In theory, all that was required of Pang was a statement

to the local police. In Sapa, however, nothing was quite that simple. In such a small and tightly-knit community, everyone knew everyone – and they were often related, even if they couldn't say exactly how. May, Pang, Zao, Chan, Chu, and Gom's families all lived near each other in the village, and Little Chu was related to Gom by marriage.

A few days after her return home, I'd taken Pang back to her mother's house for a reunion with her brother and sisters. Gathered around a low wooden table laden with meat, tofu, vegetables, and rice, they held a council of war to decide how best to handle the situation.

Gom's family was well aware of Pang's return to Sapa and, not surprisingly, it seemed they were on edge.

"Gom's family said, 'Oh my God, she's come back. Why has she come back?'" Pang said, in Hmong.

"Of course Gom's family is very scared that you've come back," her mother replied. "You should tell the police how she introduced you to those people."

Though it would clearly create tensions in the village, Pang's family was generally supportive of her desire to make a statement against Gom.

Rather than approaching the district police in Sapa, Pang wanted to go to the village police station, as she had a cousin who worked there. We went there the same afternoon – but all we found was a clueless kid in an oversized uniform and a few pigs scrounging in the yard, so we rode back to Sapa.

Most of the staff at the district police station were busy watching soccer on TV. A Kinh officer questioned Pang in a startlingly aggressive manner, taking no notes, before a Hmong officer appeared to conduct his own interview. They told her to come back the next day to make a full statement in Vietnamese.

As Pang was largely illiterate in any language, I arranged for a Kinh friend to help her make the statement. Unfortunately, with no evidence of Pang crossing the border in either direction, there was very little paperwork to support her story.

She couldn't even say exactly when she'd been trafficked, and her mother couldn't recall any further details of the trafficking gang's imprisonment. All Pang had were some photos of China on her phone which proved nothing, so it was essentially her word against Gom's.

Gom's role in May and Vu's abductions had been more subtle and easily denied: by that time, it seemed she'd learned to be more careful. Gom had made her working relationship with the kidnappers most obvious when Pang and Ling had been taken.

I felt the best thing we could do to strengthen Pang's case was to find the other survivor, Ling, and encourage her to make her own statement against Gom, regardless of any payment she might have received.

After making a few enquiries, we found Ling selling handicrafts by the church. The scene that followed felt almost like one from a spy film, as the two girls conversed in hushed tones beneath a lamppost in a heavy fog.

Ling said the rumours were untrue: she had made a statement, but nothing had happened. Gom and her sister had gone travelling for a couple of months. When Gom had returned, the police seemed to have forgotten about her, and she'd continued living in Sapa as if nothing had ever happened.

Pang and I met with Ling again the next day, far too conspicuously above the square. It was only as we were leaving that I realised that Gom's sister Ny was sitting just across the square, facing the place where we were sitting.

Pang spoke to her cousin, the village police officer, and we went back to the district police station in Sapa the following week. The police knew exactly what Gom looked like and exactly where to find her in Hanoi, and they gave us the impression that the wheels were in motion for her arrest – but nothing happened.

On 1st November – the same day that Lucky Charm injured his leg, and his threat of violence was temporarily suspended – Pang was walking down the street when, for the first time in almost four years, she came face-to-face with Gom. While I can't imagine how that must have felt for her, it clearly shook her deeply. She came to find me at the Yellow Dragon, and we called the police.

Gom had come to Sapa with her boyfriend. Pang and I encountered her – and sometimes him, too – three times in three days, once in the laneway immediately outside the Yellow Dragon. Pang was furious that the police would allow Gom to continue walking the streets when they had two victims' statements against her and every chance to arrest her.

DEPT. OF DISAPPEARANCE

Aside from the larger complex of rented rooms where Pang lived, there was a smaller and more private cluster of rented rooms on the outskirts of Sapa.

Most of these rooms were rented by the local "bad girls", and one had just become vacant. Pang and I knew that Gom's sister Ny was moving in there, we knew exactly when, and we knew that Gom and her boyfriend would be staying with her.

Pang had passed all of that information to the Hmong officer who was handling her case, and he assured her they'd go there to arrest Gom. When the police finally acted, on the morning of 4th November, they went instead to the room that Ny had just vacated, and of course found it empty.

That afternoon, Pang and I had another meeting on the streets of Sapa that felt oddly theatrical. This time we rendezvoused with the Hmong officer and two other plainclothes officers, who were all wearing motorcycle helmets, in the twisting laneways behind the market.

After a brief conversation in conspiratorial tones, Pang was sent down to see if Gom was in Ny's new room; if so, she'd summon the police.

Sending a victim in search of her trafficker (and, very

likely, her trafficker's violent boyfriend) while the police stood around chatting two blocks away hardly seemed like the best approach, but it was the most interest the police had shown in Pang's case so far.

I went with Pang. Before approaching the room, she had to prepare herself psychologically for a potential confrontation with Gom, Ny, or both, but she was also excited by the prospect of Gom's imminent arrest.

It was a tense moment. I had the sense of laying a trap for an elusive, well-camouflaged creature which lay near at hand – but the room was locked.

Pang and I shared an immense sense of frustration. For the past three days we'd encountered Gom regularly in the streets and had urged the police to do something – and now that they'd finally stirred themselves to action, we didn't know where Gom had gone. It wasn't Pang's job to keep watch over her trafficker, especially not when any contact was so emotionally triggering for her.

Ny's old room was only metres from Pang's room – and out of desperation, we checked that, too. The door was closed and we heard three voices inside, but they proved to be the new tenants who'd just moved in.

Pang took the three helmeted police to Ny's new room to be sure they knew exactly which one it was, so there would be no more mistakes. The police told Pang they'd arrest Gom later that evening – but it seemed they were too late, and Gom had already left town.

Three days later, Pang and I went to the Sapa police station to find out what was happening. The Hmong officer had a cousin who lived near Gom's family home in the village, and from the rumours he'd heard, he believed that Gom had gone back to Hanoi to collect her belongings and was moving back to Sapa permanently.

Immediately afterwards, Pang went to meet a friend at an internet café. Ny found Pang there and confronted her, calling her a liar, and claiming that Gom had nothing to do with her trafficking. Pang had been furious, and the two girls had almost come to blows.

Pang came to find me at the Yellow Dragon immediately afterwards, more angry than I'd seen her in a long time. She said if she found Gom, she'd kill her.

A week later, Gom was back in Sapa. Pang told the Hmong officer, who assured her that Gom would be arrested that evening – but again, nothing happened, and Pang couldn't reach the Hmong officer when she tried to call him the next day. It was now more than a month since Pang had made her statement, and Gom was still freely walking the streets of Sapa.

Another week passed with more empty reassurances from the police, who claimed to be making investigations in the village. Pang and I were told they were waiting for a bribe, but we refused to offer one.

The weather began cooling into winter, weeks of rain and fog sapped our spirits, and the police hardly even bothered answering Pang's calls anymore.

We still saw Ny sometimes at the *bia hoi*, which made Pang extremely uncomfortable. One evening I was there with a Western friend who knew Ny and spoke briefly with her. She pretended not to know who I was and introduced herself to me, which struck us both as extremely bizarre.

I'd spoken with Michael before Pang had made her statement. While he also wanted to have faith in the local authorities, he'd acknowledged the possibility that the police would do nothing, and that they might even refuse to take a statement.

In case the local police took no action, Michael had passed me the phone numbers for the specialised anti-trafficking unit in Lao Cai. When we called them to arrange a meeting, the officer was dismissive and had no interest in speaking to Pang, much less in handling her case.

A Blue Dragon lawyer then became involved, liaising with both the anti-trafficking unit in Lao Cai and the national anti-trafficking unit in Hanoi. Ultimately, though, it was up to the authorities to act in either Sapa or Hanoi – and they didn't.

After six long weeks spent trying to find out what was happening to the case, Pang herself began to lose interest in it. The regular visits to the Sapa police station, the endless, frustrating phone calls (often unanswered), and the pervading sense that the authorities simply couldn't be bothered had all drained too much of Pang's emotional energy at a time when her life was still filled with so much uncertainty. Her fury against Gom's betrayal had guttered into a sense of helpless resignation.

When the police raided Pang's housing complex and seized her identity card, she seemed to lose her last shred of faith in them. We were both left with a strong impression that the police would happily conduct a night raid to squeeze some drinking money out of a group of illiterate girls, but didn't want to trouble themselves with any actual criminals like Gom or Lucky Charm.

Two weeks after I left Vietnam – almost two months after Pang had made her statement – the Sapa police finally picked up Gom, only to release her immediately. They said there was insufficient evidence, and claimed to be looking for more.

Having seen how the police in Sapa operated, I could imagine just how hard they were looking. As far as I'm aware, they never took any further action against Gom, and she never received any punishment for betraying her friends to the traffickers. It's very possible that she'd paid the bribe that Pang and I refused to.

POISON

During my last days in Sapa, I spent a lot of time with Chan and Sung – and on my second-last evening in town, they invited me to their rented room for a huge dinner and a few drinks.

Rice wine was typically unflavoured, but other varieties were produced locally – including plum, Chinese apple, and even opium, if you knew where to ask. Some bottles of rice wine contained wildlife, which was typically bottled alive and drowned in the alcohol.

I'd recently heard the story of a cobra which had supposedly survived the process – it was believed to have consumed a full meal shortly before it had been caught, and there had been enough air at the top of the bottle for it to breathe. It was said to have remained in a dormant state – and, when a local woman had opened the bottle, she'd been bitten on the face by a very drunk and angry snake.

During my first stay in Sapa, my Kinh friends and I had progressively emptied a large container of rice wine containing chunks of honeycomb and countless dead bees.

Chan and Sung, however, had a bottle of rice wine like no other I'd ever seen. It was crammed full of "murder hornets"

– giant wasps with bodies as thick as your finger and almost as long, whose stings were said to be like hot knives. A single sting could rot your flesh, while a hive attack could very easily kill an adult. Murder hornets were even known to spray their venom into the eyes of their prey.

Sung explained that his father was one of very few locals who had both the knowledge and courage to lay siege to a hive. Sung's father and his friends would approach a subterranean hive by night, when most of the wasps were sleeping. Without any special clothing, they'd use spray to kill the few guardian wasps, then plug all entrances but one.

To this final entrance, they'd attach a round, metre-long wire cage with a one-way valve at its opening. When they banged the metal, the wasps would come rushing furiously out of the hive and find themselves trapped in the cage.

The hive itself could weigh forty kilograms. When it had been emptied of wasps, it would be broken open so that the young grubs could be cooked and eaten as a delicacy.

The live wasps were transferred into bottles, and would release their poison as they drowned in rice wine. The resulting concoction was considered medicinal, though it was safe to consume only in small quantities.

Sung's bottle contained a murky liquid peppered with dozens of orange wasps' heads, their dark thoraxes and striped abdomens less distinct in the darkness. He broke the seal and the three of us drank together to mark my departure. It was a little surreal drinking alcohol that Sung's father had actually risked his life to produce.

As Chan, Sung, and I sat eating and drinking, we spoke of the past and future, of Chan and Sung's coming child, and of my plans for the documentary. Most of all, though, we spoke of Pang.

Thankfully, Pang had realised I had no romantic interest in her or had lost her own interest in me, and she'd now moved on.

There was a chance that Lucky Charm was also moving on.

After a month of relentless harassment, he'd written a letter which one of his friends had hand-delivered to Pang at her work a few days earlier.

Pang said the letter had rambled on and on and she'd thrown it away without reading it all. Given her low literacy levels, I'm not sure how much she would have understood in any case, but Lucky Charm seemed to be saying that he'd realised she didn't love him and he was going to leave her alone.

Pang didn't believe it, and remained fearful and wary. The very fact that Lucky Charm had taken the time to write her a letter showed he was still obsessing over her, and it seemed more likely he was merely changing tactics.

When Pang and I saw Lucky Charm walking in town the next day with some of his friends, Pang insisted on hiding from him – twice – and was very relieved that she'd seen him before he saw her.

Over the past week or so, Pang had fallen for someone new: another young Hmong man named Lao, whom she'd recently met on Facebook but never in person. Lao was from Dien Bien province but was now living and studying in Danang, in central Vietnam. Pang and Lao spent hours calling each other every day, and already claimed to love each other.

Pang was constantly bugging Chan and me to use our laptops and internet connections so that she could video chat with Lao. He'd skip classes to chat with her, and she became insufferable one day when a power outage prevented them from speaking.

It was barely a week since Pang had first mentioned Lao, and I'd already heard his name more than enough for one lifetime. I found it especially irritating when Pang asserted that her interminable conversations with Lao were more important than the trafficking awareness work I was doing on my laptop.

I had the impression that Lao was a genuinely decent guy, but who could tell? In any case, Pang's moods were never predictable – and if Lao wasn't playing games with her, she seemed to be playing games with him.

Lao was planning to visit Sapa soon. Just that morning, he'd bought Pang a new skirt, and matching jackets for them both, with their names embroidered amidst birds and flowers. Bizarrely, Pang had responded by telling Lao he should only do that for his girlfriend, and that the two of them were just friends.

Then just a few hours later, Pang had gone to Chan's house and spent so long video chatting with Lao that she'd missed her shift at work. Chan had told her off, saying that work and family should always come before anything else.

While Pang had softened on her views towards marriage, she still insisted that she'd never marry a Hmong man.

"If someone love me for sure, for real, I can be marry with them," she told me. "But not local guy. Local guy they don't understand about lady, they just want to leave the lady working. If you get some not-very-good boy, when you have baby they just go to play with other girl. 'No, thank you' for me."

Pang's attitude towards her work fluctuated just as wildly as her attitude towards Lao. Some days she loved working at the café: she enjoyed learning how to cook and make coffee, and said her employers were very happy with her because she could speak both English and Chinese.

There were other days, though, when Pang was ready to quit. She said the customers weren't very nice to her and she didn't like to be inside all day.

"The people like me don't like be inside very much," she said.

Between shifts, Pang began guiding trekking groups to her village – but she didn't enjoy that much anymore, either. Like Vu, she seemed lost and drifting, with no real sense of what she wanted in either her personal or professional life.

MOVING ON

Though Pang and I no longer spent as much time together, we still went walking through town on most days. We'd go and buy ice creams from a little shop near Aart's house, no matter how cold the weather might be. They were cheap and delicious, and some days we'd sit there and eat four or five between us.

Chan said that Pang hadn't really changed since her trafficking: she was still an extremely stubborn, moody young woman who refused to learn from her experiences or to listen to anyone else's advice.

Chan's assessment was basically correct; in some ways, though, I knew that Pang had changed. Behind her wild mood swings, I'd gradually seen a new and unexpected side of her emerge.

Pang had always been a social, moody, and somewhat dramatic person. Now, though, she'd begun discovering a new delight in solitude. She related small moments of joy to me, telling me of her newfound happiness in spending quiet evenings alone at home, washing her hair, listening to music, and embroidering by her little electric heater. It was lovely to see her find a source of happiness that wasn't dependent on our friendship or on the flattery of young men.

For two weeks in the middle of November we'd barely seen the sun: it had been damp, grey, and miserable as the temperatures fell away towards winter. While Pang had been surprisingly mellow and content at home, I'd been the one getting moody and restless, as I looked forward to leaving the mountains of Vietnam for somewhere warmer.

During my final week in Sapa, though, we'd had a series of magnificent days like sparkling gems, and I'd taken Pang out to visit her mother and sisters in one of the villages. She wore her mirrored sunglasses and as we rode out through the mountains with the music pumping, it felt just like being back on our roadtrip again.

On the morning of my dinner with Chan and Sung, I'd been to visit Pang at her rented room. When I arrived, Pang was sitting on a plastic stool in the doorway of her unlit room, embroidering the headband she was making for me.

Pang's phone lay on a second stool beside her, and she was in the middle of a speakerphone conversation. For the first time since her return home, I was surprised to hear Pang speaking not in Hmong, English, nor Vietnamese, but in Chinese. The voice on the phone was male, and I couldn't guess who it might be.

I sat on the steps outside Pang's door and enjoyed the late autumn sunshine. When Pang finished her call we chatted.

Pang said she'd been working at the café the day before when a Chinese tourist had nervously come in wanting to use the bathroom. When he realised that Pang spoke his language, he brought a group of twenty other Chinese tourists inside to eat and drink. They were so pleased with Pang's service that the guide said he'd come back the following month with a group of seventy.

Both of Pang's employers had been present and saw it all, and they were delighted with her. What's more, the tour guide wanted Pang to start taking his groups on village treks, too, even though she'd quoted him an inflated rate. She was thrilled.

I didn't know what might happen to Pang in a broader sense, but in that moment, everything seemed wonderful. She was happy with her job, with her rented room, and with Lao, and her misplaced affection for me had receded back into a comfortable friendship between us.

Pang didn't expect to keep working at the café forever, but said she'd stay at least until the Lunar New Year. She wanted to try again to get her trekking licence.

Though I knew Pang's life would always have its ups and downs, it was a beautiful moment, and that's where I would have liked this story to end: but it didn't.

While the Chinese tour guide story was true, that wasn't who Pang had been speaking to on the phone: she'd been speaking to May's "husband". May's "husband" been calling Pang for months, just as she'd suspected – and, curious to hear what he had to say, Pang had finally decided to pick up.

May's "husband" said that May had told him everything that Pang and I had discussed with her. He demanded to know why we'd encouraged his "wife" to go back to Vietnam. He reminded Pang that May was married now and had a child, and said we should leave her alone. He told Pang he'd never bring May back to Sapa, and there was no reason for her to go.

It had been less than five months since I'd stepped off that train in Delhi. In those months, there had been a series of figures who had taken centre stage in my life, whether momentarily or for much longer periods. They'd included Isabela, Mike, Marinho, Dung and Dinh, Bao, Pang, Chan and Sung, Lucky Charm, Zao, Cho, and Gom.

I'd expected May to play the central role in that story, but she'd been almost entirely absent from it. She'd remained offstage throughout, nothing more than a distant voice in the wings, and sometimes not even that.

May was the person I'd most wanted to see back in Sapa, but now it seemed she'd accepted her "husband's" authority and had given up any real hope of ever returning home.

Perhaps he was no longer her "husband", I thought: perhaps he was simply *her husband* now.

In any case, it was time for me to move on.

EVERY NIGHT MY TEETH
ARE FALLING OUT

On my final evening in town, Pang and I went for ice cream before joining my Kinh friends for a farewell hotpot and drinks at the Yellow Dragon.

The next morning was crystal clear. I awoke at dawn and, for the first time, noticed the newly-installed cable car pylons beginning their long march up the face of Fansipan.

Pang had asked me to visit her before I left. We said our goodbyes, and I told her I was going to miss living in Vietnam.

"Be careful you don't lose your teeth," Pang replied, cryptically.

"What do you mean?"

"When you miss something so much you're sad, you walk around without seeing where you're going," she told me. "You can fall over and lose your teeth."

Pang gave me the brightly-coloured headband she'd been stitching for me over the past month: I have it with me here as I write. I don't wear it, but it reminds me of her – and in an odd way, it also reminds me of Mike.

Mike and I had once joked about how wearing a headband could suspend all rules of normal social interaction. It was just a bit of senseless banter to laugh about and be forgotten, one of the countless tiny moments that make up our lives.

Later, though, when that person is gone, you find yourself remembering funny little things like that. Or like Pang telling me not to lose my teeth.

I hadn't eaten and had only a few minutes before my bus was leaving, so I ducked into Sapa's central market. Instead of going to one of my regular spots, where the women knew me, charged me local prices, and even gave me a little extra in anticipation of my appetite, I went to the closest, quickest places where I didn't normally buy food.

Unaccompanied by any of my local friends, I suddenly found myself being treated as a tourist again. It was a timely reminder that I'd never really belonged there in Vietnam, and that my home awaited me elsewhere.

Chan and Sung had both come to the bus stop to wave me off – and then Sapa was behind me once more.

It was a glorious sunny Sunday – and, as ever, Pang had wanted to go to the "love market".

However, she was still afraid that Lucky Charm and his friends might kidnap her, and she knew I wouldn't be there to accompany her, so she'd told me she might just stay home and relax instead.

Ultimately, though, it was such a magnificent day that Pang simply couldn't resist. She'd dressed up in her best Hmong clothing, and had gone alone.

Just hours after my departure from Sapa, Pang was grabbed at the "love market" – not by Lucky Charm and his friends, but by May's mother Dung and sister Dinh. They'd been waiting for me to leave town.

Between the town square and the lake in Sapa was a small park, which on Sundays was filled with local people promenading in their traditional costumes. Pang had been sitting by herself on a bench by the large round fountain at the centre of the park. She was enjoying the unseasonably warm sunshine and the sight of the large Sunday crowds it had attracted.

Then Dung and Dinh had appeared, grabbing Pang suddenly by the arms and holding her down so she couldn't move. In front of everyone, they began shouting at her, telling her she was a "very shit girl". They wanted to know why she'd ever come back from China when she'd had a good husband and a baby there.

Dung and Dinh told Pang she'd only gone to Dien Bien Phu to have sex with me, and claimed she was now selling her body in Sapa. They'd said I'd only been in Sapa to have sex with her and mocked her because I'd left town without marrying her. Nobody was going to marry her, they said, and it would have been better if she'd stayed in China.

They threatened to kill Pang if she told me any of this, and threatened to have me killed if I kept speaking with May or tried to meet with her again in China. Then they'd let Pang go, and they left.

From our first meeting, May's father had been consistently opposed to my work – it was May's sister Dinh I found truly incomprehensible, as she wavered between assisting me, apologising to me, and behaving atrociously on behalf of her family.

After threatening to have me killed, Dinh sent me a friend request on Facebook, a fact which seems to encapsulate how truly bizarre and erratic her behaviour could be.

Being assaulted and threatened by May's family would have been a horrific experience at any time – but what hurt Pang the most was that it had happened on such a beautiful Sunday, at the very heart of the "love market", where so many of the locals had gathered and borne witness to such a monumental shaming. That, of course, had been the whole point, and what had given the assault so much of its power.

I might otherwise have expected Pang to respond with fury, as she had to the encounter with Gom's sister – but this was simply too much, and it broke her.

Pang went straight back to her room and stayed there for two days, crying constantly and barely eating. She knew that tongues were wagging, judging her mercilessly, with no interest in the truth or anything she might have to say in her own defence.

If May's family ever spoke to her that way again, Pang said she'd tell the police – but May's family never had to say another word. The damage had been done. Pang sank into a deep funk, convinced that everyone in Sapa now saw her as the lowest and most despicable kind of woman, one for whom there was no place in her community.

Pang spoke to her mother Bao who approached Dung in the village, asking why she had treated Pang that way when she'd done nothing wrong. Dung denied everything and walked off.

Somehow it hurt me almost as much to think of the sweet and gentle Bao mustering the courage to stand up to May's family for the sake of her daughter, and being so callously brushed aside. My heart broke at the thought of the helplessness and pain I could so easily imagine in Bao's large liquid eyes.

In China, Pang had refused to participate in her own "wedding" feast, and had instead remained alone in another part of the house. Eventually, though, she'd decided it no longer mattered and there was no point starving herself. Pang had walked into the middle of the celebrations and begun gorging herself with as much food as she could hold.

That pattern now repeated itself. Pang emerged after two days alone in her room, having decided that she longer cared about anyone or anything. If people were going to talk about her, she'd give them something to talk about.

She went to one of the bars where the "bad girls" went, determined to get drunk. Lucky Charm was there and he grabbed her at the entrance, warning her not to go inside.

"I'm not your girlfriend, I'm not your wife," she told him. "It's not your business, go away from me."

Pang gave Lucky Charm three or four quick slaps across the face. He'd released her, and the other girls had taken her inside.

Lucky Charm never touched her again, and when he saw her in the street, he behaved as though he didn't know her.

Pang quit her job at the café, began living off occasional unlicensed trekking work, and embraced her role as one of Sapa's "bad girls".

If you see me missing any teeth, you'll know why.

SPRAWL II
(MOUNTAINS BEYOND MOUNTAINS)

The previous year, after a long cold winter in the Canadian Rockies, summer arrived and I finally had a chance to climb some of the mountains that had surrounded me for so long.

Early one morning, I'd set out with two friends to tackle one of those peaks – and, after several hours' climbing, we reached the top sooner than expected.

From the summit, we could see a larger and more formidable mountain looming above and beyond the one we stood upon, so we decided to continue along the connecting ridge and attempt that one, too.

Hours later, as our small group approached the second peak, we lost any hint of a trail amongst the masses of broken rock fallen from the crumbling cliffs around us. We turned one way then another, hoping to stumble upon any kind of path that might lead us to the top, but that path failed to materialise.

Although the summit was just metres away, we didn't have enough time to safely negotiate the climb, and we turned back without ever touching the top of that mountain.

We'd already gone much further than our original goal, and knew there was nothing more we could have done – yet the three of us were left with a lingering sense of disappointment and failure.

In finding May and Pang in China, I'd climbed a peak far higher than I'd ever expected to – but beyond it lay the much greater challenge of helping them reclaim their freedom and power. Beyond the monstrosity of human trafficking loomed a colossal range of even more formidable issues including poverty, a lack of education, and the cultural mistreatment of women, each of which is deeply rooted in communities around the world.

China alone holds countless thousands of Mays and Pangs. While its "one-child" policy has now been abandoned, its colossal gender imbalance – involving some thirty million surplus men – will take decades to resolve, ensuring enormous continued demand for trafficked girls.

Is the war against human trafficking one we can ever hope to win, or are we simply wasting our time? Had all my efforts to help May and Pang been for nothing?

In Quebec, I'd asked myself what success meant to me, and decided that it meant being a good person and doing whatever I could to help May. I feel that I succeeded on those terms.

Against all odds, I'd found not just May but also Pang in China. I'd done the best I could to help them, and they'd each made their own choices.

In trying to help May, though, I hadn't merely set myself against her family, her "husband", Cho's "husband", my own cameraperson, the traffickers, and the authorities in both Vietnam and China: I'd also unwittingly set myself against the stories that stand at the very heart of both Hmong culture and our own.

We're forever telling each other endless variations of our one great myth – the story of an individual who overcomes all adversity to attain a satisfying, successful conclusion.

In an ever more populous and unequal world, that myth splinters us into individual units, misleads us with unrealistic expectations, and encourages us to trample each other for our own ends. That myth blames us when we fail to meet its impossible standards, and too often makes our lives a process of painful disillusionment. What it deems "success" all too often demands a predatory ruthlessness, while too many good people are crushed by the weight of their supposed failure.

The culture we've built around that myth has failed us. The myth itself is, ironically, one of the few things we still hold in common, even as it drives us apart. Hooked on the addictive comfort that the myth offers us, we've lost our ability to grasp the much larger and far more important stories that surround us.

The story of human trafficking is one of those stories. It doesn't fit the pattern of our myth: it's far greater than that. It's not a neatly-contained story with a typically small cast of characters, focused on any particular individual: it's a messy story happening everywhere at once, with countless intertangled threads twisting in all directions.

It's not a simplistic, good-versus-evil story of conflict and competition: it's a story of complex truths that call for patience and understanding. Nor is it a story with a passive audience: each and every one of us plays a part in this story, whether we realise it or not.

The story of human trafficking isn't a story that ends happily – because it doesn't end at all. It's an ongoing struggle, and a deeply challenging one, but it's one of the most meaningful struggles we'll ever be part of.

Human trafficking is a vast darkness that invades the secret spaces of the world and swallows the most vulnerable among us, reducing them to mere objects to be bought, sold, and abused in every conceivable way.

To fight human trafficking is to fight the darkest parts of human nature, and it's a fight that calls for all the light we can bring. Whether for profit or pleasure, there will always be someone willing to abuse and exploit those less powerful than themselves. There will always be uncontrolled lust and greed in the world.

In a sense, the war against human trafficking is a war for the very soul of the human race. Our species will continue in some form or other – but what kind of species will we be if we knowingly tolerate such horrors?

YOU ARE NOT ALONE

There are two styles of mountaineering.

Alpine style involves a small team moving fast and light, striking out rapidly for the peak. It's the quicker, cheaper, and more flexible of the two styles – but when things go wrong, it can be incredibly dangerous, and climbers can easily find themselves stranded without support.

Expedition style, on the other hand, involves much larger teams building a series of basecamps at increasing altitudes. Climbers can then rely on that infrastructure to rest and resupply as necessary, to make a far safer and steadier progression towards the summit.

'The Human, Earth Project' had been run alpine-style, and I'd learned just how challenging that work could be without the proper support systems in place. By finding May in China, I'd succeeded against incredible odds, and we all enjoy that kind of story – until we have to live through it.

I'd gone as far as I could go, but the mountains I'd faced were too much for any one person alone.

Our one great myth had formed a fundamental belief that had comforted and motivated me since childhood – but it had failed me spectacularly when I'd most needed it. Without the comfort of that myth, I wasn't sure what to believe, or how to understand the world around me.

When I finally saw that myth for what it was, I was left wondering how many other harmful behaviours I'd unconsciously absorbed from the culture that had raised me. It's easy to criticise other cultures, and much harder to examine your own.

Ultimately, this isn't just a story about May or Pang – it's about all of us, and what kind of world we choose to live in. We make that choice every day. Our cultures exist to serve us – the people within them – and if those cultures are harmful to ourselves or to others, then it's our responsibility to change them.

I've visited Hmong communities in Laos where the elders have spoken out and effectively stopped the destructive tradition of marriage by abduction. Yet that tradition persists in many places – including Sapa, and the Hmong diaspora communities in the United States and Australia.

All cultures are continually changing, being shaped and reshaped by the people within them. After all, a culture is merely the sum of our individual behaviours and the collective habits they form. The question is not *if* our cultures will change, but *how*, and which forces we'll allow to drive that change.

If an ordinary, working-class man like May's "husband" has the power to change so many lives without even realising it, then how much power do we have? How far do our actions reach, and how many lives do we touch? Which systems do we support and which do we starve each time we open our wallets? How much better might our world be – for all of us – if we came together to use our power consciously?

Four years earlier, on my first journey through China, I'd begun picking up litter each time I went hiking. I quickly realised that even this simple action had a ripple effect, and that its greatest impact came not from me, but from the way it inspired others to act.

I'd noticed that many of the world's problems were created in individual measures and could be solved the same way – but some problems went far deeper than that, and could only be solved by communities working together.

It's vital to have positive role models – just as Michael, X, and Georges had been for me, or as Chan and Sung had become in the Sapa Hmong community – but these individuals are merely the beginning of something far greater.

I'd been so focused on trying to help May and Pang that I hadn't dedicated enough time to creating or connecting with the kind of community I needed to do my work most effectively. I've since come to understand that my rapid, alpine-style technique wasn't the best approach for the mountains before me.

Organisations like Blue Dragon and Alliance Anti-Trafic have been building and supplying their base camps for decades. Their expedition-style approach means they're better positioned not just to help victims and survivors of trafficking, but also to help each other when necessary.

In Vietnam and China, I'd sparked a series of events that changed lives in Vietnam and China. Ultimately, though, my main role was just as I'd originally imagined it: not that of a search and rescue worker, but of a storyteller, sharing what I'd learned so we can all push forward together.

Those of us in supporting roles rarely meet the true heroes like X, who still sleeps with his phone on his chest every night, ever-ready to help those who need him most. We rarely meet those who are brought back from the shadow world of human trafficking, and we may never see the true impact of our support in the lives of those who ultimately receive it: but that impact is very real.

When I first met with Michael in January 2014, he said that Blue Dragon had rescued only two forced "brides" from China, as compared to about eighty girls from Chinese brothels.

In the eight years between that meeting and the writing of

this book, those proportions have changed dramatically. Blue Dragon has now rescued over six hundred Vietnamese girls and women from forced "marriages" in China – double the number they've rescued from Chinese brothels.

One woman was rescued after thirty-four years in a forced "marriage", becoming a grandmother in China before she was finally able to come home. Another spent twenty-one years being sold over and over again between brothels and abusive men. At the other end of the scale, girls as young as eleven have been rescued from forced "marriages".

Alliance Anti-Trafic and Blue Dragon are both working towards systemic change. As I write, Blue Dragon is preparing to unveil an ambitious ten-year plan to end all forms of human trafficking in Vietnam. The success or failure of that plan will depend largely on the support of ordinary people like you and me.

There are few happy endings in Sapa, but there is hope. As Kimya Dawson said, it's time to decide what success means to you.

YOU REALLY GOT A HOLD ON ME

The attack on Pang proved to be the first in a series of disgraceful attacks that, in my absence, damaged and destroyed many of my friendships in Sapa.

I'd left Vietnam on 1st December 2014. Just three weeks later, I found myself returning to spend one final month in Sapa, for very different reasons and under very different circumstances. My work with the Hmong people there began leading me in new and unexpected directions – but that's another story.

Pang and I remained friends, though we didn't see each other as often as before. After being assaulted and threatened by May's family, Pang wanted nothing more to do with May, and refused to speak to her anymore.

Nor did May want anything to do with Pang. May believed her family's bizarre story that Pang had started the rumour of May's second pregnancy, and she was furious about it.

"Pang, she liar too much," May told me. "She liar to my family a lot. She say to my family I have one more baby so I cannot going back to Sapa. I don't want to meet her anymore."

The original group of ten friends had come apart, and their lives were now moving in very different directions.

I kept calling May, though I wondered why I still bothered. May was forever telling me how much she wanted to go home, and assuring me it would happen soon. Despite all evidence to the contrary, I still wanted to believe her, and I held onto that faint hope.

May said she dreamed constantly of Sapa and her friends there.

"Every night when I sleeping, I dream a lot," she told me.

I felt it was important that May return to Vietnam, if only to decide what she wanted from a position of freedom and safety, but it seemed very unlikely to ever happen.

As much as May wanted to go home, it was clear that she feared the judgement of the Sapa Hmong community, and especially feared how her father might respond to her return. She said he drank too much and was angry with her all the time, because he didn't get any money when she married.

On some days, May spoke of a permanent return to Sapa; on others, she just wanted to visit her family and friends. In either case, she was still determined to do things her own way, without any help from Blue Dragon.

Sometimes May spoke of running away to some other part of China to find a new husband and start again with a clean slate, believing that would be the best way to escape both her "husband" and the judgement that awaited her in Sapa. One of the trafficked girls she knew had done exactly that: she'd escaped a forced "marriage" in Anhui province and now lived in Guangxi province with her new Chinese husband. May wanted to do the same.

Month after month dragged by as I waited for something to happen, but nothing happened. Following my final departure from Sapa in January 2015, my life took a turn for the worse, and I left Asia feeling defeated.

By June 2015, I was living in a village half a world away. More than a year had passed since I'd met with May in China. I no longer felt there was any reason to continue my work, and I had very little means to do so.

While I was deeply reluctant to break the promises I'd made, I'd begun seriously considering shutting down the project without ever finishing the 'Sisters for Sale' documentary.

In any case, I didn't know what to do with the shapeless mess the story had become. I couldn't pretend that Pang's return home was the end of the story – but there was no real conclusion or resolution beyond that, and certainly not a happy one.

Each of our lives has countless possible paths branching out in countless different directions. I just wanted to find a path that might lead me back to the world I'd known before my friends had been kidnapped and my life had fallen apart.

After all I'd seen and heard in Asia, I didn't think anything could shock me anymore – but then something incredible happened.

May's "husband" actually gave May permission to visit her family in Sapa, even allowing her to take their baby – and that proved to be the least remarkable part of a truly amazing series of events.

THE TWIST

With her "husband's" blessing, May took her baby girl and risked a bus journey of three thousand kilometres without an identity card. She travelled southwest for two days and two nights from Shandong to Yunnan province – but May didn't go straight back to Sapa.

May had been in contact with her middleman, and he'd given her directions to come and find him in Wenshan. Wenshan was the same city where Cho had once escaped her own middleman.

May had last mentioned her middleman the previous October, when she said he'd been caught by the Chinese police. His wife had also been arrested four months before that.

The middlemen tend to run family operations – and if any of the family members are caught, others take over while they rotate in and out of prison.

Vu's middlemen were a good example: while waiting for their elder brother to be released from prison, two younger brothers had continued trafficking girls. With the brothers operating from the family home in the absence of the parents, it seemed very likely that the parents had first involved the family in trafficking and were also in prison for the same crime.

Likewise, when the husband and wife who had held May captive were arrested, their adult son took charge of the family business in their absence.

It wasn't clear what had happened following the capture of May's middleman in October, but he wasn't detained for long. He was soon back home and back in contact with May.

The last time May had been inside the middleman's home, she'd been held captive there, and the middleman had been threatening to kill her. I can only imagine how she must have felt to voluntarily return and step inside that home again. The presence of May's baby – the very reason she'd been brought to China in the first place – only made that scene more heartrending.

The middleman had the connections to arrange a legitimate Chinese identity card for May, and had promised to do so. May's "husband" was aware of the arrangement, and had presumably given May whatever money the middleman had demanded as payment.

A legitimate Chinese identity card would not only give May the legal right to live and travel in China, but would also allow her to cross the border without danger. The only place to get one was from the local Public Security Bureau – that is, the police. The fact that May's middleman could acquire legitimate identity cards by illegitimate means meant that he had a corrupt friend or relative within the local police force, just as Pang's "husband" had.

Life in China without an identity card was precarious and left May highly dependent upon her "husband". The card represented a freedom that May had been denied for four long years, a freedom that she desperately wanted. It was a momentous occasion – but it was also a deeply surreal moment for her.

For four long years, May had also desperately wanted revenge against her middleman: yet here she was doing business with him. Once his victim, she'd now become his client.

To the middleman, May had been just another piece of merchandise, and her trafficking had had no particular significance to him. May, however, had taken it very personally. It was ironic that her former captor was now helping May regain some measure of freedom, that he was opening this door to her after closing so many others.

As excited as May was to finally be receiving an identity card, her middleman was the last person she wanted to deal with.

"He very mean," she said. "He sell everybody."

When May arrived at the middleman's home, she saw two other teenage Hmong girls there waiting to be sold into "marriage" and motherhood. No doubt May saw her younger self in their eyes: terrified, uncomprehending, a world away from everything and everyone they'd ever known.

Sometimes we make choices that take us down new and unexpected paths, moving in directions we'd never imagined. May made her choice immediately and without hesitation.

May's freedom was at last within reach – but as much as she yearned for it, she wouldn't take it while other girls were being stripped of theirs. She decided to sacrifice the hope of her long-awaited identity card.

We all dream about what we might achieve should we only be given the opportunity – yet how many of us have the courage to seize that opportunity when it finally presents itself, especially when it carries so much personal risk?

Over the course of years, May had feigned friendship with the middleman, and had gradually won his trust – but she'd never stopped watching and waiting for an opportunity to betray him, and that opportunity had come at last.

May had discovered where the middleman kept his own identity card – and when he left the room for a moment, May seized her opportunity with both hands. That card held all of the middleman's vital details: his full name, date of birth, address, photograph, and citizen identity number.

"I see him sell many Hmong girl, I not very happy," May told me. "So I steal his ID card!"

Rather than physically taking the card itself, May had photographed it using her phone. It was a small act, but an incredibly courageous one.

"I have he ID card, I know where he from, what he family name, so I know everything!"

When May left the middleman's home, she had the middleman – almost literally – in her pocket, her baby on her shoulder, and one last trick up her sleeve.

If May could convince the local police to act, and act quickly, then they could catch the middleman redhanded and save his two most recent victims.

But how was she to convince the police to act at all? How was she to win their support, when she herself was in China illegally? May's story was a horrific one – but how was she to prove it?

Under any circumstances it would have been risky for an illegal alien to approach the Chinese authorities, and the middleman's connection to the local police made it especially risky for May.

When she'd first been brought to the middleman's home, May had been stripped of anything that might connect her to Vietnam: her clothing, her jewellery, her money, her phone, her handicrafts, and even her name. When she'd been forced into marriage, she carried no evidence of the life she'd left behind.

But May remembered something I'd forgotten. She did have proof of her story: I'd given it to her myself.

During my time in Shandong province, I'd sent May a series of photographs from the Facebook account she'd kept before she was trafficked. These small reminders of the life she'd left behind included photographs of herself as a child wearing her traditional Black Hmong costume in distinctive locations around Sapa.

While they weren't conclusive evidence, they were proof

enough. May showed the police those photos alongside others of her "marriage" in Shandong province, and was able to convince them that she had indeed been trafficked and held captive by the middleman.

"I take all my photos what before you send to me – [photos of] you, me, Pang, Sebastien, all the Hmong girls. I say, 'I speak English! Because I am Hmong girl, I from Sapa. Because he steal me coming to sell in China.'"

Thanks to May, the middleman was caught with the two trafficked girls in his home, and their own testimonies added to the weight of evidence against him. May had saved those two girls from the horrific ordeal of forced "marriage" and unwanted motherhood that she herself had endured.

"I tell to the policeman, 'He take many Hmong girls coming to sell in China. He not the good man.' And the policeman go to take he. The policeman say, 'You are clever,' he say that."

May spent almost two weeks in Wenshan, before and after the arrest, providing the police with as much information as she could to ensure the middleman would be imprisoned. The police assured her that he would be.

May had done what we couldn't do. It was her idea, and she'd done it all herself. She'd never lacked for courage: I was the one who'd lacked for faith and patience.

It was a dramatic illustration of what even the most powerless among us could do with enough determination. We can't do everything, but we can always do something – and sometimes that's enough.

NO MAN'S LAND

It wasn't clear where May stayed during her two weeks in Wenshan.

I can only assume that the police assisted her with accommodation, as May's lack of identity card would have otherwise prevented her from taking lodgings. Bizarrely, the police seem to have otherwise overlooked May's own illegal status, neither helping nor hindering her. After working with May for two weeks they simply let her go, taking no responsibility for her.

May continued south towards the border, making the same journey in reverse that she'd made four years earlier, on her first terrifying night in China. She was still determined to go home – but without an identity card, she'd have to pass through the borderlands illegally, as Pang had done.

May made it as far as Nanxi, a small town that lay just a stone's throw from the border and was surrounded by Vietnam on three sides. Marinho and I had gone to Nanxi the year before in an attempt to meet with May's sister Cho, who lived somewhere in the mountains outside the town.

Having spent years living in the flatlands of Shandong province, May now found herself in landscapes reminiscent of those she'd known in Sapa: rugged mountains stepped with rice terraces, and splashed with brilliant green cornfields. These were the landscapes she loved and had long missed.

After having come so far, May was just two hours' journey from her home and family in Sapa – but the border still lay between them, and May didn't know how to cross it or even approach it without getting caught.

May spoke to some of the locals, who told her that vigilance had increased along the border and it was no longer so easy to cross without identification. She heard horror stories of others who had been captured while attempting illegal crossings.

As May hesitated, she received a call from her "husband". He knew what May had done to her middleman, and he approved of it. May's "husband" saw the middleman as someone who'd deceived and cheated him, and he felt that May had now taken revenge also on his behalf.

But May's "husband" had now changed his mind about allowing May to go home, and he ordered her to come back north immediately. If she came back, he said, he'd find some other way of getting her an identity card, and she could visit Sapa legally at an unspecified future date.

May was torn.

For the first time in years, May's "husband" had no physical power over her: he hadn't even kept their daughter as collateral. May could now disappear from China, and from his life, forever. She could slip across the border, make her long-awaited return home that very same day, and begin a life of her own choosing.

But of course, it wasn't quite that simple. May feared being caught at the border, and feared that if she didn't return to her "husband" immediately, that option would no longer be open to her. Most of all, May feared that in disobeying her "husband" she would incur the wrath of her father.

In many ways, May's dilemma was the same one in which she'd been entangled for the past year. For the first time, though, May was now making her decision from a position of freedom, and she had complete custody of her baby girl – but the stakes had been raised, and the clock was ticking.

I spoke to May as she was trying to decide what to do.

"Right now, no good for me," she said. "I have very big problem. If I go back to Vietnam, my Chinese family will be hate me a lot."

"You don't need to worry right now about your husband's family, or about your father," I said. "You need to think about what's good for you."

"So I thinking about good for me, you know?"

"And what's good for you?"

There was a long pause.

"To love my baby," May said – but the connection was poor, and I wasn't sure I'd heard her properly.

"Sorry?"

"Just love my baby, nothing else," May told me. "I think I need to going back to my family in... China."

If May's "husband" had been hitting her and treating her like a dog, she thought perhaps she would have left him. Despite the many ways he'd abused her and the perpetual uncertainty of his broken promises, he was still more reliable than May's own father, and her own community.

May had never wanted to be his "wife", or the mother to his child: but she was. She wanted to take care of her daughter and didn't want to be separated from her in the same way that May had been separated from her own mother. For all his flaws, and all the horror of her situation, May's "husband" had at least provided food and shelter for both mother and child.

I'd seen this as a major decisive moment for May – but facing the opposition of both her "husband" and her father, May didn't feel she had any real choice in the matter. I'd wanted her to make her decision from a position of freedom, but I now realised that no such thing existed for her. There never had been a dilemma: it was May's duty as a woman to do what she was told, and nothing more.

No matter where she went, May would never be free of

the myth she'd been raised with. After years of captivity and a lifetime of subservience, she was unable to see beyond the walls that had been built around her.

With a heavy heart, May began retracing her steps back north that very night. She left Nanxi without even seeing her sister Cho, just as Marinho and I had.

"I hope one day I will go back to Sapa forever," she told me. "I thinking that."

But after fulfilling her duties as a loyal daughter and an obedient wife, there seemed little space left in May's life for her own hopes and dreams.

GETTING AWAY WITH IT
(ALL MESSED UP)

There was another reason I'd hoped May wouldn't go back north.

May said her middleman had sold many girls in Anhui, while she and others had been sold in Shandong. Only now did I understand why his sales had been concentrated in those two provinces.

The middleman had a daughter living in Anhui, and a son living "very close" to where May and her "husband" lived in Shandong. These adult children helped find customers for the girls the middleman held captive in Wenshan.

Now that May had orchestrated the middleman's arrest, I was concerned about potential reprisals from his son, but May assured me there was nothing to worry about.

"He don't know where are me," she said. "He never come to my house before."

In any case, May and her "husband" had now cut all contact with the middleman's family, and were moving to another city in Shandong. I wouldn't know where to find them, either. I'd only needed May's location as a means to a potential rescue, but I realised now that May would never be rescued. She'd made her choice, such as it was.

May's "husband" seemed to have belatedly realised how much power May had held over his future when she'd been at the border with their child. After May returned from her journey south, her "husband" began giving her small freedoms at home so she'd be less likely to run away.

May was permitted to unlock her SIM card and, for the first time, was able to call her family and friends in Vietnam directly. She was also allowed access to Chinese social media, which she used to video chat with Cho.

To my surprise, May's "husband" followed through on his promise of buying a legitimate identity card for May. She said it cost a "lot of lot of lot of money – like four million dollar." Given May's habitual confusion with numbers, I imagined she meant four thousand yuan ($600), a considerable expense for her "husband".

The details for the card had presumably been taken from someone else's birth certificate, as Pang's had been. It wasn't merely a new identity card, but a whole new identity for May: a new name and date of birth, which I didn't know. I wondered if May still thought of herself as "May", or if she'd already slipped into one of the Chinese personas she'd been assigned. What name did she respond to at home?

Scared that May would use it to run away, her "husband" kept possession of the identity card. He used it to legally register their "marriage", four years after the fact. I asked May if he still wanted another baby.

"If he want, he [can] find new wife!" May said. She hadn't wanted her first child, and refused to have another.

May said she missed her family, and missed the mountains of Vietnam, and still planned to return permanently to Sapa. She swore she'd go home in early 2016, before the Lunar New Year.

"For sure," she told me. Perhaps I'd sounded a little dubious.

I'd once seen a tattooed phrase which has always stayed with me: "A bird in a cage is not a bird".

May's "husband" had bought her, kept her in his home for

years, and forced her to bear his children. He'd seen her merely as a means to an end, as a womb on legs, and had established their relationship dynamic as a tense ongoing struggle along lines of control and abuse.

If he'd ever glimpsed May's incredible courage, if he'd seen how clever she could be, May's "husband" would have seen these qualities only as a threat to his own power. By putting a price tag on May, he'd never seen her true value as a human being.

I remembered the May I'd first met in Sapa: a sunny, sociable girl with a big heart and a sparkling sense of humour, always surrounded by her friends.

In all the years he'd known her, May's "husband" had never known that May, and he never would. What opportunities did May have to laugh, joke, and smile in the company of her rapist who held her captive? How was he to ever see her immense charisma when he kept her locked away from the world? How could he see her generous spirit when everything had already been taken from her?

This, perhaps, was the greatest tragedy of May's story: that May's "husband" had erased so much of who she was, and had rendered her invisible – perhaps even to herself. I wondered how much of the girl I'd met in Sapa still existed after all that had been done to her, and if May still remembered those parts of herself.

May's "husband" had bought a teenage girl for three thousand dollars – but he'd never imagined, and would never know, what a treasure he truly possessed.

The middleman's wife had been sentenced to two and a half years in prison – a seemingly typical sentence even for larger-scale traffickers in China. It's almost certain that the middleman himself was imprisoned for a similar length of time: significantly less time than May herself had already spent in China against her will, not to mention the countless years of captivity spent by all the other girls the middleman had trafficked.

In any case, both the middleman and his wife will have long since been released. I have little doubt that their children continued the family business in their absence, as they'd done before, and that there are trafficked girls being held captive in their family home even today.

Soon after May returned to her "husband", she and I were chatting about her baby.

"She's a very cute baby," I said.

"You want?" May asked. "I give to you!"

"It's okay, you keep her there!" I told her, laughing.

"Sure, I give to you!" May said. "You know before, when I go to Kunming, I say to her, say, if her no listen to me, I'm gonna sell her."

A MESSAGE FROM PANG

On 14th October 2014 – five days after Pang came home from China – she asked me to share this message via 'The Human, Earth Project' blog for everyone who had been following her story:

"Thank you to everyone who worried about me and helped me. I'm very, very happy to come back to Vietnam and hope one day to see you all here."

I remembered the way that Pang would suddenly disappear when she and I were walking together in Sapa, and I'd turn around to find her there behind me. In early 2017 – two and a half years after she came home – Pang disappeared for the last time, and was no longer anywhere to be found. She returned voluntarily to China, though not to her "husband" and child. I lost contact with her, and don't know where she's living now or under what circumstances.

A MESSAGE FROM ANEMI WICK

Journalist and author

I first heard about Ben's work through a friend, and considered writing an article about it. As it turned out, Ben and I were both present for Pang's first days at home in Sapa. I can still remember very well when we were hanging out with Pang in the square in front of the church. She was wearing a traditional Hmong costume, the dark blue indigo still shiny and new. Pang's mother had given it to her on the day she returned.

Now Pang blended in, visually, with the other Hmong girls who were gathering around her. First there were at least twelve of them, then more and more joined. They talked and talked, and Pang repeatedly pulled her smartphone out of her bag, scrolled through a menu with Chinese characters, and showed the girls a picture of a small child sitting in a baby chair.

After about two hours of constant chatting, Pang suddenly started to look very tired. She sat down on a small stone wall, slowly slumping down more and more as the other girls kept on talking.

During these first few days after Pang's return, I got to know her as a person who stands and sits very straight most of the time. Pang is someone who often puts her fists on her hips with a disapproving snort if she gets annoyed with something. It was only her knees she could never keep still. They were constantly bouncing, as if she wanted to run away. But she had already run away.

In Sapa, there had been a lot of talk among the Hmong women since phone contact with Pang and May in China was first established after years of silence. Were their Chinese husbands good-looking? One of the Sapa girls pointed out to me that neither Pang nor May was being beaten by their husbands. And there had been a lot of talk about what future would await Pang and May should they return to Sapa. The quality of that future, it seemed, would mainly be determined by the chance of finding a husband back in Sapa. "If they return from China after a short time, and if they are still young and beautiful, they might still be able to find a man", one of the girls explained to me. "But if they already have a child, they look too old." The girl had seen a picture of May holding her little daughter. May looks old, she said. When the picture was taken, May was still a teenager.

That reality, and the generally tough life the Hmong girls lived behind the façade of lush rice terraces and picturesque mountains, wasn't new to me. But in that moment, as I watched feisty Pang sitting on that wall holding on to her phone, appearing estranged and even smaller than she already was, I felt a sting in my heart. I don't know with what hopes and dreams she had returned to Sapa, nor do I know what expectations she had of life before she was taken away, and I will never know. And I can only vaguely guess her reasons for taking yet another drastic turn in her life more than two years later. Sometimes I think about her, and I wonder if her knees are still bouncing, wherever she might be now.

Maybe what Pang was craving, maybe all we are ever chasing, as human beings, what keeps us going, is validation. I don't know what it is like to be sold, to have a price tag. No one should ever be sold, it's that simple. There were moments when this whole story left me overwhelmingly sad. But most of the time, I was aware that it didn't really matter what I thought and felt. I was simply observing reality. That's what a journalist does, after all. What difference does it make if I care, if I write down what happens to one girl in a small remote town somewhere in Vietnam's Northern Highlands?

I started writing that article, but I never finished. I found the unfinished story on my computer years later. It's a strange phenomenon that I've experienced several times, with stories I'd put all my heart into and then couldn't quite finish, stories that never really stopped haunting me, and maybe even changed the way I see the world. I still can't fully explain why; maybe too much heart, maybe too little distance, maybe too many profound doubts around my purpose.

Later, however, I did write several stories on human trafficking. I also interviewed Michael from Blue Dragon, and even that interview felt partly like I needed those answers for myself.

And there was Ben, and for Ben, doing nothing was not an option – even though the question whether or not he was doing the right thing must have kept him awake many a night. I know that his motivations were questioned by some of the people in Sapa. My friend Chan, who has always been a sister to me, told me about it. All I could say was that in my heart, I truly believed and trusted that Ben did what he did for the right reasons.

I still believe in Ben's work. He has my greatest respect for never giving up, no matter how difficult his journey has been.

A MESSAGE FROM MAY

Claire Bannerman is a Californian anti-trafficking advocate who had a personal connection to May and had been involved with 'The Human, Earth Project' since it first launched.

In July 2015, Claire interviewed May for her Masters dissertation, a comparison of human trafficking in Vietnam and in the United States. By chance, Claire's phone interview took place exactly a month after May returned to her "husband". The following text has been edited from Claire's transcription of that interview.

"I miss my family a lot. It makes me very sad and I cry a lot. I stay inside all the time and only get to go out sometimes. I don't know many people. My family and friends were not at my wedding and that makes me very sad. [My husband] said I can go back to Sapa to visit my family, but he worried I not come back.

I went to make [the middleman] go to jail. He will be there for two or three years, but I think that not long enough. He sold lots of girls and that made me very angry. I get police on him.

My husband was a bad man and I didn't like his parents.

They were very controlling, but they're better now. Some husbands in China are very bad man, but mine is good, he not hurt me. I have trained him. Some girls don't train their husbands. I now have legal ID card in China so my husband and I proper marry.

I will go back [to Sapa] in the New Year and if I am happy I will stay there forever and not come back to China. I want to go back to my family and go to school and get a job. I want a new husband in Vietnam but I am scared there will not be a good one. In Sapa, if I go back, people will call me naughty, bad girl. It's hard to go back.

Going home would make me happy. Right now I am only happy when I sleep because I am dreaming of Sapa and my family and friends."

Claire's interview ended abruptly when May's "husband" arrived home unexpectedly and May hung up for fear of what he might do.

Rather than going home at the Lunar New Year, May fell pregnant and gave birth to her second child – the little boy her "husband" had always wanted. As I'd imagined, the country in which May gave birth was the country in which she remained.

May is still in China. While she and I have stayed in contact, I haven't seen her since our 2014 meetings there, and I've never been back to Sapa.

AFTERWORD

Since 2014, the headline of this story – the fact that I'd found my kidnapped friends in China – has reached millions of people around the world. It's only now, almost a decade later, that I've finally found a way to tell that story properly.

What began as a small story about May grew into something far larger: a story about all of us.

Some people believe it would have been a more accurate and authentic story coming directly from May and Pang themselves. Beyond the barriers of guilt and shame that prevent them from sharing their stories honestly, these women have never had the luxury of an education, of literacy, nor even time, and have little grasp of the larger forces that have shaped their lives. The alternative to my telling this story was not to have it told by May and Pang, but to leave it untold.

There is great power in storytelling, and it's important to hold our storytellers to a high standard, especially those who tell other people's stories. Ultimately, I believe the key question is not who tells a story, but why. Whose interests do they have at heart, and how much effort have they made to truly understand the issues involved?

Some people have questioned May and Pang themselves.

They weren't perfect, they weren't always honest, and they didn't always act in their own best interests – but the same might be said of any of us. This is the human element of human trafficking.

Like the Hmong, we have a fault-finding culture. We love to find someone or something to blame, as if that's somehow a solution in itself. Nobody deserves what happened to these women, and the fact that abuse has been normalised within a culture only makes the need for change more urgent. A healthy community is one that supports its most vulnerable members rather than preying upon them. If you find yourself seeking out flaws in those who have been abused, it's time to question that impulse.

Some people have chosen to interpret this as a white saviour story. It might seem that way superficially, and race does play a role – but it was never the story's defining feature, and I'm wary of anyone who chooses to view it primarily through that lens. My involvement was driven by the very human desire to help my friends, not by the colour of my skin or theirs – and, in any case, I never saved anyone. The most courageous parts were played mainly by locals, including May, Pang, Chan, Cho, Zao, X, and Thanh. The foreigners – including Aamir, Aart, Charlie, Georges, Michael, Sebastien, and I – ultimately played supporting roles.

I was wrong about many things in this story – but if I hadn't pushed forward, I never would have understood nor have been able to explain the true mechanisms driving Sapa's human trafficking crisis. We all make mistakes. I've shared my experiences honestly here so that we all might benefit from them.

Life is a learning experience, and our knowledge will always be imperfect – but in the face of an issue as vast and horrific as human trafficking, complexity and the fear of making mistakes should never become excuses for inaction. We're always in the middle of the mountain. We do the best we can, we learn from it, and then we do better.

In China, I'd met May's "husband" – a man who'd bought a girl, held her captive in his home, and raped her until she became pregnant. He was a man whose money had perpetuated a horrendous trade in human lives.

I'd also met X – a real-life hero who rescued girls like May, and who did everything he possibly could to end that trade and keep communities safe.

These two men were, in many ways, polar opposites – and yet what struck me most at both meetings was what otherwise ordinary people they seemed to be. You could meet either one of them without ever imagining the things he'd done.

The key is awareness. It's awareness that divides these men, and it's awareness that helps us understand the roles they play in the world of human trafficking.

In that world, education is crucial – including our own. Our work at 'The Human, Earth Project' is to help people understand the global human trafficking crisis and what we can all do about it. That work is never over: there are always more mountains to climb.

While I couldn't help May and Pang in the ways I most wanted to, their story – in the form of the 'Sisters for Sale' documentary and books – now resonates around the world and is making a very real difference.

You might remember all the way back in the first book, when I left my home and full-time job in the Canadian Rockies to dedicate myself to this work. That was nine years ago, and I took with me the last paycheck I've ever received.

Since then, 'The Human, Earth Project' has survived only thanks to the support of people like you. Our team members are all volunteers and we make the most of every dollar we receive, though it's never enough.

There's a power in stories: they become a part of us, and we carry them with us. They help shape who we are, how we feel, and what we want in life.

Whoever brought you to this story believed you were strong enough to make it through and smart enough to make sense of it – and, if you've come this far, they were right. It's time for you to decide what your role in this story will be.

Take a deep breath. Drop your shoulders. Take care of yourself – we need you.

The movement to protect girls like May and Pang needs your support. At sistersforsale.com, we collect donations which are shared between Alliance Anti-Trafic, Blue Dragon Children's Foundation, and 'The Human, Earth Project', and your financial support will make a very real difference in the fight against human trafficking.

Join our mailing list at sistersforsale.com and follow us on social media to be part of the continuing conversation.

Explore Sapa with Chan and Sung at Hmong Family Trekking Adventures: www.hmong-family.com

This is not the end

ACKNOWLEDGEMENTS

Technically and emotionally, this has been the most challenging story I've ever written or ever expect to write. I thought I was writing a book but quickly realised I was wrestling a beast.

Thank you to those who played a positive role in this story – including Aamir, Aart, Bao, Big Zao, Chan, Charlie, Cho, Ingeborg, Isabela, Joeri, Krista, Leng, Ling, Mike, Qiuda, Sebastien, Sung, Toan, Vu, Zao, and Zhe. A very special thank-you to Michael and 'X' for your collaboration; to Anemi and Claire for your written contributions; to my first reader, Brittnay Mayhue, who gave me the early encouragement I needed to tell this story my own way and to say the things I most wanted to say; to my other early readers Judith Cooper, Kim Miller, Ian Tymms, Sharon Tymms, and especially Dr. Michelle Imison who went through the manuscript with a fine-tooth comb; to Katie Carriero, Debbie Lee, and Kim Miller (again!) for getting behind my work; to Sussie Walker for your emotional support through what became a long and challenging writing process; to Tracey Smith for teaching me those magic words; to my mother, Susan Randall; and to May and Pang for your strength and courage.